Three Tides

Writing at the Edge of Being

Other works by Cecile Pineda

Face

Frieze

The Love Queen of the Amazon

Fishlight: A Dream of Childhood

Bardo99: A Mononovel

Redoubt: A Mononovel

Devil's Tango: How I Learned the Fukushima Step by Step

Apology to a Whale: Words to Mend a World

Three Tides

Writing at the Edge of Being

Cecile Pineda

WingsPress

San Antonio, Texas

2016

First Wings Press Edition

Print Edition ISBN: 978-0-930324-92-6
ePub ISBN: 978-1-60940-162-7
Kindle ISBN: 978-1-60940-163-4
Library PDF ISBN: 978-1-60940-164-1

Wings Press
627 E. Guenther
San Antonio, Texas 78210
Phone/fax: (210) 271-7805

On-line catalogue and ordering: www.wingspress.com
All Wings Press titles are distributed to the trade by
Independent Publishers Group • www.ipgbook.com

Library of Congress Cataloging-in-Publication Data

Pineda, Cecile.
 Three tides : Writing at the Edge of Being / Cecile Pineda. -- 1ˢᵗ Wings Press ed.
   p. cm.
  ISBN 978-0-930324-92-6 (pbk., printed edition : alk. paper) -- ISBN 978-1-
60940-162-7 (epub ebook) -- ISBN 978-1-60940-163-4 (kindle ebook) -- ISBN
978-1-60940-164-1 (library pdf ebook)
  1. Pineda, Cecile. 2. Women authors, American--Biography. 3. Hurricane Katrina,
2005--Biography. 4. Environmental responsibility--Drama. I. Title.
  PS3566.I5214Z46 2016
  813'.54--dc23   2011023988

CONTENTS

To my students from whom I have learned much

The difference between literature and its imitations might be defined in any number of ways, but let's be reckless, even elitist, and propose that a literary novel requires new reading skills and teaches them within its pages, while a conventional novel—whether it is about lawyers or professors or smart single girls—depends on our ingrained habits of reading and perception, and ultimately confirms them as adequate to our understanding of the world around us.

—Jay McKinerney

Introduction

Three Tides was conceived with the writer in mind—someone, you perhaps—who may find craft manuals ultimately unsatisfying because none of them ever seems to address the matter of origination, the mysterious *how* of Making Something Out of Nothing. *Three Tides* aims to fill that gap.

That said, although there are probably as many ways to read a book as there are readers, before starting out I would like to share—with you, the reader—a simple map, a navigational chart if you will. There is a fundamental reason this work is presented to you in three sections. Each subtitle draws on the unifying water image of the title, and each section develops the underlying theme, namely, how does a work come to be made? (At this point you might ask: why water?) This writer's process suggests a cycle in three stages: Emptying ("Watershed"); Gathering ("Out of the Whirlwind"); and Making Something ("Like Snow Melting in Water").

A word about "Making Something." I prefer explicitly avoiding words like "create" or "creativity" because they seem hollow to me, overused and overrated. I prefer the expression "Making Something." It's a word choice favored by six-year-olds. Its full expression might go: "Don't bother me. I am making something." It carries with it the full assurance of mystery, surprise, and above all of commitment, of uncompromising non-negotiability. It is that level of commitment that distinguishes both the six-year–old and the true artist, including the artist-of-words, the writer. You.

I began life as a theater maker, the director/founder of an experimental theater company whose performance works originated in collective (through the medium of improvisation) creation. Or collective Making Something, the expression I prefer. The theater taught me everything I know about the art of words. The wellsprings of our theater practice was the impulse, allowing risk to flow uncensored from bodily sound and movement. Above all else, the theater (similarly to film) privileges the visual over the verbal. Primarily, mine is a right-brain, visual imagination. There are no craft manuals that I know of that outline a program for freeing the visual imagination. I know only of theater exercises designed to awaken and free sense memory. As Clarice Lispector and Luisa Valenzuela urged (see Bibliography), I write with the body. Just about everything I write originates in visceral sensation, exactly like the sound and movement impulse which lay at the root of the style of theater I once practiced.

Three Tides is designed to offer a pathway. It is a pathway you the writer are invited to follow—as you might follow a trail of bread crumbs in the great forest of possibility—only one modest path. I offer it as one casts bread on the water, hoping it may return the riches of reward to your own shores.

Making Something

Nothing. That's how it starts. It can't start any other way. Before you make something, there has to be Nothing, and all the uncomfortable, fearful feelings that come with it. If there's any doubt about that, just check out the creation story. First there was Nothing. That spirit of god moving over the waters, that's the good news. That's the unconscious, that shadow creature of anarchy and disobedience rippling the surface of the waters.

Three Tides begins with Nothing. The first section, *Watershed*, depicts a period in this writer's life when nothing really seems to be happening. A time of emptying, of grasping at straws, letting the tides sweep me to and fro, and out to sea. A time when I felt disengaged, marking time, first with a journal of daily practice, later piling up mileage, frog leaping from one dot on the map to another: West Coast, Malaga, Granada, Madrid, St. Jean de Luz, Les Landes, Rennes, Ile des Moines, Paris, Milan, Vienna, back home, letting things happen to me in no particular order, and without much rhyme or reason, all the while keeping haphazard track of the days, of daily experiences, travel adventures, reminiscences maybe, but asking myself: what exactly are you doing here? Trying to ignore what was happening to my body, not writing about it much. Leaving much of the pain—and fear—unsaid. Because almost from the start, something out there slammed me harder than a stampeding elephant and that's what I mostly didn't want to write about, the thing that wore me down until at last, walking—the act of walking—became impossible. But what you read here—at least at first—is mostly avoidance, camouflage. It's the way a certain kind of writer prepares. Call it Emptying. Then things start to happen. They make their demands, exert their pressures. And completely unexpectedly, a storm hits New Orleans, people swim for their lives; they wash up far from home.

Without recognizing it at first, Katrina turned my life upside down. I began Gathering stuff, doggedly at first, but without any thought as to where it might lead. And when at last I came to be ready to Make Something, what appeared was nothing close to anything I might have imagined. Without realizing it, I was still responding to the reverberations imprinting me some months beforehand: Julio Llamazares' *The Yellow Rain*. And partly it came about because I'd clipped an article from *The New York Times*, one that must have resonated personally even more deeply than I cared to admit, so that I tacked it to my bulletin board to make sure it wouldn't disappear.

What separates the writer from the dilettante has to do with taking writing seriously, with the kind of attention and care that lends ferocity to the writing commitment. Call it engagement. Living is no spectator sport, and writing isn't either. Not good writing, not writing that comes from the very marrow of a writer's bones. To people who look to me for writerly advice, I like to say, What do you love? What kind of world do you want to see? Where do you see yourself in that world? What are you willing to do to get there? What impossible task will you set yourself? How far can your imagination take you—if you let it?

No one can really teach anyone how to write. Someone can teach you how to spell, how to diagram a sentence, identify the parts of speech. And that is what your grade school teacher should have taught you, if that teacher really cared enough to teach you the necessary nuts and bolts. But that's not writing. That's mechanics. Then there's composition: topic sentences, paragraphs, rhythm, sentence variety, narrative arcs, organization, and so on. But when writers refer to it, they take composition to an entirely different level. Composing is the act of sitting down and putting something on the page. It comes from that elusive seat of the imagination: the right brain, the non-verbal place that sees the world in images.

Over a brief career teaching creative writing, the best writing guides I've found are those that do not so much talk of craft, as demonstrate craft through textual analysis and close reading, usually of short fiction. Of all such texts, one of the more outstanding for me still is *Narrative Design: A Writer's Guide to Structure* by Madison Smartt Bell, published by W.W. Norton.

But guides with their single-minded emphasis on craft leave out any discussion of the writerly impulse—that Right Brain leap some like to call "creativity." Bell decries programs that focus exclusively on craft, agreeing with me that such programs most often result in paralysis. "The great defect of craft-driven programs is that they ignore the writer's inner process. Creativity, the inner process of imagination, is not discussed...[it] is sealed in a black box.... [Such] workshops [tend] to exercise the left brain at the expense of the right, with craft consciousness becoming so dominant that creativity is squelched.... [Craft] is indispensable for talking about texts, for finding their flaws and...their merits.... But critical intelligence *originates* nothing." The thrust of this book aims to correct that omission.

Given the national culture of the United States of Selfies, few writing guides raise the issue of why write, let alone what to write about—beyond the Self. Most writing programs disdain paying any attention to "politics." I heard this opinion unequivocally voiced by Jack Leggett, director of the Iowa Workshop, 1969-1987. (He elicited some heated words from me.) Beyond the self, and preoccupation with the self, to what, in the chaos and disintegration of the greater world around us might we want to give voice? *Undoing the Silence: Six Tools for Social Change Writing* by Louise Dunlap, published by New Village Press, fills this glaring need. Underlying the process of offering explicit, practical suggestions for organizing thought on the actual page, it essentializes the basic question of why writers write.

Reading is the graduate university of writing. The best writing program I know is found between the covers of books. This morning found me doing research at the Berkeley Public Library (which, like many public libraries nationwide, suffers from the new trend in library science to pulp books—39,000 of them—some last copies, many of them out of print). I found myself scanning the carts outside the Friends of the Library store, which I rarely find open. And there I pounced on that rarest of treasures, *Daisy Bates in the Desert*, a book by Julia Blackburn (it can be found in the Bibliography at the conclusion of this book). *Daisy Bates* has more to teach about the writerly imagination than almost any other work I can think of. Daisy Bates herself was a historical character, but she was also a compulsive liar. Very little is known about her remarkable life and work (she wrote an amateur ethnography, *The Passing of the Aborigines*, a people she called "the oldest, most interesting people in all the world") and much of that is unreliable at best. Yet Julia Blackburn has reconstructed a character and a life, much of it drawing on pure imagination alone! Her point of entry into such a demanding project is a simple stalk of green cabbage. From such an unpromising beginning, she has pieced a life together stitch by stitch from her own imagination. And a compelling and extraordinary account it is. At the same time it offers an amazing example of a unique literary strategy which combines fiction, biography and autobiography, all within the covers of a 232-page book! (Why did I buy this treasure when my home overflows with so many books I need to pass on? Because now, whenever I rave about it, I can actually place it in my skeptical listener's hands: "Here. Borrow it. See for yourself!")

Franz Kafka, the writer whose vision, more than any other's, allowed him to see the darkest future in store for the 20th century, wrote: "A good book should serve as an ax to the frozen sea within us." Nothing less will do. A reader needs to feel compelled by the breadth of a writer's vision, by a writer's words, a writer's images, surprising choice of words, the variety and rhythm and sheer music of the sentences, the power to make the reader laugh, the passion to make the reader feel something.

When you're lucky enough at last to have found the writer who speaks like that to you, who blows your world wide open, keep coming back for more. Notice things like energy, the energy that makes you turn the pages, that packs the material with the kind of drive that makes every word sing, every sentence count. That keeps you reading way past lights out. That might even keep you up all night.

Over a lifetime of reading—dramatic texts, fiction and non-fiction—I've put together a short bibliography of some of the books that have stayed with me over a lifetime. It can be found as an appendix at the back of this book. Besides bibliographies, keeping track of reviews is another useful way of finding writers whose work is as yet unfamiliar. The *New York Times Book Review* sometimes leads to amazing discoveries. It doesn't have to be this week's book section. Hiding inside may be the discovery of a lifetime, particularly inside the weekly feature called "Editor's Choice: Recent books of particular interest." Of course it's hidden way in back. You might miss it if you blinked. But that's what the good sleuth is supposed to do: work to find that original voice, that treasure that becomes all yours, and which you won't be able to stop yourself from sharing with everyone you know. It's especially important, at least to my way of thinking, to discover what writers in Other Parts of the World are writing. How do they see the world? Contrary to received opinion, the United States is not the Center of the World, let alone the Culture Capital. Anyone who's done a bit of foreign traveling soon discovers that there's lots more to being in the world than hotdogs, football and self-satisfaction.

When you get really lucky and begin finding those writers whose work stays with you years afterwards, that's when you begin to ask yourself what is it exactly they are doing? And what are they doing to you, the reader? And how are they doing it? Are they laying in the groundwork for what is to come? What foreshadowing may they have laced through the pages? How do they bring surprise to your heart?

Do they lay it out all at once? Or are they given to slow unpacking? What is their narrative strategy?

How vast is their world? And how multifaceted? Because every writer creates a world. If it's a persuasive world, the reader trusts that world. Notice how you, yourself, lend your trust to a writer. Notice if there are developments that take you aback, that don't quite "wash." How might they diminish or challenge your reader's trust? Because that's what a good writer does: draws up a contract with the reader, inviting the reader to trust the writing. Allowing that reader to inhabit that writer's world.

When you have found that treasure, that writer who really speaks to you, you might imagine for a moment that what you're reading is a letter, a letter meant exclusively for you, one that's calling to you personally with a call so powerful, you can't help wanting to write a responding letter back. This one, this writer you've discovered after a serious search, this one is going to get a letter from you today. And this is how it starts:

(Materials: one lined notebook, blank book, or lined note pad. One really cool pen that slides over the paper in the most sensually pleasing way. Because that friction of writing tool on paper is part of writing. Because the best writing is coming—not from some electronic technology—but from your very own body, from your very own breath.)

Maybe your "letter" is a story you want your writer to hear, one that somehow resonates with what you may have read. Maybe it's a confidence, something so secret, you wouldn't want to share it with just anyone. Whatever it is, it's something so compelling you cannot *not* have the power to share it. When you're ready, you don't have to think about it very much any longer because it comes of itself, maybe in a way you would never have imagined possible, but that's for you to discover once you get to some kind of stopping place. Never before.

Writing takes forgiveness. Why? Because when the baby is ready to come, it shouldn't be expected to crawl before it's ready, it shouldn't be blamed because it's not ready to stand up. At first, it just needs to be allowed to do what it's doing. No judgment as the *I Ching* says.

Just the good stuff slowly filling up the page, the words, the sentences. There are plenty of people all too ready to harp and carp and criticize, but you are not one of them. You are not going to choke that baby before it draws its first breath. Judgment comes much later.

But while the pen spills the words onto the pages, that nagging, inner voice that wants to convince you your work belongs in the recycling bin has no place. Do whatever it takes to throttle it. A good approach calls for finding what I call an "as if." Write as if no one else was ever going to read it. Write as if you had to get something fully out on paper so you could put it in a drawer and forget about it till tomorrow morning. Write as if you damn well mean it, every word, and no one's going to stop you! Write as if the strongest hallucinogen just swamped* your mind.

Applied more widely, "as if" allows the writer to inhabit a variety of personae. There is no reason a writer's work needs to repeat itself in terms of tone, voice, or any other of a number of otherwise signature components. Actors inhabit multiple roles. Why not writers?

During the course of my own career teaching creative writing, the technique of textual response cited above was to yield the most astonishing results. It revealed to students that they could approach writing from a multiplicity of voices, and through a multiplicity of narrative strategies. More than any other technique, it allowed them to become aware that their imaginative range was infinitely broader than they might initially have realized. Perhaps the most noteworthy example of a student's use of the textual response technique is a sadly overlooked work of literature published by Riverhead Books in 2001: *Three Apples Fell from Heaven* (soon to be released as a feature film) by Micheline Aharonian Marcom, based on her response to Juan Rulfo's *Pedro Paramo*. While *The New York Times* review (https://www. nytimes.com/books/01/04/22/reviews/010422.22liveset.html) refers to this narrative approach as "wandering," the reviewer overlooks its place in the tradition of the poly-vocal novel.

---

* *Word choice: I could have written "affected," but "swamp" used as a verb lends more color and dimension.*

Letter writing was my way of getting ready to write fiction. I had no way of knowing it would be my way of preparing for something not yet manifest. It was a time before computers, before e-mail; my friends were—some of them—very far away. I wanted to let them know how much I missed them and what I was thinking and doing with my days, and what was happening in the world around me, and how it seemed to be changing. It may have been no accident that my own early fictional works came in response to writers whose letters have broken the ice of my own frozen seas. Eduardo Galleano, whose work, *Memory of Fire*, colored the novel-within-the-novel in *The Love Queen of the Amazon*; Kobo Abe, whose *Woman in the Dunes*, in which almost nothing happens, and whose indeterminate ending influenced *Face*; and Bruno Schultz' portrait of his mad, mad father in *Sanatorium at the Sign of the Hour Glass* found companionship with my own father in *Fishlight*. Once I had completed and published *Frieze*, my novel set in 9th century India and Java, I wrote to J.M. Coetzee, whose novel, *Waiting for the Barbarians* had offered me the seeds of inspiration: "My protagonist is your Magistrate, negotiating the mine fields of his own uncertainties, but in a much more innocent time."

My more recent fictional works are "mononovels" (meaning they take place inside one all-encompassing consciousness). My approach came from asking challenging questions: What if a solitary pilgrim were forced to revisit the 20th century, setting fire to almost everything he touched (*Bardo99*)? Could my narrator be someone still unborn (*Redoubt*)?

Sometimes apprentice writers misunderstand good advice, that old saw that goes, "Write what you know," for example. (Try writing what you don't know. Please!) That may be because they have yet to discover that there are many ways of knowing. Writing fiction is not like journalism; it involves intuition, imagination, but above all, it draws on the writer's best friend: the well of your unconscious, that unruly place, rife with anarchy and disobedience that resists sitting in neat rows. It visits you when it's good and ready. There's nothing you can do to force it to deliver when you may not be pregnant yet, although there are things that can be done to encourage it, such as keeping a dream journal.

Writing takes time. Which is why ideally, no one should have strict deadlines or fall victim to writing assignments. You assign your own project. You let it ripen over days, months, and maybe even years. All that time, you are "gathering," collecting thoughts, ideas, images, making the connections that may have eluded you at first.

Writing takes habit. Like meditation, it needs a calm quiet place for it to happen; and it needs a place in the writer's day. Everyone has that time in the body's day when you are most available to your unconscious, when the words flow the easiest. When I am in the heat of composition, my time starts at 4:00 AM, before allowing any routine daily distractions to take over, before the telephone—or e-mail—start to exert their tyrannies. I use pen and paper to write past sunup into the freshness of the morning. I don't sit more than three hours; then and only then, I use a keyboard to post what I've written on the computer, make minor changes, maybe correct a thing or two. I don't write for the rest of the day. I leave the work unfinished, so I can come back to it next day. Not every writer agrees with me, but for a writer to reflect what's going on in the real world, living is part of the process. A day richly lived is grist for the writer's mill. And you can't make that day happen if you're stuck to a chair, working at a writing desk all day.

There are days when nothing comes. You have a skeleton sense of where the writing needs to take you, but you're stuck. Those are the rough times, but if you let yourself just tough them out, often they yield the most spectacular rewards. You literally Make Something out of Nothing. Psychiatrists, when they have someone hemming and hawing on the couch, like to say, "Stay with that, stay with that for a moment." What they're calling on is a thing called staying power. Stamina. Not being too quick to toss in the sponge. Sit there. Nothing comes. Stay with that. Let yourself get to know what emptiness feels like. For a good long time. Emptiness. Allow yourself to feel alarm. Discouragement. Despair! Maybe you stay like that three hours, facing the wall. Then, all of a sudden words well up, a phrase, a small sputter of words. There you have it. Those few words give you all the

Permission in the world. Caught on the lined paper by the pen that moves so deliciously over the page. A small string of words, a phrase. It sings like no other phrase. It spurs you on.

In the long view, permission might be described as any event that allows the writer to take what previously might have seemed like an impossible risk. For example, *Bardo99* could never have been imagined had I not spent two months at the bedside of a dying friend, aware in all that length of time that his expiring mind was firing with endless and extraordinary hallucinations (which I gathered from the constant movement of his eyes), although his state was comatose. It lent permission to make an entire mononovel (*Bardo99)* of an end-to-end dying hallucination.

Juan Rulfo, who wrote a remarkable short novel, *Pedro Paramo,* one of many titles that figure in the bibliographic appendix, was the first writer I know to have used the phrase to open his sections (those small intervals writing programs like to refer to inelegantly as "crots," presumably from the French meaning turds). Whereas prior to Rulfo, most fiction starts by "locating" the reader, i.e. giving a sense of place and time where events are about to occur, Rulfo used actual spoken phrases, repeated each time to mark his character's entrances, much the same way medieval sculpture identified saintly martyrs by what they carried, the tower placed in St. Barbara's hands, or the wheel in St. Catherine's.

Many of my chapters, in fiction work especially, begin with a phrase. (In non-fiction, I use title headings.) They help jump start me. And they serve the important function of setting the tone. They get me though the days, months and years it sometimes takes to write anything that really counts, the thing that distinguishes literature from routine fiction (see the epigraph by Jay McInerney). And coincidentally, I add the phrase to the wealth of things I learned from the theater. Use of the phrase was the transition point we used to move from the non-verbal sound and movement impulse to reach the uttered word.

Here are three phrases from *Face,* my debut novel, one that's still winning recognition 29 years after publication:

"Wait outside."
The door is closed now.
He has become a creature of the night.

I listened for three hours for that last one to come, all the while facing the wall. I add listening to my collection of personal writing tools along with drawing on the visual imagination, and writing with the body. From the start, during the three years of composing *Face*, I heard my father's voice, characterized as I came to know it by a kind of Levantine fatalism. Listening allowed me to find the Voice the narrative of *Face* required. Another aspect of listening comes into play from time to time. I ask myself what does the narrative itself require? What is it asking for? In such instances, I listen for what the narrative itself wants to tell me, almost as though it were an independent agent. There is yet another, even more valuable aspect of listening, namely, allowing yourself to read your work aloud to colleagues, a technique that allows writers to hear the harmonies (or disharmonies) of their own sentences in a way no silent reading ever permits.

Three Tides documents three stages in this writer's process, a three-part cycle: Emptying; Gathering; and Making Something. It is intended to offer a topography of one writer's creative process—a process so mysterious, it tends to collapse on analytic examination. For example, how do I do "emptying?" A colleague posed that question recently, and I admitted to some bafflement, but on balance, I suspect that absent being directly swept up by an actual writing project, there are life intervals when I allow myself to wallow in the world of the trivial. And I put things in boxes before I even know I'm moving out.

Three Tides offers no prescriptions for awakening "creativity." Rather its intention is directly to invite readers into that idiosyncratic black box—one that belongs to the writer alone and inside of which no one but you has the right to trifle. This book won't tell anyone how to "be a writer." For that you have to put words on the page. Any help you may find here starts when you begin to write. Because with something like writing, you don't decide it; it decides you.

FOREWORD

On memoirs in general and this one in particular

"Watershed," which occupies the following pages, presumes to be something of a memoir: a memoir of war, lost years, and national catastrophe, a memoir of a period in this writer's life. To imagine a memoir has much resemblance to the truth, at least in the way truth is understood, probably amounts to a sort of delusion. Memoir may be no more reliable than autobiography, which undoubtedly shares with it some equally fictional characteristics. But this short memoir concerns itself less with questions of truth. Rather its intent is to raise questions having to do with the play of forces at work in the life of a writer, and to examine some of their unforeseen results.

On the 800th anniversary year of Beckett's martyrdom at Canterbury Cathedral, my experimental theater company staged its debut performance in the sanctuary of San Francisco's Grace Cathedral with a production score based on the words of T.S. Eliot's *Murder in the Cathedral*. At the conclusion of one performance, a member of the audience approached me. He posed a question, which has intrigued me ever since: "How did you do that?" he wanted to know.

The how of what artists do is never easily explained. Even artists themselves find the alchemy of their art inexplicable. We live a little, things happen to us and to those about us for whom we deeply care, but the how and why of what emerges remains a mystery.

This work is intended to present a period in a life, a watershed if you will, where out of a crucible of personal challenge and under the pall of my own country's McPolitics, something emerged which I could neither plan nor foresee.

Cecile Pineda
Berkeley, California

I.

Emptying

WATERSHED

A process memoir of the years 2002 - 2007

In memory of Walter Raine

I

Limping through Europe

More and more lately, I have caught myself wondering what my own life has amounted to. What good has it put into a world, which my very existence has burdened by its unconsciousness—by all the years I lived and encouraged others to live on a planet whose bounty most believed to be inexhaustible, lived as part of a great churning feast that would never end. I can place the time exactly (I was thirty-five) when I collided with the idea that all the comforts I took for granted: a roof, three meals a day, paved streets, running water on demand, cars to take me wherever my unthinking impulses might dream up, even sidewalks to walk on, were enjoyed at the expense of a world where other people lived on less than one dollar a day.

I don't remember when I first learned about *ashanas*. According to the teachings of Hinduism, there are four life stages: the way of the student, celibate and disciplined; the life of the householder, burdened by career and family; the later life of renunciation, of the "forest dweller," given to meditation and good deeds. And last, a life of retreat from the noise and fury of competition, polluted cities, a path back to the solace of nature, of empty spaces, a place given to contemplation. By now I've lived a number of lives, that of a student apprenticed to a master; the life of what in Spanish is called "ama de casa," the heart of the household, the one to raise the children, to provide a comforting roof to those immediately around her; a life in art as director of an experimental laboratory theater; later as a person of letters, some of that time as a mentor to young writers bent on discovering their own voices. But a life of devotion to the greater good of others not of one's immediate blood, bound to my world solely by the bone and sinew of our common humanness, by 2002, this was a phase I had not yet lived. True, as I promoted myself, advanced my career, practiced my art, I have lent a hand here and there, raised money for causes, helped people find jobs or housing—as my father had before me—but always on the fly, never with a singleness of purpose for which all around me I had shining examples: my friend Marc Gold for example, whose father had set him on a bathroom stool high enough for him to see his seven-year-old face. "By the time you are my age," his father said, "if you have done good in the world, you will be able to call yourself a man." Through his non-profit, 100 Friends, Marc raises thousands of dollars year after year to distribute to perfect strangers, people he meets whose eyes can be saved for a simple $200 operation; school children whose future would otherwise lie scavenging in the garbage dumps of vast Asian cities. Marc has reached his father's age.

Marc Gold showed me the face of that other world—a smiling, bright-eyed Indian fifteen-year-old who made his home under a water trough in an Indian produce market. His smile shone infinitely brighter than the pinched White faces of privilege I'm used to seeing all around me. A paradox: how could there be such dissatisfaction in the home of untold privilege? How could there be such joy in the face of someone living under a water trough?

I was living at that time in a house overlooking San Francisco Bay, surrounded by four gardens at the cardinal points, and one more in the inner courtyard, at its heart a burbling fountain, which could be turned off at night. Oh, I was about to forget the swimming pool, on the side which caught the sun. On a clear day I could see 50 miles to the south, as far as San Jose. The living room was big enough to swallow up a concert grand without so much as a hiccup. My writing study had a built-in desk 15 feet wide, room enough to let me work on three projects at once—something I came eventually to do—and a bedroom so vast it could gulp down two king-sized beds with room left for dessert.

The luxury of its ambience afforded appropriate support for the composition of my novel, *The Love Queen of the Amazon,* a conflation of prostitution and politics.

Not long ago I received a letter. I knew I had seen that handwriting before—but whose could it be? I opened the envelope.

The message read "Are you the author of *De Liefdeskoningin van de Amazon*??? I came across this novel in my bookcase with the inscription 'for Dini with love and happy memories of snow.' Signed Cecile Pineda. Is that you?"

It was from Dineke, my old friend, one-time high-jump contender for the Netherlands, whom I'd lost track of years ago. She knew me not by my author's name, but by an ex-husband's name. She is one of my few Dutch-reading friends. I'd sent her *The Love Queen of the Amazon*, in translation because *klickklacken*, the sound made by the gaggle of floozies trotting over the cobblestones of Malyerba in their spike-healed shoes sounded infinitely more delicious in Dutch.

I jumped at the chance to reconnect. "Yes, it's me. I have such good memories of snow; one time when my short legs wouldn't let me cross a ditch, you carried me on your back.... I hoard that memory."

I wrote "it's me." And yet, not exactly me. Not someone who wrote a comic novel nearly twenty years ago, carrying on in a life style as if the feasting would never have to end, living in my party house, parlaying its unreal ambience to write about unbridled luxury, and corruption—the lifeblood of whores and politicians:

> It was on one such rare occasion that as Ana Magdalena sped past her aunt Ofelia's establishment in mid afternoon she saw an enormous wooden van parked in the street outside. Workmen were sweating and struggling to move vast objects down the improvised ramp and out onto the street. Imposing canvas screens were stacked against the villa's walls. La Nymphaea's doors were open wide, but there seemed to be no one in view from the establishment. She parked the car and went inside. She found Ofelia directing the crew as they unloaded the last items from the van.
>
> "Cretins," she mumbled under her breath to Ana Magdalena, "every one of them cretins and sons of cretins, big hulking dummies with sawdust for brains. Their mothers must have tried to pry them loose with knitting needles and sadly botched the job!"

"Ofelia, *que pasa?*"

"Oh, *niña*, it looks like I'm finally going to do it. We're going to open The Screw. Isn't that the perfect name? I'm so proud! Imagine the luck! The Manaus opera house auctioned off all their old sets. I even bid for a swan boat, and just in time to beat out Gulbenkian, too...! We're going to have our own gala blast-off like Malyerba has never seen. But there's so much to do! I can't imagine how it'll all be done in time."

"In time?"

"For the Inauguration. Haven't you heard? Everyone will be here, all of our old customers. The councilmen, the lawyers, the municipal judges, even the parole officers. And the Chief of Police is lending us a contingent of armed guards. The mayor has even invited El Magnifico himself!"

"*El Señor Presidente?*"

Ofelia nodded. "I'm not supposed to know about it, but I have my private sources." Ofelia's laugh rattled the roof beams. "God's little kneecaps, I can't wait!"

This was the comic novel that came to be titled *Love Queen of the Amazon*, the one in Dutch translation my friend Dineke was asking me about. Was I that same Cecile Pineda?

I said I was, although I knew already then I had become someone different, someone farther along in time, a collector of memories, of traces laid down by passing years, reminders that once I passed that way. That I chose one path and not another. Or that the path chose me. Living with a feeling lately of somehow having lost my way, keeping a *Book of Joy*, a daily journal to mark my days of emptiness:

April XX. The first robin. The first spring robin making the fallen oak leaves of last winter crackle, the soft, downy feathering of its rust colored neck, haloed in sunlight. Darting this way, that way, still. Now inclining its head, gulping the unsuspecting worm. And I, sitting here under the oak tree, writing in a rain of inch worms.

April XX. Stopping Time. No matter that my footsteps announce my way along the path, in the mottled sunlight of early morning, nesting bird sings to nesting bird. And now the chorus weaves its net of sound in the quiet air. No sound but this and the softly chuckling brook. The wayside green, shot up from winter's shoot, unfurling its minion flags of green, and at the finial, the smallest of small star lilies unfolds its sweetness. Leaves proliferate on stems still red with remembering the winter's cold and wet. Concealed beneath their shelter, twin blossoms hang, half hidden, bowing their tiny heads. Sunlight. Stillness. The quiet of early morning, the shepherd trotting at my side.

April XX. We Are Still Here. You can still find us here, our faces sometimes shaded from the hot sun by the peace signs we carry. Snow has visited our hair, pallor dimmed our cheeks, etched now with the contour lines of time. But we are here. As long as we have breath to walk, to stand, we will find each other here, in these places, some of us half hidden in the crowd, some silhouetted in the noonday sun.

Do I know this one? Does she know me still? Is it really her? I hesitate, groping across unrecognition brought on by time, my first steps hesitant as I approach to get a better view. And now I recognize the familiar head thrown back in raucous laughter! the same laughter! the sweep of hands! the gesture that has always been her signature. I push through the wave of separating years.

April XX. Face of the Woman of Palestine. Her look takes my breath away. As if she has been waiting, counting the years of her oppression, lost hopes, raising her children in darkness, persevering, hanging wash out to dry, pounding out the dough, kneading it to make flat bread, her eyes that luminescent amber you discovered once when, as a child, you painted that veiled Madonna of your formerly Catholic days. But now in her eyes the look of homecoming at last, the sign at last, some meaning to the journey. And I look in her eyes, and she sees me looking. I have to shut my eyes not to cry out and because no words come close to this acknowledgement. When I open them her eyes have become luminous, and I nod to her because I share this moment, this moment in her eyes. I have seen her in her time of perfect beauty and she has seen my eyes reflecting hers. And I continue, elbowing my way through the crowd, protesting yet another war, through a multitude of 110,000 faces.

I think this multitude, these 110,000 faces are as one face in the eyes of the plain woman, the transfigured face of Palestine.

April XX. The scratch of pen on paper. Swirl of letters dancing on the page, rough language of Pict, of Dane, of Jute, a rabble crowd, mouthing syllables of their dailiness, marking millennia of vowel shifts, and now you write in this tongue become a crossroads of the world. Layers upon layers of time like glaciation, before time, of writing before writing, inscribing itself, scratching to be let out from the surface of this page.

April XX, 2002. A Calendar of Time. Time past, time present, time yet to be, all flowering at the path's edge: a humble flower, one bud, still green, curled tighter than a tiny fist; one already showing off its stunning spiral order; one efflorescent, its snowy bracts shedding pollen in the soft spring wind. Is this joy, this calendar of time's caress? Time past, time present, time yet to be. And for the traveler, time now.

The letter comes clear out of the blue. An invitation from Vienna to read from my work in Europe. The second invitation—the one in Malaga—I finagle. Two conferences, six weeks apart; and in the interim, four intervening weeks, a vacuum I will have to try to fill, renewing old friendships, exploring the back roads; weeks that will take me across Spain into France and Brittany, and by rail to northern Italy and Austria. The thought of home comes like light at the end of a tedious tunnel; it makes contemplating such a detour in time and space barely possible, but possible nonetheless. Still I feel lost, looking to the detour of four weeks' travel, during which, somehow perhaps, something will happen to me, something to shake me back awake.

~~As to my essential self, that's quite another matter. For all my confusion, that self still lives with me. For that I go back to the age of seven. The occasion was a children's birthday party, the game: finding some small hidden object with some precious prize awaiting the lucky winner. Perhaps I considered the prize in some way desirable, although of course by now I have long forgotten what it was. I only remember seeing the expression on the face of a small blonde girl, much younger, more vulnerable than I, more intent than I on clutching that prize at any cost, and how it seemed perfectly right for me to point out to her the place where already I knew it had been hidden.~~

Critical Note: The last paragraph hit the cutting room floor. Why? Because although I may find flattering the self-image it describes, it does nothing to advance the narrative, the thing writer's programs like to refer to as "**profluence.**"

Mine had become the post World Trade Center world—and how ironic that the *walpurgesnacht* of globalization would be announced by the implosion of twin towers, its very emblem—a perfect storm. Had the landscape shaped by history been other, I might have seen in such an opportunity an unalloyed gift, but I am a writer after all, and writing comes with some obligation. It comes seen through the eyes of an outsider, one fated to live always on the margins, taking the measure of life as it is lived by people in relation to one another and to the world about them, taking cognizance of the depredations of my species, its basic drives dictated by its impulses to greed, destruction, and an insatiable need to profit at another's expense. These were the roiling waters into which I presumed lowering myself, traveling to Europe in a time of war to advance my own obscure career. Is it any wonder I felt at loose ends? Is it any wonder that only catastrophe—personal and public—could bring me to my senses?

My plane arrived in Spain eight hours late, held up in Heathrow by a flock of hapless birds sucked into its engines. By the time I reached Malaga, the airport had shut down for the night. A clutch of groggy passengers waited for their luggage. Predictably, mine was the last to appear. I wheeled it out into the night. At the curb a lone taxi waited. I climbed in.

"Casa Diocesana," I said. It was the seminary in which, starting the next day, the conference was to begin. He eyed me uncertainly.

"El seminario." I tried my chancy Spanish.

"Ah, sí." We drove through the streets of Malaga, deserted and chill at that hour. We stopped at traffic lights. We heard them click as we idled. At last the driver took a sharp right onto the cobblestones of a terraced street. He came to a halt at the crest of the hill.

"Aquí," he said. I paid and, given the late hour, I tipped generously. I watched him drive off. From the terrace where I stood I could see the lights of the deserted city asleep. I turned to face an imposing carriage entrance two storeys tall shrouded by dark velvet portieres. I brushed them aside. A person stood behind the desk ready to receive me. He was young enough to manage cheerfulness despite the hour. He led me down long, darkened corridors to a room, a cell really, its dimensions barely wide enough to hold cot, table, and a crucifix fixed immovably to the wall. There was a bathroom with sink, toilet and stall shower.

I waited, barely able to keep my eyes open while he reviewed the sparse amenities. I knew he would be brief. The door closed behind him. I threw myself on the bed fully clothed. The moment my head hit the husk pillow, I remembered nothing more. Checking for the stray spider, which might have made its home in the corners or the crevices of my cell was the last thing on my mind.

At 70 years of age, with no effort I could hoist myself up onto a four-foot high table—as I did when my turn came to read in Malaga. If I was to read from a memoir I had cast in the voice of my five-year-old self, I wanted to dangle my legs, to feel again the joy of swinging my child's feet, back and forth, back and forth, to re-enter the happy and punishing world of my own childhood. I refused the microphone, hubris made worse by my introductory remark: "Today I want to dedicate this reading to our great prophet, Martin Luther King, Jr. I quote from his Vietnam speech: 'A nation that continues year after year to spend more money on military aggression than on programs of social uplift is approaching spiritual death....' Now look...."

I waited. I scanned the blank faces of my audience. I wondered what they must have been thinking that day, nine months before, when the twin towers collapsed. Did they accept the received narrative that nineteen for the most part Saudis had brought their steel framing down? Did they wonder how it was that the FBI could identify all nineteen hijackers the day after, but couldn't forestall them the day before?

In 1937 when I turned five, not even World War II had taken place. At the conference in Malaga I read from the introduction to *Fishlight*, my childhood memoir:

> My father always believed in memories. Memories live in the places they happen, he explained to me. That's why you always have to be very careful where things happen to you. The winter before my father had to go away, it was always snowing and it never ever stopped. My mother said it was the worst winter New York ever had. Anywhere else they would be sending out the Saint Bernards to rescue all the people that got lost in the snow the way they did in Switzerland when she was growing up.

My mother and father said when they were growing up people always got tuberculosis. They were always scared I was going to catch cold. They said I was delicate. That's why they made me wear high shoes all the time and eat my supper in bed, even on the days I had to go to school. At night when she helped me to undress, my mother told me all about Babette, her baby sister, and how she got so sick nobody could even hear her crying, and how her older sister, Blanche, kept asking for oranges, only when she got diphtheria, it was winter, and where they lived they didn't have any oranges.

My mother used to light the lamp and tuck me in, and let me sit in my pajamas looking at the picture books my father always brought me, or coloring with my crayons while she was getting supper ready. Sometimes if I got sick and didn't have to go to school, my mother took her special book down from where she hid it in the closet. Its cover was all shiny, like patent leather shoes, except you could see the weaving underneath. All the writing had fancy curlicues and bubbles popping everywhere and tiny spurs on it my father said were serifs. Inside were pictures of things like roots, and the cells plants have that look like little boxes, and all the hungry baby lips leaves have to help them breathe, and branches with numbers on them so you could tell where all the stems and leaves were going to pop out, and flowers like daisies and eglantines and pinks. My mother even glued an edelweiss inside and when you touched it, it felt all soft and velvety. She said it grew high up on the mountain where she climbed to pick it once. Then came the silver apples and golden pears, but I liked the plums best of all, all purple and frosty with summer bloom, and the sunlight shining through the leaves just like it did the day long ago when my mother painted them in her mother's orchard. They pushed my mother's writing way into the corner. Maybe that's why after the plums, the rest of the book was empty and my mother didn't write in it anymore.

When my mother brought me my tray with my supper on it, I had to close the book and give it back because she didn't want me getting any sticky stuff on it. She said I had to eat without spilling anything because cockroaches were always hiding in the walls, just waiting till they could jump on any stray crumb. After she put the light out, I would lie in bed shivering, worrying that maybe some tiny crumb escaped. All the spots on the wall started to jiggle, like cockroaches running everywhere, hunting for the greasy thumbprint my mother said was all they needed to live on for a year.

I lay in the dark waiting for my father to come home, listening to the cars chugging up the hill, fanning light beams across the ceiling, counting the footsteps ringing on the sidewalk, and hearing the street doors squeal open and bang shut and the scrape of garbage pails getting put out for the night. Sometimes I got out of bed so I could see way down the hill outside, but the window curtains gave off a rusty smell, and when I pushed them aside, pieces of soot scattered all over the window sill and got stuck under my fingernails. I would stand a long time by the window, watching the snowflakes flutter and swirl like moths trapped inside the street lights, but when I heard footsteps coming down the hall, I jumped into my bed and threw the covers over my head and breathed loud like people do when they're supposed to be asleep. Out of the corner of one eye, I could see the door opening, and the shadow of my father looking at me in the doorway. After a while he would tell my mother I was asleep. *Elle dort*, he would say and he would close the door softly. Underneath the blankets, I could feel my cheeks get fat because, maybe in the daytime my mother still used to call me baby names like Fifinette, or Babette, or even Cecilola, but at night, when they thought I was asleep, they called me *elle*. It made me feel grown up, almost like I didn't belong to them at all.

One time, my father caught me standing barefoot at the windowsill. He said I was supposed to be asleep, it was cold and drafty in my room, and if I kept getting up like that, I might catch cold and have to stay in bed. He said if I ever tried getting up again, he was going to have to smack me.

That's when he first told me about memories. Memories live in places where they first happen to you. Some memories could stay long after you jumped inside the covers, maybe even for years and years, my hand brushing against the window curtain, for example, or the sound of my bare feet. But when you least needed to remind yourself, there came the dusty smell that warned you that a memory was about to replay itself and that's how he could always tell when I wasn't in my bed, because he could still hear the slap of lost footsteps on the floor or even the sound of a misplaced cough. He said there were no secrets, no way of hiding from him because there wasn't any kind of box, or place—not even where we lived in our big apartment house—where you could lock a memory away safely enough to make sure it wouldn't come back some time and give you away.

Although I subtitled *Fishlight* "A Dream of Childhood," throughout my childhood years, both my parents subjected me to a nightmare of constant punishment. They left their mark: welts on my hips and legs that would vanish with time, rage in my psyche that has lasted a lifetime. It is a rage which has spilled over onto those close to me whom I have loved, but from it comes the material I have forged to make my best writing, my most electrifying theater. It is a blessing and a wound, and I have used it—to bless and to wound. It is the stuff that keeps me resisting, protesting the predations of empire in the Age of the Bad Father, of torture and warrantless wiretapping that, in shredding the Constitution, have become "normal," accepted practice in the world in which I live.

He said there were no secrets, no way of hiding from him because there wasn't any kind of box, or place where you could lock a memory away safely enough to make sure it wouldn't come back some time and give you away.

My father was Harvard educated. He had two advanced degrees. Although my parents came from educated stock, they never reached beyond their narrow inherited mindset. Both were teachers. They must have felt that what they did was the best and only way to raise a child, beating me as they had probably been beaten, and as their mothers and fathers and their forebears had been beaten. It was what they knew, part of a European education. This, after all, is the same continent where indigenous people referred to their White conquerors as "the people who beat their children." At a world congress in Recife many years ago, perplexed by a White man's arrogance, an Amazonian Indian reproved him: "Your mother must never have held you," she said. This savaging of children has been with Europeans probably since the Kurgan invasion, starting in 3,500 B.C., its ultimate wave the scourge of the so-called "Age of Discovery," including the conquest of the Americas.

I have never cared for microphones, for the sound distortion they produce, the way they separate the speaker from the audience. I have noticed that somehow the voices of men always manage to be heard, but that, for the most part, the voices of women, still now in our present century, remain the well-behaved voices of girls who early on were taught their place so effectively they've never been moved to forget it. I seem never to have suffered from such deficiency. Already by the age of seven my wild guffaws were raising the hackles of the good nuns to whom my disapproving parents had consigned me in the hopes they might break me of what they took to be offensive laughter.

"Get your hairbrush," my mother ordered. I guessed she must have read or heard somewhere that this was how American parents whaled on their children, the tougher the bristles, the rosier those rosy cheeks. Having surreptitiously padded my backside with a pillow, lamb to the slaughter, I submitted to her lap. She whacked and smacked, but the more she got into the swing of it, the more I couldn't help laughing. She came to a stop, felt my backside and succumbed to her own convulsive mirth. It was one of the few times I ever heard her laugh.

My mother was a Protestant from Calvinist Switzerland. When she married my Mexican Roman Catholic father, she agreed to sign a paper pledging that I would be raised within the fold. We lived next door to Corpus Christi Church where my parents had been married and where I went to school. Riverside Church where my mother worshipped towered—all 24 storeys—dwarfing the hill on which we lived. It was the pulpit from which Martin Luther King, Jr. preached his Vietnam sermon, a year to the day before he was assassinated. Our hill in Morningside Heights was the site of the Revolutionary War's turning point, the eponymous battle where George Washington's Continental Army turned to face the Red Coats who had made the strategic miscalculation of sounding the fox hunt bugle call to mock the Continentals' retreat. As a child, when I climbed the hill towards the looming tower before me, I imagined what the land must have looked like two hundred years before: grassy farmland, the hills inno-cent of buildings of any kind. It was home. It was where one day when I was five years old, I received the most frightening punishment of all. My father held my legs jackknifed over my body so I could no longer breathe. I wanted to tell him to stop, but nothing came out of me. I had no voice. I couldn't breathe. That was the place when panic came to keep company with my rage. From then on I determined I'd never run out of air.

The last day in Malaga the weather turned unusually hot. On the eve of our departure, I stayed up late in conversation with a colleague, enjoying the cooling air of the patio while we sipped the wine which has made Malaga famous. At eleven, I went to bed. In the morning I woke late. In the mirror I looked like I had mumps. On each cheek, a welt the size of a silver dollar bloomed an angry red. A third swelled on the hand that held the toothpaste tube. At breakfast, my colleagues stared at me. "What happened to you?" I flipped them a wise crack: "the kiss of the spider woman!"

Within forty-eight hours, although I didn't know it yet, I would have difficulty walking. And I'd have trouble drawing breath.

My friend Michelle was waiting for me where she lived in Madrid. Our friendship goes back to college days. Following graduation in France she accepted a Fulbright to come to the United States. I listened while she addressed our Cercle Français, describing the rather closed culture of her country, expressing the hope that she would find "you Americans" more open and generous of heart. I pictured myself far from home, in the midst of strangers in a strange country. Barely eighteen, I had little else to offer but friendship.

Over the many years we've known each other, we've vagabonded through campgrounds from Galicia in the west of Spain, across Europe through Greece and Macedonia as far east as Turkey. We've rendezvoused in improbable places, one year on the steps of the Cathedral of Albi in the south of France. We've shared dark times, too. Just out of school she took up with someone whose past must have been troubling enough to haunt him. Two years into the marriage, with two children, a third on the way, he took his life. We were still part of a group then, some of us still students. We called ourselves *La Bande*. Now we came to her rescue. We bargained on the Lower East Side's Hester Street for steamer trunks which we crammed full of her belongings. The day came when we drove her to the docks to put her and the children on the boat back to France.

On our camping trips, those first hours when we re-discover one another, we always give ourselves up to miming and clowning and dissolving in hilarity, perhaps to keep the dark shadows of the past at bay.

I phoned her from Malaga. "J'arrive!" I warned her, "but this time riddled with pimples." She was used to my mysterious rashes, but somehow in French my announcement rang especially absurd: *"j'arrive cousue de boutons!"*—literally sewn up with buttons, like a costermonger's vest. We gave way to helpless laughter. It would be another couple of days, I told her. I was making a stopover on the way, two days in Granada to pay my respects to Al-Hambra, which I do not expect to see again, at least not in my present lifetime.

How much living does it take to call a place home, how many years of walking the paths, of breathing in the dust, of gathering pine needles for mulch, or learning those places in the forest and what grows there in what season? How many years does it take to inhabit a land so that the red hills, the forests are inscribed with the intimacy of a lover's touch, so that the minute particles of soil embedded in the crevices of fingernails burrow underneath the skin? How many years of breathing the wind that blows over the sea and the hills until its smell settles in the snake brain that recognizes home? How many generations of living?

Exiled by their Catholic Majesties from Al-Hambra in 1492, the Moors wept. And for centuries afterward, they mourned Al-Hambra's red walls, its fountains, its courtyards, the filigree stalactites of its archways, the wrought iron clasps of its doors. Like today's Palestinians, they kept only the great keys to remind them of the wordless beauty they had lost. Minute particles of their tears water the parched land, which still cries out for them. The pines in the hollows still bear witness, the many generations of birds still remember in their bones the crumbs of Moorish flat bread scattered in the hills. The red stone weeps. Al-Hambra, its name means red—red for the tears that watered the hills, red for the hills, for the soil, for the walls formed of red soil, the red of the heart place that calls me home.

I first laid eyes on Al-Hambra after my mother died, some 30 years ago. I went there in the company of my son. We were on easier terms then, or perhaps those terms were not so much dictated by time as by the claims of place—the Sierra Nevada, Granada cradled in its snowy embrace. Al-Hambra laid a spell on me; it was as if I had always lived there, for all my generations. I recall walking the pathways in the surrounding woods, committing, trying to commit each tree, each branch to memory. Pacing the courtyards, at dawn, at noontime, and at night, gathering in the cast of light, each wave, each particle, burning them behind my eyelids. Pondering the arcane mathematics of each dado, committing to memory the color and pattern of its tiles. Inhaling the scent of the rose gardens, drawing in the burble and chatter of its fountains, as if, so doing, I was trying to re-member my own self. It was as if the place—when I first saw it—could knit what had been the living of my past with the future not yet lived. Al-Hambra became for me the link fusing time together.

Sometimes people talk to me about their home place. Sometimes the plainest countries claim their hearts, countries devoid of hills, home to unrelenting winds, places shorn of trees, all but the sentinel poplars that edge the distant roads. Sometimes they play their songs of home for me and weep. I weep with them. Ask me how I know this pain? My mother's mother kept an orchard in vanishing countryside soon to be engulfed as Neuchâtel spread amoeba-like, diffuse as a one-celled organism lacking any brain. My father's line lost touch with the soil twenty-five generations back. A small seaside village on the Cap de Salou 100 km. distant from Barcelona is the place from which his people get their name. I write the chapter of belonging nowhere: "Deracinated: the writer re-invents her source...." A source somewhere in earth. If I name my human origin, I name the dirt.

In the dusty scrapbook she kept, and which I found after her death, my mother kept the photographs she'd taken in the '20s when as a successful business woman—her expertise was interior decorating—she visited Al-Hambra, and struck a pose in her cloche hat and flapper duster before the lion fountain. Twelve lions whose original purpose was not only to cool a courtyard through the fierce temperatures of summer. To this day, no one seems to have unlocked the secret of the Moorish clockworks, passing round the circle, each lion in turn spilling water from its mouth to mark each passing hour.

My mother died by the spoonful. Her life ran shallower with each breath. By her bedside I watched her neck as the carotid pulse grew faint, the veins in her hands turn dark as bruises. I don't remember where we buried her. I remember only reading from the Book of

Job over her open grave, tears that would not be stemmed for all the years we missed each other.

While my mother was alive I disclaimed my work, never signed my name, as if nothing I did or made by my own hand could come from me. The competition that pulled us apart from the time of my birth no longer existed. It died with her death. I was free at last to sign my name, to claim my work as mine. Back home, I knew I would put an end to the theater I had made, would scatter everything—the blacks, the risers, the dimmer board, the light grid—scatter them to the winds, all the things I had once struggled to bring together in one place, to make my theater home. I no longer needed them. I would sign my name. And the name I would sign would be a husband's borrowed name no longer. I would re-take the name I took with me from my father's house, the matrilinear name he inherited from his father who, when he no longer had a father, had to take his mother's name.

I would begin to write.

Michelle is one of my very few oldest friends. She was visiting from Spain. We had driven all afternoon from the time we lay on our backs cooling ourselves in the shallows of a Yosemite stream.

"Why don't we visit the southwest?"

In July? With only a small tent, a two-gallon jug of water, and a Coleman stove between us, I thought she must be mad. "Give me an hour to think on it." But almost immediately I said, "Why not?"

We were on our way to the red desert, she driving. Our road followed the leeward side of the Sierras. We came to Manzanar. We stopped the car. The gravel crunched beneath our feet. A marker had been placed there. It read:

MANZANAR

In the early part of World War II, 110,000 persons of Japanese ancestry were interned in relocation centers by executive order #9066 issued on February 19, 1942.

Manzanar, the first of ten such concentration camps, was bounded by barbed wire and guard towers, confining 10,000 persons, the majority being American citizens.

May the injustice and humiliation suffered here as a result of hysteria, racism, and economic exploitation never emerge again.

California Registered Historical Landmark #850
Plaque placed by the State Department of Parks and Recreation in cooperation with the Manzanar Committee and the Japanese American Citizens League April 14, 1973

I know of Manzanar. In 1944 my classroom door swung open. A nun stood there, leading a small boy by the hand. "This is Seichi Yasumura," she said. "I want you all to welcome him." She said he was a refugee from the West Coast. All I remember of Seichi is the mural he painted of Paul Bunyan. He painted better than I did. What we didn't know in 1942 was that those round-ups only involved West Coast Japanese-Americans, not because hostilities threatened only the West Coast, but because Japanese-Americans happened to be farming the best land—their hard work had made it so. In 1942, Dole Corporation wanted it.

Already past Lone Pine, rabbits began coming out, cooling themselves from the heat of the day. As they hopped into our head-lights, Michelle swung the wheel this way, that; we left not one splat of road kill behind us. In the far distance, sheet lightning flashed over the desert. We hoped by nightfall we'd be past the low point, before any flash flood washed us away.

Fresh off the bus in Granada, I discovered my favorite hotel was booked. I'd be forced to find a pricier and less attractive substitute. A punctilious desk clerk grumbled when I claimed a room other than the one he'd hoped assigning me, cheaper by 100 pesetas. But, if I wanted to visit the Al-Hambra that day, he could fix it for me: it would cost an extra 100 pesetas. He pinned me with an unctuous smile.

It was not the Alhambra I remembered. Twenty years before there hadn't been the lines of people waiting to buy tickets at the kiosk, spitting the husks of sunflower seeds till the ground was thick with them. The museum, little more than a souvenir shop, was housed in a structure which had all the grace of a U.S. ranger station. Past the gates, the noise was deafening. Guide vied with guide, describing minutiae to crowds of gawking tourists in a Babel of languages. I ran an obstacle course, my camera making war with other cameras, craning my neck, peering past the backs of sweaty tourists as they paused for another shot. My hips began to hurt. I noticed I was limping. Bent on lining up the hitching rings fronting the Palace of Charles V in my viewfinder, I tried hoisting myself up onto the basement molding. I found I lacked the strength. And later, in my hotel room tub, after a good pre-dinner soak, I discovered I couldn't haul myself back out. I was alone, the phone beyond my reach. I reasoned if I had lowered myself in, there must be a way to get myself back out—which I managed at last by scrunching my body around 180 degrees to grab the towel bar. Happily it held.

We sit around the coffee table, some nine of us, sharing our stories. In June of 2001 the United States began conducting naval exercises with Israel and Turkey in the Mediterranean. I emailed my list, "Anyone watching? Anyone noticing what's going on?"

"I can't remember a time when we weren't at war," observes my colleague.

As these many years drag on, these many years of war, I try coming to grips with exactly how I feel, exactly what I think. A feeling of deep undifferentiated unease has come to roost. I recognize the deep humiliation, the personal feeling of violation, which Arundhati Roy's words pinpoint so explicitly:

"Each of the Iraqi children killed by the United States was our child. Each of the prisoners tortured in Abu Ghraib was our comrade. Each of their screams was ours. When they were humiliated, we were humiliated. The U.S. soldiers fighting in Iraq—mostly volunteers in a poverty draft from small towns and poor urban neighborhoods—are victims just as much as the Iraqis of the same horrendous process, which asks them to die for a victory that will never be theirs."

It is a feeling I associate with the desperate punishments I received in my childhood at my father's hand. Of my rage—and my panic.

Besides paying my parting respects, my impulse to re-visit Al-Hambra may have had to do with feeling I needed to return to a place of healing, a place of making whole. By the time I reach Madrid and the welcoming hugs of my friend Michelle, I can barely walk. I have developed flu-like symptoms, and a wracking cough. Michelle puts me to bed where for three days I cough and sweat. Amplified by the steep canyon of the street outside, traffic noises, the sounds of human voices remind me that Madrid's animated life goes on at all hours, but all I care about is sleep.

I wrote my first short story one night I couldn't sleep. Although by now insomnia is an accepted part of life, in 1980 it was unusual enough to notice. Night after night I lay awake, tossing, churning. All my life I've had recurring dreams of drowning but as I've grown more at home in my skin, the water level has tended to recede. I began to think there was some dream waiting for me that I didn't want to dream. One night I sat at my typewriter, determined to dream the dream awake.

Listen: A man wakes to discover that his city has been evacuated. He has missed the last trolley out. On foot he proceeds, past the place of the theater, making his way to the outer boulevards, and to the bridge, which will take him across the river to the other side, past the palisades into the woods. From the far distance he watches as his city burns. At sunrise he feels an iron vise grip his leg: he has walked into an animal trap. He has little else with him but a pen, a journal. He begins to write, to describe the pain he's in. How many days can he live like that, without food or water, just writing about pain?

He dies. In that instant, stage hands move in, shouting commands, hooking all the trees to guy wires. Hauling the whole forest up into the flies.

"Cut the lights," the stage manager roars.

Written before computers, the story is lost somewhere in my files. My executors will probably be the ones to find it. They won't know it marks the year when making theater was no longer possible, the year I began to write. The administration had seen to that. Reagan had been elected, funds for the arts were drying up.

We cross mountain ranges, Michelle and I, canyons and the high mesas where Hopi keep their villages. We set our tent up in dry river beds, in abandoned campsites, foreboding in their atmosphere, where one night Michelle is startled awake by some nocturnal creature whose blood curdling screams sound like a woman being stabbed. Much later we learn these are the calls of the mountain lion. We visit Acoma, the longest settled city in the hemisphere, famous for its black pottery. And all along the way, when the heat becomes unbearable, we tip our two-gallon water jug over our heads till our clothes are drenched. In the absence of air conditioning, it's the only way to keep cool on the road. We enter the Navajo nation. Visitors are allowed to travel in the canyons only when accompanied by a Dineh guide. John Johnson takes us to Canyon de Chelly. On the way he describes the campaign of 1864 led by U.S. Army Colonel "Kit" Carson who invaded the canyon, killing all Dineh who were either too young or too old to escape by climbing the canyon walls, rounding up the 150 starving survivors who joined 8,000 more of their people on the Long Walk across New Mexico to Fort Sumner where they were held captive for four years before being allowed once more to return to their homeland, the place they called heart of the world.

This is Indian country. Perhaps it is no accident that we catch sight of its inhabitants only rarely. One evening we observe an old Dineh couple sitting propped against the wall of their hogan, peacefully enjoying the evening cool. A young brave rides his pony nearby. In a government station bordering one of the monuments, an old Dineh couple enters, very reserved and dignified, he in dentalium shell necklaces and formal black felt hat, she in the crimped velvet skirts and petticoats of her tribe. They have come to ask the White man behind the counter for help reading their electric bill. We watch aghast as a French tourist thrusts his camera in their faces and snaps away.

We reach Santa Clara Pueblo in time for the corn dances, but more tourists than squash and turtle people mill around the kivas. Discouraged by the throngs, we continue up the Rio Grande to San Felipe Pueblo. We park at a respectful distance, edge our way quietly to a place where we can see the dancing ground, sunk three feet below the plaza level by centuries of pounding feet. We watch the rows of dancers, hundreds of them, chant and shake their antelope-hoof ankle rattles. Although we laugh at the mud babies clowning in their pock-marked body paint, mocking the contradiction between the White man's ways and his religion, no one looks directly at us. In all the time we stay there no one speaks to us, neither in English nor in Tewa. We leave quietly, hoping not to give offense.

In Madrid, the sweats disappear, the cough subsides. I don't exactly know when I began to make the connection between my state of health and the now slowly subsiding welts on my hand and cheeks. They are some kind of bites, but of a vector unknown, although the symptoms are beginning to suggest Lyme disease. After three days I am well enough to roam the Madrid streets in Michelle's company preparing for our trip through France, destination Brittany. It's a perfect day. Martins swoop in bright sunlight, exploding from the dark eaves where they weave their nests. On the way, we pass the weavers of baskets, and the sellers of wine, of cinnamon and saffron; the rope makers' shop, the makers of espadrilles, hemp-soled shoes older than civilization itself.

It's the start of the World Cup. Sissé plays for Senegal. We watch them on the TV, the young warriors of Africa, permitted this one indulgence. Game over, they celebrate their victory, dancing together in a ring, oblivious of the screams and shouts, of the commentators' chatter. And now a great shout wells up in the street outside; every-where the doors of Madrid discharge their exiled Africans. Down the canyons of the streets they press, surging toward El Bar Africano to the beating of the drums. Opposite our windows, the roofers pause, happy to watch them pass. But we stay indoors, avoiding the noon-time heat, packing for our dawn departure.

The old may lie in the dark, unable to sleep, pondering the end of life, awaiting the verdict, the vise-like grip in the chest, the tingling in the extremities, the bloody stool. But I'm not there yet. This limp, this incapacity to walk without pain is only a temporary inconvenience, to be ignored like all inconveniences, one that can be trusted to retreat after a healing night of sleep. Except this one doesn't go away.

It's barely light when we leave Madrid, the trunk packed with our provisions, our ultimate destination far to the north where we will join other friends in their summer place on a Breton island off the coast, that scattering Chaucer described as the *blackes rockes* of Brittany. We make good time. We've booked a place for the night in St. Jean de Luz, which we need to reach by nightfall. The road winds towards San Sebastian and Hendaye; we pass through a narrow can-yon of exfoliating shale where road crews have hung retaining wire from battens to contain the falling rocks. At the lip of the canyon, reaching for the rays of sunlight, the young grasses force their way through the wire. We continue through the Basque country, through towns with deserted streets. People stay indoors deterred not so much by the heat as by the threatened violence of the separatist movement, the ETA, afraid to venture out of doors—although we catch sight of a lone woman improbably wheeling a baby carriage through a deserted plaza at high noon.

Our first day's drive is a long one. We are early to bed, waking next day to an overcast sky and a lushly decorated city. It's *la fete de St. Jean*. Oriental rugs spread their opulent colors at each of the many fes-tive shrines dotting the streets and alleyways. Over the cobblestones women unroll great lengths of white linen and scatter them with rushes. But with many kilometers ahead of us, we decide to tarry only long enough to grab the quick croissant.

By noon we reach the Arcachon basin where the beach front town of Gujan-Mestre is home to oystermen whose cabins line the road. We stroll past their storage sheds where oyster farmers keep their rolls of wire mesh, bobbins of white and black discs, and steel frames in pursuit of the generously breeding oysters. Beyond the cabins stretches a strand so vast the oyster flats, and the bay of Arcachon itself, lie virtually beyond the horizon. Along the path, the occasional table is set up, its umbrella open despite the overcast.

I can't resist a pair of oysters on the half shell. An oysterman shucks them as I watch.

"Only two?" He waits expectantly for a better answer.

I sit at a table under the uncertain sky. A very young girl approaches. She's missing two front teeth but her smile is not any less beguiling.

"Aha! You must be the oyster princess," I tell her. She shakes her head, spins about and vanishes inside the family's darkened quarters.

"Maman, there's a lady who says I'm an oyster princess!"

She ventures back outside, this time with a smaller version of herself in tow.

"What's your name?"

"Valentine!"

"What a promising name."

"And this is Kami, my little sister."

I appraise Kami's red framed eyeglasses, her myopic eyes, the generous wad of snot nesting beneath her button nose.

"Aha! You must be the other oyster princess, a princess for each shell. Do you like oysters?"

Both shake their heads emphatically. "Non!"

"It doesn't matter. You're princesses all the same. If we asked you very nicely, would you let us take your picture?"

The princesses pose for us, their small arms wrapped around each other, but no image can capture the happy sounds of their affectionate murmurs, more delicious than the mewing of kittens, than the coo of mourning doves.

In the picture we retrieve later from the photo shop my cheek shows a large plum colored bruise where the swelling has subsided. It is ten days from my midnight encounter with whatever it was that bit me.

Throughout my childhood, we lived near my godmother, no more than one or two blocks away. When I was a small girl she had little use for me—I was too rowdy, too willful; we discovered one another when I turned eighteen. It was to her house I ran when violence overflowed at home. It was there after I dried my tears I first discovered Beckett, Genet, Ionesco, and Nathalie Sarraute. For years she wouldn't believe that my parents beat me.

She had family in France, but she lived her adult life in the United States from the time just after World War I when she left her country on a liberty ship to join her American soldier husband in Arkansas. She was unprepared for Little Rock, for a mother-in-law who wanted to know if French babies were born with teeth.

For seven years her husband beat her. He beat a wife who had never learned to cook. She came from people who had servants. He beat a wife who left home by day to teach French in an upscale Baltimore girls' school. In the eighth year of her marriage she left him when she remembered she had teeth.

As she lay dying I promised I'd see her through.

"Get me some pills," she ordered.

"How many?"

"Enough," she said. Although we weren't blood, I was her only family in the United States. I found a way to commemorate her passing:

They're in my suitcase, 100 phenobarbital tabs, enough to do the job. The prospect overwhelms me. New York can wait. I travel to Israel instead. An Arab taxi drives me outside Jerusalem's golden walls to the tomb of Jehoshaphat.

"Wait for me," I tell him.

I walk down the path. Old stones line the roadway. The earth here is packed hard with centuries of human traffic. The path is white. It drops into the gully. The tombs are carved into the rock. They're supposed to date back to the First Temple. Ancient olive trees twist, their leaves shimmer silver as they have shimmered for a thousand years. The air is filled with light. There is a faint, paling winter sun. It turns the sweet grass emerald.

I sit on a stone dreaming. *Where does the spirit go when the spirit flies? Does it fly into the sun? Is it forever suspended in the eternal night of space? Does it hum for a long time afterward? Can it see us? Does it hover still?*

Three Arab boys herd a flock of sheep into the hollow. "Hey, hey, hey," they shout. The sheep trot briskly, their bells quicken the afternoon air.

They greet me as they pass. "Shalom," they say.

"Salam aleikum," I say. Peace be with you.

They laugh. "Aleikum salam."

"Did you bring them?" She's waited to ask till the last day of my stay.

"Yes," I say.

"Enough?"

"Enough."

"Put them in the desk. In the little drawer."

It's the drawer where she keeps her keys. The key to paradise, I think. I slip the vial inside and quietly close the drawer. When I return four months later, she's still there greeting me from the chair where she spends her days. But the pills are nowhere to be found.*

---

* From "Notes for a Botched Suicide," published in 1999 in *580 Split.*

Set in the meadows between the gently rolling hills of Brittany we catch sight of the granite monoliths of Carnac, a set of razor teeth devouring the landscape. In the grass, sheep graze, their woolly coats blending with the stone, but as we approach the fenced off area, a pre-historic site dating from before Stonehenge, row upon parallel row of stone monoliths acquire more distinct definition, their bases buried upright in the ground, some taller than the height of two men, set straight, thousands upon thousands of them, ranging through hill and vale of the countryside, mingling here and there with thatched Breton cottages, dropping past the shore into the deep blue tides of the Atlantic. What was once sacred ground is now fenced off from human traffic, grazing land for the occasional flock, here and there a dolmen, its rounded dome shaped like a huge boletus, place of burial (or some think, sacrificial altar) of the Druid folk who inhabited these coasts millennia before the arrival of Saint Columban. Yet however cowed by missionaries or conquerors, by the wildness of the moors or their menacing skies, clad in their fleece skins, their shoes woven of hemp, they're our ancestors all the same. We stare down the wrong end of a telescope at a past so distant, we cannot begin its decipherment, and yet I can't help thinking these ones, our blood, lived here once; birds darning the clouds in darting flight are offspring of those, which long ago must have animated these same skies.

We lunch beside a reconstructed galleon in the Port of Auray, place of debarkation of Ben Franklin, come to solicit France's aid for a bourgeois, slave-owner's revolution, and the hearts of willing French ladies—preferably ones past their prime. He praised their easy virtues: "they don't tell, they don't swell, and they're eternally grateful!" Under the shade of canvas umbrellas, we savor a variety of crepes made of the dark grain here called *saracen*, historic trace of the Arab conquest that, before it was repelled, reached as far west as Poitiers. Made of buckwheat, they're variously filled with ham, egg, mergueze, andouille, champignons, onions or tomatoes.

Sitting next to us, unabashedly staring at these strangers busily stuffing themselves, sampling morsels from one another's plates, sits one of those curly-haired English children, flat of face and wondrous of eye. Watching her now, perched in her high chair, touching nose to her mother's nose, butting forehead to her forehead, I wonder did those ancient ones from a past we barely fathom, did they, too, know the delights of touching noses, butting brows to their children's brows?

As my godmother lay dying in a hospital, I began to clear the apartment she'd lived in nearly 30 years, first the surface things and as I found a place for them, the recesses of closets where the daylight never shines, the bottom of bureau drawers that began to yield their secrets.

My godmother came from Tours in the region of the Loire, but the people on her mother's side had Breton in their blood. They came from that region to the north, bound by the Atlantic, the place of dark legends, the pre-Christian, Old Europe mysteries of its people, belief that lingers still in spells and magic, in spirits, ghosts that haunt the land—the "snakes" not even Patrick could drive out. The cult of the Druid, of a people who stepped across the sea to share a language with the men of Cornwall and of Wales, Brittany, my godmother's heart place.

As she lay dying, I packed her clothes, many articles made by her own hand. I gave them where I thought they might be needed most, to the African National Congress, to the people of Stephen Biko, cruelly murdered by South Africa's apartheid regime, by its truncheon bearing minions. I was late to our appointment—20 minutes late. In the front courtyard two Black women sat. They had waited for me. Yes, they assured me, South Africa was cold. Folks would be glad to have my godmother's winter woolens. My godmother was a racist. It was our only disagreement. She never knew to whom I'd given her clothes, the suits and coats she'd labored to make; it was my way of making up for her.

Still now, somewhere packed away, I have the tiny albums, some no bigger than my palm, with photographs of my godmother's travels. One pictures Nuremberg in 1938 where one day in a biergarten seated at an adjoining table, she snapped Hitler's picture. But it was her pictures of Brittany and all her books of Breton legends that I keep to this day, photos of peasant women spinning distaffs in the shadow of their doorways, fishermen in their wooden clogs mending their nets. Processions of townsfolk, banners held high, their headdress ribbons streaming, making their way through the countryside to pause at the calvaries, stone carvings that celebrate the passion of the Christ, sites of the Breton pardons where in pre-Christian days, Druid priests held blood sacrifices.

As she lay dying her closet shelves yielded the dark skirts, the starched lace headdresses that the peasant women wore and that she had collected, the bodices of crimped velvet, embroidered with seed pearls in the somber colors of the north. I recognized the costumes from the time I was in first grade. I must have needed to go to the lavatory. Making my way back to my classroom, I heard singing, music, Lorelei sounds which cast a spell on my child's heart so that I forgot where I was meant to go, forgot everything as I peered inside through the crack between the auditorium doors, too short by at least two feet to see through the porthole windows. I pushed them open. I tiptoed down the balcony aisle to take my place on a folding wooden seat, much too large for my small frame, to peer under the brass safety rail at children older than I, speaking not English, but a language I could nonetheless understand, wearing dark costumes, lace headdresses, in what I took to be a peep show, a magic box with backing blue as the sky. It was my first time ever in a theater. Many years later I would discover what it was that I had seen. In my godmother's effects I found the hand painted program. It read: "L'Oisseau Bleu." It was a high school production of Maeterlinck's "The Blue Bird" that my godmother had directed.

When she could no longer walk or stand, I cooked for her, shrimp, her favorite, and while we ate she told me her stories. When she was a child her father failed at a string of businesses. When she was ten, he tried establishing a hardware store in a small village outside of Tours. She went to the village school. Her classmates were all children of the peasantry, people who worked the land and who had worked it from before history. She played with them, their families took her in. They embraced her in a way she couldn't imagine in a home where children had to address their own father formally as "Monsieur." She herded cows with them, and learned to call them home at night.

"How did they call them?"

My godmother lowered her voice: "Quo, ma belle," she growled, "Quo."

They had been calling their cows in Latin at least from Roman times. What happened to these people who had taught her love? Had she kept in touch with them?

"Oh, no!" she said, "they died of tuberculosis. By the time they reached fifty they were dead."

It took my godmother two months to die. Had she died at home, I would have been the one to wash and prepare her body for burial. When I reached the hospital I found she had been laid out on a gurney under the cruel light of a fluorescent bulb. It lent her skin a terrifying color. I washed her face and combed her hair.

While she lay dying in the hospital, I catalogued her library. I held a two-month-long garage sale. Day in, day out as I sat reading the proofs of *Frieze,* my new novel, people wandered through the apartment, buying books, costume jewelry, furnishings, slowly moving things out, paying me until I had enough to fulfill her last bequests.

She had left nothing to chance. Her arrangements were in place—all but the dereliction of an undertaker who forgot to come. By the time of her death, I had all but emptied her apartment. In the depth of the most remote closet just one box was left. I had been saving it till last. When I opened it, I discovered ceramic figurines smaller than my hand, priests, and bishops, bearing the heavy banners of the Breton pardon—the *Tro Briez* of Brittany—choir boys, fishermen, the statue of Mary resting on their sea-roughened shoulders, village women in their high lace headdresses, bugler boys, tiny lace-capped village girls. I had not cried till then.

From the shore of Brittany we board the ferry to Isle des Moines. There are four of us now, including Marie Claude whose Breton house we share on this island whose name suggests it may once have given refuge to monks fleeing the French Revolution. Early morning sees us walking the narrow streets, looking for the open market where we will shop for shellfish, fruits and vegetables. We pass the bookstore that serves the 610 souls living on this island. Today in the window it displays copies of best-selling Transtromer's *Volleur de Bibles*. Past the post office and the green grocer, we come to the little square. It's not so much a square really as a place of indeterminate function. Today, an outdoor market squats under the shade of white canvas umbrellas displaying squid, crabs, their long claws bunched by rubber bands; mussels; clams in their baskets, giving off scent of the sea. And here is Françoise, her red hair frizzled, a stout Breton woman, with her smile of welcome. She greets all who come, and all come now to Françoise, to her little truck, to her green and shining vegetables, to her bee-seducing fruits: melons, and white peaches with their poignant smell of spring. She used to be a fixture at the green grocer's stall down the street. Everyone knew Françoise. And everyone was outraged when, good capitalist, thinking to maximize his profits, the green grocer fired her. But Françoise is not one to be defeated lightly. With her frugal savings, she buys a truck. Every Tuesday and Thursday, she parks it in the Place where she displays the gentle fruits and benign vegetables of the season. And people come; they come for her vegetables, her fruits, and most of all for her welcoming smile, and her gossipy good nature. Down the street, the sign in the green grocer's window reads **Business for Sale.**

While she was still well enough, we went through my god-mother's photographs—hundreds, thousands of images of women in dark Victorian dress, garden party hats, with the obligatory gloves and parasols, photo studio children solemnly posed, families, here and there a *pater familias* leaning commandingly on a photographer's lectern. She must have destroyed the picture of Hitler—too gruesome, she said. Resting at the bottom of the heap was a color photograph. She picked it up.

"*Ah, ça c'est Jeanne!*" she smiled.

I studied the image of this woman who bore the same name as my godmother, a countrywoman, her sleeves rolled up, who stood against a background of enamel basins and shiny copper pots. In the foreground a rolling pin lay on the chopping block. She looked like a woman well into her sixties, possibly even seventies. Thinning straight white hair framed her face. A ruddy complexion accentuated sharp blue eyes. Her hands were roughened by decades of service, washing, cooking, setting fires, airing mattresses, beating rugs, trimming the wicks of oil lamps, cleaning their chimneys of lampblack. This was Jeanne, the family servant who came from peasant stock, from a small village, to enter into service with my godmother's family just after she turned eighteen. It was she who wrote the simple letters that brought my godmother news of home. What stays with me now, many years later, was the light in her eyes, her generous smile—signs that at her age she still allowed life to feed her curiosity.

It has taken me some time to see that what we imagined to be Europe or European history is entirely misleading. Europe was never anything such as history imagines it. Europe was quite simply a colony, an internal colony to be sure. Its kings, princes, and lords colonized a peasantry whose history remains largely unwritten to this day, whose languages remain regional and vanishing because traditionally peasants were never allowed time to learn to read or write. They lived and died of forced labor, of providing the crops that would feed the aristocracy, the linen, cotton, and wool to clothe them, the quarry stone to build their castles and palaces, the cannon fodder to fight their wars. They labored to place food on their tables, empty their slops, while the lords paraded their power and magnificence into the grown-up fairy tales of history books. In some of the films of Olmi and Rossi, memorialized and celebrated, we rediscover their lost faces. The face of Jeanne, the servant who could share my godmother's given name but never her destiny.

We roam the moors of Ile des Moines, this small, cross-shaped island and its woods with names as romantic as those of Venetian canals: *Bois des Soupirs, Bois d'Amour, Bois des Regrets*. I join my friends on the first of these jaunts. The winds blow in from the sea and the Bay of Morbihan (Breton for "Little Sea") bringing storm clouds and promise of rain. We walk through the wild grasses of the seaward shore, braving the wind, the scattered raindrops. The trails take us through windswept meadows, stands of moaning trees, high places from which we scan the surrounding hills, steep terraces where we look out over the thatched roofs of the few Breton cottages here and there dotting the road. But I discover my hips cause me such pain during the next few days, I am no longer inclined to join the others. I stay at home reading. I have brought along Seamus Heaney's translation of the *Beowulf*, apt reading for these windswept shores. From the porch under the lash of storm clouds I watch the sea moods change. At sunset, the day decides to take a turn. The skies clear, the blue vault melts to rose at the horizon. And the sun makes its last play, casting diamonds on the restless waters. It's the eve of our departure. We outdo one another, transforming Françoise's leftovers into an evening feast. Tomorrow we will part ways. Michelle will return to Spain. With Marie Claude I will venture on to Paris.

Seen from the Paris autoroute as we speed by it on our way, Chartre's verdigris roof, its spires golden in momentary sunshine, must have prompted me. Once we arrive, my first impulse is to make my way to Notre Dame, Paris' ancient heart. Perhaps because my physical discomfort makes me feel increasingly unsettled, I'm looking for some anchor, something like home ground to center me. I take the familiar subway route, emerge through the art nouveau arches of the Cité station to limp my way past the tourist lines waiting to cram the Sainte Chapelle and on toward the rue du Parvis de Notre Dame. Something tells me this will be the last time I'll see its portals, gaze at its saints, its bishops, its humorless kings of France, its seven prophets, its monstrous devils aflame with glee as they pitchfork the damned—all clerics and princes of the earth, each one recognizable in his day—into their designated cauldrons. Aside from these devils, I find very little joy, or comfort in this stern orthodoxy. But central to these portals, next to Adam and Eve who cower in the shame of their nakedness,

Lilith smiles in the innocence and sheer delight of her lubricity, as appetizing as a '30s Pagnol heroine, the same Lilith one can see today bending over the zinc of any neighborhood café.

But I'm heading for the series of bas-reliefs in the side street, discovered on a previous trip, which, even though they have now been cleaned of their decades of soot, still mostly go unnoticed. It's their small-scale informality that draws me, especially the scene of the Virgin's birthing bed, not just because by Gothic times this quaint iconography had largely gone out of fashion, but because of its feeling of intimacy. Lying supine, Mary holds the child in swaddling clothes. Working people surround her, shepherds, animals, all share what nowadays is viewed as a private event, restricted to all but near relations and medical personnel. But here on this side street, its depiction is quite public. The feeling is real, down-to-earth, no doctor in attendance, no fuss, just the humble manger, a woman resting, the child placed in its mother's arms. A peasant birth, one the common folk, who slept on straw, could readily understand.

At the island's tip, I discover a crypt dedicated to those rounded up to be sent by Paris' Nazi occupiers first to the Vélodrome d'Hiver where they were kept for five days without food, water, or sanitation. It was a journey whose next stop would be Drancy, a way station on the road to Auschwitz, the concentration camp from which few would ever return. I let myself down the steps with some difficulty. Although I am visiting it only today, the monument's been here since 1994. The subject of its history is not unknown to me. My husband, now deceased, was born in Paris, Jewish son of Jewish parents, hidden during some years of his childhood in La Bourboule, "free zone," territory unoccupied by the army of the Third Reich. I read engraved on the walls the names of the deported. They are Jewish names—many of them familiar. Enumerating them becomes a kind of a pilgrimage of atonement for the taint of a race—the human one—of which I, too, am an uneasy member. At last I am ready to leave. I pull myself up painfully, step by step until once more the watchman lends me a helping hand.

More recently I chanced upon a site-specific performance work that joined movement, theater, spoken word, and music to present the history of the Japanese, over 100,000 of them, almost all American citizens, who were relocated to concentrations camps during World War II. As the performance began, four women appeared, moving in slow motion at the far end of the outdoor driveway which served as a performance runway. Each was dressed in the fashion of the '40s, each carried one suitcase. They were battered suitcases, held together with straps, the kind of luggage my husband had once carried when he left France for the United States in 1949. So much has the suitcase become for me the emblem of displacement that from the moment the performers first came into view I wept.

I first saw Paris through other eyes when, newly married, I roamed this city in the company of my husband and some of his close friends, exploring the Marais, gleaning from the very few medieval buildings left standing how this district—and much of Paris—must have looked in the Middle Ages, and adjacent to it, discovering the Jewish Quarter, where their mother, the family matriarch, Mamie Rodgold, still lived in the apartment the family had occupied from before the war. And as we walked, I heard our friends' stories: how Serge narrowly escaped the SS pursuing him by jumping on a Metro train, open on two platforms, in one door, out the other, just as the doors closed on his pursuers, allowing him to escape up into the street. When we came abreast of the Conciergerie, his sister Lucienne remembered how under the German occupation, it had been a staging depot where the Jewish population of Paris had been summoned to report for deportation. And later when we passed the offices and bookstore of France's leading publisher, she recollected a sign posted on the front door reading: "Closed to dogs and Jews." Much later, when I was to visit the Holocaust Museum at Auschwitz, I would recognize the names of all those Paris streets from our first walks: rue du Rosier, rue du Roi de Sicile, rue Bassano—from the most humble to the most exalted in the 16th arrondissement—on the dusty and abandoned suitcases of the dead.

Our every footstep that day incised my husband's history alongside mine. To my own history of the Harlem-Morningside Heights neighborhood into which I had been born I added another layer, that of Paris-under-the-occupation. I wonder now if all the blurring of American history isn't reflected in the a-historic numbering of our urban streets: One Hundred Twenty-First Street; Two Hundred Forty-Second Street of the New York where I grew up, Main Street of Charleston, S.C., where my first son was born. Americans don't have to discover who Copernicus was (rue Copernic in Paris, where the synagogue was bombed); they don't have to remember the battle of Austerlitz (or Bassano for that matter); they don't have to real- ize that a street named Chalmers—or for that matter Pennsylvania Avenue—was once the location of a market which sold human beings to other human beings. They wipe their history out block by numbered block through all their anonymous, undifferentiated streets. In some countries there are streets named El Grito, signal- ing that country's first cry of rebellion against colonial rule. In such a country the street of my childhood might well be named Street of the Bugle Call, yet if such a street exists nowhere else, it still lives in my imagination.

The afternoon is not quite over but the pain in my joints makes walking difficult, especially on the cobblestones of the Ile St. Louis. I take a side street where a hotel sign stops me short: Hotel du Jeux de Paume. Curiosity piqued, I peer inside the darkened lobby. To my astonishment, I discover what I suspect may be the last remaining 17th century tennis court in Paris. I mount the stairs, hoping for a closer look and a friendly seat to ease the clamor in my joints. A doorman bars my way. Alas! (*malheureusement!*) the lobby is reserved for guests only, and clearly *Madame*, with her nosiness and her pain-pinched face, is not one of them.

Happily, I *am* the guest of an old friend and collaborator from my theater days. Michel and his partner, Chantal, and Fidji, their cat of haughty and sullen disposition, live in the tenth arrondissement in a six-storey turn-of-the-century apartment house with a seventh floor tucked under the mansard roof, originally intended to house the influx of girls who migrated from the villages in the 19th century to serve as maids to the middle class families living on the floors below.

My friends insist on giving me their bedroom, a room lined with books, where I can live out of a much too congested suitcase, but my muscles no longer obey in their habitual way. I have to resort to giraffe-like contortions to get out of bed. Rolling on my stomach, placing both feet on the floor, pushing myself into a jackknife position, then slowly walking my hands up my legs and torso, I manage to stand upright. Every morning, Fidji, the drama queen of the household, watches my antics through the glass panels of the French doors. Ever the actress, her facial expressions range from perplexed to disgusted.

Michel is that rare animal, an intellectual-without-portfolio. His father and mother hailed from la Creuse, an area of France corresponding roughly to Georgia or Alabama. A good Saturday night entertainment might be pouring kerosene on an unsuspecting dog to light it up and watch it run. Come to Paris, his father found work as a butcher. His ambition is a fairly narrow one: "If I'd had your smarts," he tells his son, "I could have been a postman." As a ten-year-old Paris schoolboy, son of a tradesman, already Michel's been placed in a technical school track. But every afternoon on his way home, he passes the Armenian bookseller who keeps a shop downstairs. He presses his nose to the bookseller's front window. One day the old man steps out into the street.

"Which book do you like?"

"That one," points ten-year-old Michel.

"Very well then, take it home with you. And when you're done reading, bring it back. I'll trade it for another."

In school, Michel is assigned mechanical drawing. With compass and protractor, he labors over his assignments. When the instructor is less than satisfied, he smacks Michel on the knuckles with a convenient ruler, seizes the offending drawing, which he rips to shreds and tosses out the window. An unpromising start for an intellectual career, but by the age of 20, Michel will have completed his studies with Pfeiffer, chief exponent of a study called chromatology, whom he will join, teaching with him at the Sorbonne. But a year of its ballets and minuets are dance enough. He abandons the academic life to create an exhibition in a prestigious Paris gallery. "Bullet" invites the public to go wild over his collection of nearly 50 motorcycles variously painted in vibrant day-glo colors. Paris has never seen anything the like.

When I first meet him in 1975, with my company, I am developing an ensemble piece based on Kafka's novel, *The Trial*. I am working with Bill Young, a modernist composer who has been my collaborator since my company's inception in 1969. One day Bill arrives in the studio accompanied by Michel. I am struck by his generous head of wildly frizzled hair. His wardrobe, as I will discover, consists of an assortment of tops and pants (or for variety, jumpsuits) and high tops. These he mixes but never matches. The high tops might be pink one day, the jumpsuit orange and yellow. In San Francisco he is known in the outer Fillmore district where he lives amidst antique machines and rusting parts as "The Colors Guy." When he tires of a pair of obsolescent high tops, he tosses them overhead so that they hang suspended in all their vibrancy from a power line.

Michel reveres Kafka; he's eager to lend a hand to our enterprise. He joins our first production meeting. He carries a canvas student's bag from which he extracts notebook and pen, a reassuring sign. What can he offer? Well, for one thing, he knows how to design lights. He can create costumes. Our production concept stresses menace. Under his guidance we shop the salvage stores for survival gear. We buy bright orange hazard jackets; for the priest we buy a khaki rain poncho and a Coleman lantern. We buy respirators from emergency equipment stores, Plexiglas welding helmets, ironworker's spats. And we dumpster dive for junk. Our biggest coup is a near truckload of discarded cardboard tubes, castoffs from a yards goods store, repurposed as sound devices, and used by the suppliants as canes.

Besides designing costumes, Michel proposes improvisatory exercises in which the company invents a movement language for the scenes located in the bank. The actors become frozen automatons, springing to life randomly, with split second delays, moving always in straight lines, and always at right angles. Only one figure moves diagonally on this corporate chessboard: the janitor with his wide push broom and his cry of "Coming through!"

Evocative of Kafka's threatening world, Michel's light design makes use of flashlights, cigarette lighters, miner's head lamps, candles, lanterns, all of them hand held, although others, such as the blank TV screen, its blue light bouncing off a convex shoplifting mirror, will be controlled by a light board built out of many salvaged parts, some from his personal collection. It is housed in a large but portable wooden box that can be folded up and carried like a suitcase. Once we move into the theater where our final pre-performance rehearsals take place, he connects the overheads to it with zip cord. In the midst of rehearsing the office scene, the bank manager pulls on the chain controlling an overhead light. *Poof!* It's too dramatic to miss. *Poof* goes the zip cord, *poof, poof, poof,* little bursts of smoke at precise intervals of 2 3/4 feet. Transformed into a human bullet, Michel races along 90 feet of floor, vaulting the balcony stairs, cutting power to the light board split seconds before the traveling puffs ignite and blow it up.

In his fifties now, Michel makes his home in Paris, although for a number of years he returned to renew his visa—and our acquaintance. Each visit revealed a different facet of his many pursuits: one year, insects and the social life of insects, another year the face and the 18th century codification of stereotypical facial expressions associated with different emotional states. Through these past years, I perceive myself to have been the proverbial blind man, with each recurring contact acquainting myself with yet another facet of his prodigious curiosity, which like the fracturing of a geode, reveals the nature of the precious gem within.

Today is no different. The subject is Paris, time and space mediated by its streets, its buildings, its pedestrians, its smells, and flavors. Michel proposes our first stop this morning will be a surprise visit to the Empress (*L'Emperatrice*). He amuses himself by keeping me guessing, but refuses to explain. Finally he concedes, but only on one point. It's not really the Empress we are going to visit, so much as the Empress' dear friend and confidante, Madame Bourrienne, like the Empress Josephine, in exile from her Caribbean girlhood. We turn the carriage bell of #58, an ordinary looking building in a row of ordinary buildings on a rather ordinary street. We are admitted through the carriage door by a snobby factotum. Beyond, the sun-drenched courtyard reveals a country pavilion, *La Maison Bourrienne,* a small jewel of surprise. The factotum numbs us with stupefying verbosity—the high price we pay for admission—as he guides us through its mirrored *style Empire* salons and draped bedrooms. But Michel manages to ignore him; his attention is focused on the state of technology of the period, the mirrors, for example, indications of a period in which the technique of casting full-length plate glass was as yet unknown. And he's fascinated by the 19th century *hammam*, the salon of its time, where Madame could discretely lounge in a bath which concealed most—but not quite all—of her ravishing anatomy while entertaining the visits of however many ardent gentlemen might care to call of a given morning. And how clearly, there being no plumbing at the time, she expected the maid to carry pail upon pail of boiling water from the basement kitchen, up the stairs and across the courtyard to prepare the bath for Madame's more frivolous disportments.

"*Comment vont les pattes?*" Michel wants to know. It's my legs he's making light of, treating them like paws. "Why won't you visit a *toubib?*"

"Because doctors wouldn't know what to do." And I ought to know: I was married to one once. But curiously, although one would expect the day's rain and wet to affect them, the pain in my joints takes a perverse holiday, and a good thing too, because our walk will take us through the many districts of Paris, underneath whose misleading façades and threatening skies, Michel will point out a phantom city whose building corner stones hide their former names—engraved palimpsests of Paris' forgotten self—covered over with newly enameled plaques as little by little, the streets suppress their old identities as in Mexico, the churches mark the repurposed foundations of Aztec temples. Walking through them now, I'm overcome with a haunting of the past, of the throngs which may have passed through these thoroughfares, of events to which these blind facades still pay silent witness: the tumbrels with those dead of the plague, the execution carts, the burnings at the stake, the guillotining, the cries of revolutionary outrage, the great human drama whose voice has been silenced with the passage of time and by the distractions of a consumerist society.

Michel tells a favorite story of two reclusive sisters whose curious obsession to mark events in time shaped their collector's impulse. Following their deaths, their bureau drawers yielded nothing but egg shells, all carefully labeled "eggshell," including the dates of their original archiving.

We reach rue Montorgeuil. All along the cobblestone street eateries offer their tantalizing variety of smells; crowds flit from shop to shop, frenzied bees seeking the nectar of that perfect gastronomical flower. We agree it's time for lunch. We dine, sheltered from a momentary downpour under the terrace umbrellas of "The Flying Pig." Michel allows me a sampling—just a tiny one—of a crisp pig's ear swirled in tartar sauce, part of a tantalizing pork and sausage mixed grill billed as *La Tentation de Saint Antoine.* It's more than enough temptation to corrupt any St. Anthony—and his arteries—no matter how ascetic. But, no matter how distracting, none of these savories dilutes a conversation, which centers on a recurring theme, namely the less visible historical processes, which mark subtle shifts in the sharing of ideas. A case in point is the emergence in the 18th century of the daily newspaper, which provides the first possibility for instantaneous response, predating the blog (and the current newspaper collapse) by more than 300 years.

Lingering over after-dinner Armagnac, our conversation turns to what he calls *le pourrissement de la société,* literally the rotting away of the social order. He describes a documented incident of the late Middle Ages, foreshadowing the immolation of two towers some 600 years later, wherein a lord was forced to grant a charter to the commoners. But following an unfortunate fire storm which burned the town to the ground, and reassuring himself that the charter, too, had been incinerated, the lord felt free to take back each of his concessions one by one.

Our conversation lasts from its start in the promise of Paris' early morning sunshine, through the rain squalls of midday, to the rain slicked streets still a-drizzle following the afternoon's downpours; it continues in the gathering dusk with the lighting of the street lamps along the Grands Boulevards, which trace the ancient city walls, to the Place de la Republique with its monument to the French Revolution and its terrifying liberation, and through the 18th century district near the Porte St. Martin, where in passing we pay our respects to the Theatre de la Renaissance and the Theatre St. Martin. But we never again hope to see a theater such as the one we practiced long ago. Michel thinks the circus with its vast budgets and resources, may be one of the few places left able to address the poetic language of the archetypes as we once did—and perhaps skirt the banality that pervades our present cultural life.

During the twelve years I directed theater, some of it with Michel, I made visits to New York only very rarely. Whenever I dropped in on my godmother, she always asked me what kind of work we were doing, what were our projects. During those same years, my mother never asked me anything. Thirty days after my godmother died, we held a memorial in an apartment so very nearly empty we had to borrow chairs. Mostly women came, former students, colleagues, some of them from the old days, the few friends whom age had not yet silenced or deprived of mobility. And David, my life-long friend and long-time reader, now deceased. People told stories about my godmother's life, how she coped with despair when in 1942 at Toulon, French sailors scuttled their own ships rather than allow them to fall into German hands. That day my godmother went out to buy a hat. How, as a young girl growing up, more than anything she had wanted to join the theater, to become an actress, a path denied her by the strictures of her bourgeois family. That was the story that stunned me the most. It made me realize there were things I never knew about her. I understood in a way I never had before why she questioned me so eagerly about my theater work, how thrilled she was on the one occasion I showed her my portfolio.

Back in the apartment he shares with Chantal, Michel and I recall each twist and turn of our day-long conversation theme by theme, by following on the map those particular streets we traveled, starting from our visit to the Maison Bourrienne. But this day of walking, with its peripeteia of stories told one to the other by way of determining the exact page in this four-dimensional chess game in which ideas intersect with our passage through specific streets at established times (and weather changes), is finally about more than the sum of its generous parts. About even more than the disciplined insistence that questions themselves must be linked to the mind of the questioner, or about the notion of reciprocity on the part of the inter-locutor, whose ethical bent must be to help the other arrive at a more precise and conscious articulation; about even more than the historic memory emblematized by the story of two reclusive sisters who pre-serve eggshells in their bureau drawers—this day is a visit to that city of marvels, the labyrinth of my friend's mind temporarily open to me for a visit. There is no admission charge to this particular city that consists of side streets of listening and intersections of response. This day marks that rarest of joys—the nearly forgotten art of true conver-sation, that generous give and take in which two friends, beneath the dense and sometimes elaborate surface of negotiated ideas, partake in a deeply marked appreciation one for the other and of a friendship seasoned by time.

The weather has cleared. Perversely, the pain in my joints returns tenfold. It takes me a full week to summon up enough courage to visit the Louvre. If not today, I think, probably never. In the galleries, vast crowds press forward, flash bulbs ignite; like ants devouring sugar, her groupies attack the Mona Lisa in such numbers one resists the impulse to run to her defense. Against this onslaught, I hobble back and forth, zigzagging my way across the parquet corridors, seduced now by Da Vinci's Madonna of the Rocks where the Giaconda's enigmatic smile echoes once again, now by Mantegna's crucifixion, its opulent palette warring with its feeling of stark austerity, to stop at last, dumbfounded at the radiance of the Botticini Madonna in Glory, surrounded by cherubim and seraphim, soaring weightless for all eternity in a cerulean sky, the whole curtained in the trashy drapery of the cartographer's art! On reflection, such kitschy conceit may have been deliberate, Botticini's way of suggesting a celestial atlas showing off the Terra Mirabilis of a Madonna transfigured in glory, surrounded by her archipelago of angels.

From an unknown 13th century master all the way to Titian, my afternoon in the Louvre feels four centuries long, and nearly every bit as painful. The ache in my joints prompts me to collapse at the gallery's exit on the isolated chair placed there for the guards to take their rest. I sit motionless with my eyes closed. A young and very kindly attendant approaches me to ask if I am all right. I smile reassuringly. Of course I am all right! I want avoid thinking about what's happening to me, or at least defer the moment when, on my return to the States, I will have to confront what I can ignore no longer: my body's playing tricks on me.

I have barely enough energy to limp back to rue d'Hauteville. But when the turn of my key lets me in, the sight that greets me banishes all feeling either of discomfort or exhaustion: Chantal is pouring a cup of tea for Michel from a translucent porcelain tea service. They sit opposite one another, intent on each other, absorbed in their conversation, which inevitably my arrival interrupts. Will I have a cup of tea? Chantal wants to know. Very happily, of course I'll have a cup of tea. What more civilized way to punctuate an extraordinary afternoon? I collapse in the nearest chair, too tired even to remove my raincoat.

I raise the feather-light cup to my lips. The steam rises, its scent promising a faint suggestion of orange. The taste is tantalizing: a deep blend of black tea, a hint of jasmine, a soupçon of orange. "Why not take our supply back with you," offers Chantal in her generous way. "We'll replenish ours without a problem." I sip, pondering this idea. It's an appealing one. There's still room in my overstuffed suitcase. I fantasize the scent perfuming my clothes, pervading my possessions.

"No," I decide, "no." I want to remember the surprise of tasting Chantal's tea for the very first time. I know it will never taste quite as exquisite ever again. There is no way to repeat the discovery of the first taste, of the first time for that matter. *Never the same thing twice!* It's my Rule of One: one experience, one only. The same reason, if you've really allowed yourself to see the paintings, to let them imprint you, you'll never again be tempted to buy postcards at the Louvre.

One day before we are to leave for Avalon in the Morven district where my friends have a vacation place, I discover the Musée des Arts et Métiers. Housed in a former chancellery, a vastly imposing building in 17th century style, some four floors document the history of Paris seen through the lens of its early machines, its items of daily usage, many of them painstakingly and beautifully fabricated, objects such as barber's tools and the official scales and uniform weights mandated by the city for use by all its 18th century merchants. In the topmost gallery, echoing my accidental discovery of the only *jeu de paume* still preserved in Paris, a most spectacular surprise awaits. The 17th century supporting roof timbers are left exposed, their elegant ribs mimicking the inverted hull of an ancient galleon. In the annex next door, is a gallery housed in a decommissioned Gothic church. Its interior stone walls and pillars are painted, as such churches most certainly were originally, this one a rich ocher, with forest-green accents, stars gilding its midnight blue ceiling, and—nothing short of hallucinatory—hanging from its vault is a collection of mono-planes, fragile butterflies of the early 20th century, canvas glued to their wooden frames. Up an iron staircase, each landing houses one of the earliest motorcars. I'm curious to see if perchance my Swiss grandfather's electric car is among them. Displayed on the ground floor is a peepshow diorama of 19th century New York Harbor in which the Statue of Liberty—that much betrayed lady—occupies the central focus. All around are miniature models of Bartholdi's vast studio, demonstrating the various stages of the statue's manufacture. None are there to attest to her de-construction.

Derelict printing presses and carriages, caissons and early steam engines, shaving cups and coal-burning irons, engraver's tools and outdated retorts, all are reminders of life in the shops, the early fac-tories, the print shops, the laundries, and the streets. The afternoon and my limping gait leave barely time enough to explore a collec-tion which attests to the extraordinary vision of the museum's 18th century founder, the Abbé Gregoire, who recognized that the work of laborers and shopkeepers and engineers advanced human history every bit as much—and probably more happily—than the efforts of those who made wars, governed, or penned treatises.

Next morning I make my halting way along the Boulevard de Strasbourg to the Sebastopol Metro station to book my railroad ticket. All along the way, folks are making ready for Saturday night. Between the pedestrian stanchions lining the avenue poster boys thread placards announcing the battle of the bands—all African—from 8 PM to dawn! These folks know how to party! People swing by, chatting in any number of languages. Some sport native dress, flounces for the women, *boubous* and knitted Moslem caps for the men. A newly arrived young man calls to a woman in the street. "Hey! Your cousin told me you were here!" She turns. Dawning recognition. Great exclamations of joy, exuberant bursts of laughter. "Oh, yes, he told me you were coming!" Africa away from home, that's the Boulevard de Strasbourg on a Saturday. The windows of nearly twenty establishments display styling charts, elaborate braidings, Iroquois hairdos, all identified by number. Dealers offer wigs, postiches, hairpieces, extensions, many made of real human hair. In the dimly lit salons, clients submit to the ministrations of the hair braiders; friends and family, and even onlookers cluster to watch the slow process of transformation in the flyspecked mirrors of rooms painted a dim green. But here, in this neighborhood, beauty is a secondary pursuit. Not for nothing are these establishments referred to as parlors and salons. The easy familiarity of neighbor, cousin, once, twice removed, all engage in happy chatter, children doze, pressed against their mother's opulent breasts, their backs to the mirrors, succulent thumbs disappearing in tiny mouths. Nowhere is there hint of chrome, no one wears an operator's uniform. Over fifty people crowd into a storefront meant for twenty. Braiding is meant to be a shared ceremony. Around each chair, four, sometimes five people press, all deep in concentration. On the benches at the back, men in *jellabas* and turned up slippers bend forward knee-to-knee, exchanging jokes. Who needs Africa this morning when you can find home right here in Paris in this happy rubbing of skin, of elbow, this ritual grooming of hair? Down the street, at the entrance of the Metro station, more men cluster, gossiping, trading the time of day, waiting for the women to emerge. In this animated chatter are echoes of a more distant origin, the one they left behind to come here, the one they may not find—ever—if ever they return.

I take the station stairs one at a time. A catacomb of horizontal Babels, the joys—there are some—of the Metro would require a list as long and detailed as the moment-to-moment encounters of all the people—native and visiting—of its seven million daily riders, moments in which overheard languages can number in the hundreds, moments of verification (by the stranger) of correct directions, moments in which the affectionate exchange of two men (native) can echo from opposite platforms of the same (temporarily trainless) station, and where the performance of the Fifth Brandenburg, flawlessly rendered on marimba, comes to a close, its last harmonic fully decayed, just before the train alarms the station air with its oncoming clatter.

I am on my way to the old Jewish Quarter of La Butte aux Quailles, where Henry the Fourth went quail hunting when it lay well beyond the outskirts of the medieval Paris of his day. Mamie Rodgold receives me in her new apartment, located in the same *quartier* she's lived in all her life, one her youngest son, Serge, has bought for her. We've known each other from the time my husband first introduced us. During my last visit, some twenty years ago, she takes advantage of the intimacy of our meeting to tell me how her husband, the father of her five children, who plied his trade of a ragman, was deported, of his many letters to her written from Beaune-la-Rolande, the camp where he was held before his deportation to Auschwitz. "I'm doing all right," he writes to her. "Don't worry about me. Take care of the children (whom she will later have to support with the constant clatter of her foot-operated sewing machine). Buy yourself a winter coat." And she clasps my hands in both of hers, pleading for an answer to the question that has perplexed her all her life. "Madame Cecile," she says to me, "Madame Cecile, how can people do things like that?"—as if I, as if anyone on earth could provide an explanation for the deliberate genocidal mind that crushes whole populations as if they were the lowliest of vermin.

Today, wrapped in her years, surrounded by her family, still wearing her perennial sling-back canvas shoes, I find her as sheltering as ever. Her concern forgets no one. Lucid as always, this rabbi's daughter is the living repository of the visitor's and of her children and grandchildren's memories. She remembers each life's detail with surprising accuracy. She wants to know about my writing, she asks after my two sons, how old they are, what they're doing now, and this recital she will store in her ageless mind with all the other histories she keeps there. We cling to her as she does to time. Of all the many embraces Paris has to offer, this one of Mamie Rodgold, now one hundred years old, at an age where she describes herself as "*contente*," this one is the sweetest.

A cardboard mailer will arrive, postmarked from Paris. "Here's a work I've just had published." Serge sends me an odd-sized book, *Dear Edzia*. Until now, I haven't known Mamie by any other name. It's a compendium of the wartime correspondence between Mamie Rodgold and his father, Mordka Rodgold. Letters from Serge and his four siblings to their father, many of them illustrated in the naïve way of children, and their father's letters to them from the concentration camp of Beaune-la-Rolande from which he will never return. In the appendix, amidst facsimiles of carefully kept lists of death-train convoys, the Rodgold family tree is charted, maternal side on the left, paternal side to the right, in all 48 individuals, most with postage-stamp-sized photographs above their names. It's because there are so many family members to accommodate that the book is much wider than it is long. Of the tiny children, four met their death at Nazi hands. Of the 24 adults, 15 met their deaths in the camps. And of the oldest generation, six of ten met their deaths. All had left Poland for France, hoping for a better life, all were returned to Poland to their deaths. Below their names *assassiné à Auschwitz, assassiné en Pologne* reads their final destination.

Sunday, with Michel, Chantal, and Fidji, the family cat of cranky and jealous disposition, we board the TGV in the already sweltering heat of June on our way to Avalon, to their summer retreat on the steep hill overlooking the gorge which separates the town into sandstone (their side) and granite (the other side). It is a house acquired in a rare moment of prosperity and purchased very much on the impulse at the suggestion of a friend, without awareness that the plot stretches past the backyard boundary and up a sheer cliff face, and that maintaining it will become their responsibility and burden. The measure of the steepness of its incline is that the previous owner used to retreat to the cabin he constructed on the ridge to guarantee days free of the clamor of an overly zealous wife. Its garden is dug, spoonfuls at a time, out of unforgiving sandstone, the calcareous ground of the Morven region. It's a humble house, which overlooks the canyon road bordered to either side by the lush massing of summer green, where from first light to close of day, a clustering of songbirds celebrates the sun. What could be closer to the sound of paradise?

We spend the days roaming unfrequented pockets of the countryside, visiting its wealth of unique and decaying chapels, and eating the generous bounty of the local farms of Burgundy, drinking its wine. On our last day, we throw localism to the winds to visit the city of Autun and its great cathedral. The church itself has the dank, graying proportions of early Gothic, its tympanum depicting a severe Christ in judgment presiding over a hunched and shame-faced procession of the damned. Nine hundred years ago, attribution—and the cult of the individual artist—had not yet been imagined. Autun provides the rare exception. Its tympanum reads: *Ghislebertus hoc fecit.* "Ghislebertus made this." Inside, nearly three storeys above the line of vision the boundless treasure of Ghislebertus' twenty exquisitely carved capitals awaits. Martyred figures repose under the protective wings of gigantic eagles. Noah builds his little boat, ox and ass chew their cuds, warming a swaddled infant Jesus, Joseph leads Mary's donkey over a magical landscape cobbled in jewels as candied as Venetian glass beads, angels fall to earth in astonished majesty, devils skewer transgressors with well-aimed pitch forks, interlopers shake the tree of life, troubling Joseph's dream, and, oblivious of the laws of unintended consequences, an absent-minded Eve plucks an apple from the tree. Just as bee must breach petal's wall to reach the nectar's prize, so here, the strain of spectator, neck craned, taking in each image's stock; but without such effort, I wonder would these images yield half as priceless a reward?

On our way home, we stop to visit the little country chapel of Montreale, where the medieval order improbably known as the Giggling Fathers had its seat. Michel recollects the cautions of an early art professor to imagine these anonymous carvers of stone as they must have lived in the eleventh and twelfth centuries, robust, even corpulent fellows given to hearty eating, rowdy jokes, and raucous laughter, imbibing generous draughts of that deep red wine of Burgundy. Here at last we find them, in drunken celebration of the carver's art, these unknown masters, not just portrayed in a two-dimensional bas-relief, but boldly free-standing. Tiny Lilliputians perched improbably on the cheek of a choir stall, their chisels neatly laid out on the cloth, which only partially hides the saw-horse legs of their trestle bench. One reveler pours a generous draught into the tankard of the other. They sprawl in happy abandon at their tavern table, a hint of how the Giggling Fathers themselves may have earned their name.

On the eve of my departure, Michel and Chantal wine and dine me in a restaurant deliberately selected near the Place des Vosges to remind me that that's where Madame de Staël, essayist and literary light of revolutionary Paris, had her apartments. On the morrow they accompany me to the Gare du Nord, where my train departs and where we share a quick croissant and café-au-lait. How much I appreciate the warmth of this parting gesture, more especially because lugging a suitcase full to the brim with books, and packed with more clothes than I can possibly excavate deep enough to reach has become very nearly impossible.

My train is due in Milan six hours from now. I have plenty of time to consider my situation. Being unable to get out of a bathtub seems a rather trivial a complaint. Most of the time I am able to walk despite sometimes incapacitating pain. I deal with my growing weakness the way I usually deal with signs of questionable health: denial, and cheery optimism. Besides, I am in Europe. Three weeks remain with friends to visit, fun to be had, experiences, sensations, all of them more interesting than cooling my heels in some doctor's dim waiting room. Meanwhile I haven't yet given up faith in my own body and its amazing ability to heal itself. Even if there were some herb that could in fact cure me, certainly no doctor in Paris—or in Milan for that matter—would know what it was; and no pharmacy would stock it. Anyway, I want to put off being sick till I get back to the United States.

I am unsure when I first began to make the connection between the bites on my cheeks and hand and the onset of my debility, or why I assumed from the first that no visit to a doctor would be of much use, perhaps because I don't know the first question to ask. All the same, I can't help wondering, could this be Lyme disease? My symptoms mimic what I know of it: arthritic pain and joint stiffness, except my bites don't show the typical bull's eye pattern normally associated with tick bites, and I know something about ticks because I make my home with a large German shepherd, close to open country overrun by deer. But if not tick bites, what sort of bites are they? The culprit must have been an insect. But what kind of insect? A scorpion, perhaps? Maybe this is not the place to think about it.

We're not halfway to Milan, more than enough time to ponder the domestic situation back home in the U.S., the curious way people around me—myself included—are behaving, and not behaving. In the streets, people's eyes no longer meet. Any criticism of the government or its wars is dismissed as unpatriotic. People relate to one another only as it seems to serve them. Once service is rendered, communication dead ends. Casual visiting, getting together for hikes or walks in the park become quaint anachronisms.

People work, mind their kids, shop, stay locked in their houses watching the brainwash box, clinging to it now more than ever perhaps to shore up any wavering certainties. Congress announces implementation of the TIPs program, which encourages people to report their friends and neighbors for "suspicious" behavior. Overnight, cameras mysteriously proliferate at road intersections. Recorded messages stridently repeated on the BART platforms urge passengers to report any suspicious activity to the station manager. Where does one report suspicious activity when it emanates from the halls of power?

During the first days following 9/11, most perplexing to me was the discovery that at least one of my presumably pacifist friends heartily supported attacking Afghanistan, despite what already seemed obvious to me, namely Afghanistan's proximity to the Caspian oil fields, not to mention the unmentionable: its high-value opium crop. And even more to the point, Afghanistan had nothing to do with it. Weren't those presumed "hijackers" supposed to be Saudis?

I couldn't help remembering the time I waited for a plane to take me back to Bangkok after a day spent visiting Changmai. At the airport, I opened my bag to change some baht.

My purse was empty, all but for my passport, my airplane ticket, the numbers of my vanished travelers' checks, and the 80 baht I'd need to catch the airporter. Everything else was gone. Then I had been stranded in an unfamiliar country with no resources other than my wits. Now, adrift in Europe, I feel as though I am entirely on my own, living a sinister reality where the state through its media corrupts language, where people act more and more strangely and there's an elephant splashing in the bathtub, which no one wants to see. Tucked away in my backpack, the passport I carry reads United States, but it's the passport of a country I no longer recognize.

Heat. Stifling heat. The sun glows a sickly orange through gray, miasmic smog. As my train nears Milan, the city seems to squat in a graceless hollow, collecting the industrial smog of Italy's industrial north. Da Vinci's ferocious mosquitoes breed in the canals he engineered just to the north, waiting, season after season, to administer their coup de grâce to a smog-trapped population. The train doors disgorge me into the steam bath of Milano Centrale, onto a platform sticky with melting asphalt. The feeling is utterly surreal—as though I've landed on the moon. I can barely maneuver my suitcase and my own body through air thick as tear gas, but the press of passengers hurries me along. Striding toward me through the crowd to rescue me is my old school chum, Marianne. I recognize her loping gait, unchanged from the time the two of us raised such Cain in our good

Catholic high school where the two of us made news as the best students with the most deviltry in our veins. She learned her repertoire of tricks in Utah where as a child growing up, she enjoyed sticking lemons up the exhausts of July Fourth holiday paraders and watching their cars stall before leaping forward and nearly crashing into the ones in front.

She hasn't changed. Tall, strapping with her American good looks, long teeth and horsey laugh, I'd spot her anywhere, even though as she likes to put it, it's been "donkey's years." Each of us in our way is the poster child of good Catholic family propaganda. Each of us married, although with her nine children she outstrips my own record by seven. Her children might have something else to say, but my sense is that she's done amazingly well by each one of them, supporting their search for a life work with her steady encouragement and her keen appraisal of each one's unique gifts. Now that all but one has left the nest, her vast Milanese apartment echoes with empty bedrooms along an endless corridor.

"Come on, old thing," she urges me. All efficiency, she grabs my bag. I have all I can do to stagger after her to where she's parked the Fiat. She's all chatter as she slices her way through the choke-hold of Milan's rush hour traffic. The years have not damped her energy. Home at last, she shepherds me into the ancient lift and up we go.

She insists on installing me in the master bedroom with its 15-foot ceilings and its shutters clamped tight against the stifling heat. During the ten days I spend with her, we live in a penumbra morning, noon and evening, bargaining for a cool, which never comes.

It's not an easy stay. She's got her writing and although school is temporarily out of session, she's got a load of courses to prepare. I'm left to negotiate the subway system, to make my way along the wide boulevards and to the Piazza della Catedrale and the post office where I return the key I've mistakenly purloined from Michel's and Chantal's Paris apartment—an unconscious gauge of how much I wanted to cling to their welcoming hospitality.

The nights bring momentary respite, enough to allow Marianne to emerge from her bedroom, and to permit us the rare nocturnal prowl. On one such occasion I accompany her to a feminists' potluck. All evening, one woman dominates, swept up in her own rococo oratory, co-opting anything the others may have to offer. We eat, the orchestra of our knives and forks the only counterpoint to her self-conscious speech.

Another evening we connect with two of Marianne's friends to ride the streetcar line, ending at the canal district. Caroline brings her son along, a clamoring 11-year-old, and the self-appointed companion/guardian of his mother. He is dressed for the sweltering Milanese summer in floppies, sleeveless T-shirt and shorts. We sit in a tapas bar overlooking the canal, drinking beer, watching the fire-eater performing for the diners on the terrace outside. Caroline chain-smokes, monopolizing the conversation, interrupting herself from time to time to sip from her rum cola.

"Ma," her son tugs at her elbow.

Caroline carries on, affecting not to hear.

"Ma," he tries again. Caroline hardly pauses to draw breath.

"Ma!" he shouts.

She turns to him. "Yes, darling," she says, "mother's talking. Mustn't interrupt."

Outside the fire-eater has been joined by a juggler. A crowd begins to gather. I excuse myself for a breath of air. Inside the air is stifling, but outside the mosquitoes wait, biding their kamikaze time.

On the return tram trip, the others sit in front, attentive to Caroline's on-going monologue. I sit in back with the eleven-year-old.

"Budgies," he confides. "I have budgies, two of them. They're so sweet," he says. "When I call to them, they come, they sit on my arm, and when I take them in my hand, they feel so soft. Tweet, tweet," he says in his budgie voice. "They know everything I say."

Another evening after dinner, we hike for miles. Marianne wants to visit a neighborhood where she has been told her father used to take her on outings as a child. She hopes that by seeing it she will be able to recollect a past of which she has lost all memory. But Marianne is tall, her stride relentlessly energetic. In my acute discomfort I have trouble keeping up.

"What is it?" she asks me, frustrated by my inability to keep the pace.

"Probably arthritis." I don't elaborate. But is it arthritis, I wonder—or something even worse?

Next day we decide to drive north to Mantua. Tearing up miles of roadway in suffocating heat, we reach the Gonzaga Ducal Palace just after noon, only to be stopped from entering by a cluster of striking museum guards. "Come back after lunch," they advise us with a shrug, "the strike may be settled by then—or maybe not." Over a terrace table we linger over our garden salads, our pumpkin ravioli, buying delay and political correctness, but by the time we are ready to brave the heat to stumble back over the cobblestone streets, the doorway gapes open; there is no sign of any guards, or for that matter, any strike. Perhaps they've gone to lunch.

Today, in the absence of guards assigned to every room, we are allowed admission only if we promise to tag along with a group of tourists being herded by two guides loudly declaiming explanations clearly learned by rote. This palace complex sprawls with miles of corridors, connecting rooms, private apartments—even a hanging garden, much of it closed off to visitors. Deliberately we straggle behind. Once safely out of sight, we're free of their tyranny. In the great hall, Marianne conks out on a marble bench for an after-lunch siesta while I explore roped-off anterooms and stairways, their every wall and ceiling decorated by painters who in their exuberance did not shy away from color. Our freedom allows us to linger way beyond the usual five minutes allocated tourists admiring *la camera degli sposi,* the bridal chamber, crown jewel of Mantegna's art. Its proportions are small by palace standards. A fresco shows well-fed cupids floating a bridal inscription in midair. On the opposite wall, the Gonzaga clan, some fifty of them, pose in haughty profile, except for the family dwarf who stares directly at the spectator (as in life people probably stared at her), apologizing neither for her wrinkles, nor her apparently cranky disposition. To the extreme right, a hawk-nosed finance minister catches the duke's ear: money is to be squeezed out here, payments (perhaps to the artist) withheld there. Family retainers—even the children—sport the hose colors of the clan, left leg clad in red, right leg evenly divided in sides of blue and white. A small child attaches himself, two fingers held in a tutor's hand. All these details are carefully recorded by an artist who senses how his subjects breathe, lead lives that, however exalted, are marked by the dailiness of their routines. None displays any interest whatsoever in the spectator, neither of his century nor ours. None dramatizes an event, or an emotion. But each seems animated by some inner reality. Their faces attest to the seriousness of their purpose. That sense of inward self-sufficiency marks Mantegna's portraits more than that of any other painter. But for my taste, the most exquisite is the side panel depicting a white horse poised in a mythic landscape, against a sky the painter must have brushed with powdered cobalt. It might as well be a miniature for its jewel-like quality, although it takes up an entire wall.

On our way home, we discover a buffet offering a supper perfectly geared to our flagging summer appetites. It's the only time Marianne will allow me to treat her. We dine outside on the terrace watching the Romanesque façade of the Cremona cathedral turn to rose in the waning rays of sunlight. Back on the autostrada, miles of sunflower fields stream past us, straining to catch the last rays of the setting sun. If ever a flower could be said to possess a human face, I think it is this one. At one time in my small San Francisco garden, kissing one on the tips of its seed-pods seemed to me not an unnatural thing to do. Flower, angel perhaps, I half expected it to speak to me in a human voice. I imagine what it might have said to me. Now, homebound, speeding past these fields, I sometimes catch them fanning their straight rows at us. But the best fields are those that hide the ordering of their rows to offer the uninterrupted glory of their crowns, turning whole fields to gold in the setting sun.

It's my last day in Milan. The temperature gives no quarter. Nonetheless, we drive to the Sforza castle, a huge enclave, its inner courtyard the size of a football field or very nearly, already pulsing in waves of morning heat. Posters marking each of its many entrances advertise the various displays concealed behind the looming doors of its apartments. We chose the picture gallery. Half-heartedly we shuffle through a largely indifferent collection, but, happy discovery, hanging on one of the gallery dividers is an early Mantegna. The focus is a Virgin Mary in glory. She is depicted in an uncharacteristically sentimental style, one that, for Mantegna, is still clearly derivative. But grouped in the foreground, each one of the angel-musicians seems to be listening to some unheard music, absorbed in an inner life which, as in Mantegna's much later portrait of the Gonzagas, will become the characteristic signature of his art.

Back outside, we pass a reproduction of a popular 17th century "story board," a checkerboard depiction of a world turned upside down, its imagery meant to titillate the descendants of those same folk who must have gaped in wonder at Ghiselbertus' fiery angels and lowlife devils, their tongues protruding, giggling maliciously. In my viewer's ear, the singsong notes of the storyteller's refrain echo over the centuries, and, just for a moment, my eyes follow the teller's pointing stick as one by one he chants each image's cautionary rhyme. Here a pig roughly barbers a client, there a horse kicks a stable boy in the ribs, to the left a pair of sheep guard two humans cropping grass, and central to it all, those who are invisible and voiceless get to have their say.

Early the following morning, Marianne drops me off at the train station. I take leave of her, saddened by the feeling I have not been able to fully reciprocate her week-long hospitality, although she's given me scant opportunity. The memory I prefer to keep has her happily poking her head through the balusters on the third-floor balcony on Fifth Avenue where we attended school, craning her neck to see our physics instructor's car stall before lurching forward to expel that lemon from an exploding exhaust.

The ride north to Chiusa/Bressanone takes four hours. The tracks follow the Adige River, now edging alongside its meander, now crossing and re-crossing it. The river shapes the topography of this valley with its cover of espaliered apple trees, of young grape vines, at places so densely lush, they conceal the ground from view. Each vineyard is staked in its own distinctive way, some with an attention that surprises with its artfulness. In the far distance to either side of the tracks, great upthrusts of granite conceal distant valleys rising to yet higher peaks, interrupted briefly with a stretch of basaltic cliffs before the train starts its slow climb to nearly 5,000 feet. Along the way, villages fan out over the gradual rise of the valley floor. Here and there, at Avio for example, castles rise, or monasteries, their grounds enclosed by crenellated walls. The last lap, from Rovaretto to Chiusa, passes through a long stretch of tunnel. When at last the train bursts free, I scan the hills to the west where the starkest of towers rises on the steepest peak. How could anyone possibly get up there? And yet my first suspicion is confirmed: my friend Therese, graphic artist and painter, keeps her studio there.

It has been a lapse of some 18 years since we've seen one another. "I will meet you at the station," she writes. "It is a very small station [this Bressanone whose former Austrian name is Brixen]. I will have my dog Mira with me." I have no difficulty recognizing her: tall, her dark hair now cropped short, and I wave an exuberant greeting from far down the platform where my second class coach deposits me. Despite my limp, we run toward one another. Mira leads the way. I offer her my hand to smell.

Therese is not the sallow-complected, chain-smoking tea drinker I remember from my summers spent in Upper Austria nearly twenty years ago. Now her skin shines with coppery health. Today there are warm hugs and embraces. We toss my suitcase in her back seat, Mira waddles aboard, and we back away from the station on our way to Chiusa. The road winds along a high mountain terrace, through enchanted forests to cut through a long plateau of vineyards where at last we come to a stop in the shade of a branching adder. From up here we see clear down to the valley floor, some thousand feet below.

We walk the remaining quarter mile to Kloster Saben, the convent in whose complex Therese has her tower. The hike is steep, along a roughly cobbled mountain trail edged by a newly installed iron railing: too many people, some of them nuns, have broken too many arms and legs sliding on the scree. At its highest reach, the ground levels off, and the path switches abruptly to the left, leading to the convent courtyard where a fountain bubbles to cool the weary traveler. Its bronze bas-relief portrays a row of tiny figures from all walks of life rowing toward the spigot where one of them, overcome by thirst, strains to catch the stream from a spout quaintly bigger than his head. Therese knocks on the convent door. A sister opens. She wears the pale blue scapula and winged headdress and guimpe of her religious order. Her nose and part of her cheek show the marks of a cancerous lesion, but she greets me and extends a welcoming hand. Her smile is utterly serene. Therese leaves me outside while she and Mira pass within. After some time she emerges, small milk can in hand. We leave the enclosed courtyard with its rosy chapel dedicated to St. Michael whose refulgent statue occupies a corner niche. At the end of the rise a richly flowering garden appears over the wall. At last we reach Therese's tower. It forms one side of a walled enclosure, rising four storeys above ground. The entrance walk curves through Therese's front yard where astilbe, peonies, hosta and primrose crouch in the shade, while snapdragon, poppies and larkspur raise their spears of color to the sun. It is hidden from the outside by a no-nonsense wooden fence (on which a beware of dog sign threatens ferocity in three different languages). On the far side of the enclosure, another garden, this one with lettuce and tomatoes is edged in wattling, the kind of fencing in use since—and probably before—the Middle Ages. Here is the plainest but most refreshing fountain of all, one under whose tap we will soak our heads tomorrow after our steep climb up switchback after switchback on our return from our early errands in the town.

On our arrival Therese offers me two generous helpings of her homemade soup. It's the best soup I have ever tasted, full of home-grown ingredients, but she saves her best surprise for after lunch. We climb the steep staircase leading to the top storey of her tower. The entire floor is open space, suffused by light and air. Four enormous windows, an improvement funded by state subsidy, open on opposite sides allowing a view of the hills and valleys beyond. "I can't wait till summer," she says, "because in the winter it's too cold to paint up here:

the wind whistles through the cracks." And indeed, here and there sharp streaks of sky glint through the wallboards. One wall provides easel and display space. The fourth wall provides stairway access and storage space. Two large drawings of ocean surf occupy the easels.

Therese has been studying animals, birds, water, rocks, glaciers, all natural formations ever since I have known her, prizing open their secrets. Her re-naming of these things is her way of being in the world, of deep listening to its messages, as if in her own particular way, she's reaching for the heart of things. From time to time she paints solitary female figures. They used to occupy a central place in her figuration, as did lovers busy with each other, but now, gradually, these figures have become pretext for the study of pure light—and of darkness—these shipwrecked figures of solitary women, offering themselves to a distant dawn, their hands open, perhaps in supplication—because, as she remarks, you cannot have light if you do not have darkness also.

In all this beauty, of art, of landscape, and of place, it is Therese herself who shines at its center. She is beautiful with her savage cheekbones, untamed hair, decisive nose, and the slight droop of one eye. Everything seems to come from her hand—this steadfastness to draw things that by her own assertion people won't or cannot buy because their starkness frightens them. I photograph her studio and the view of the distant Dolomites. And despite her reluctance, I photograph her, too, posing in her east-facing window, in her studio and in her garden. But when much later the film is developed, I discover her image is absent.

Like everyone, Therese hangs by a thread, but without the distraction of western civilization's toys. She has no cell phone, no television, no CD player. But her house is lined with books. There is also a refrigerator and a washing machine, and food, things she did not always take for granted, and the food is almost all of it grown by her own hand. There are no cigarettes, no wine to speak of, but there is *Most*, traditional in Upper Austria, a drink she distills from pears. Before lunch she offers me a shot glass—real firewater that tastes more like plum brandy than anything else.

Her village friends still visit; they help her move her furniture and her heavy engraving press up improbable mountain paths, up the four flights of her tower; they're strong enough to help her sledge-hammer the stakes around which she weaves her wattle fencing. She has friends with whom she gardens and with whom she shares the abundance of her harvest, and friends who, after their hard work, liven her tower with all the songs they still remember from their village life until—in her words—they make her tower sigh with its own tower-y happiness.

Hers is perhaps the most perfect existence I know, distilling the meaning of things through her art, distilling her pears to make *Most*. The way, accompanied by her stone-catching dog, she scrambles down 1,000 feet of steep terrain (and back up again) to swim in her own swimming hole, soaks her head in the refreshing spring water of the fountain after her hike, serves us lunch on the picnic table outside her door, sheltered by the chestnut trees from the slight spring rain, prepares the chanterelles she gathers in the woods in the cream sauce from the milk she makes into cheese and yogurt, flavors the salad grown in her own garden, a garden enclosed behind the wattling her friends have helped her build.

On our afternoon walk we fill the gaps in these now 18 years. I know her through my long-time partner, Peter, who believed so much in the power of her art, for seven years in Austria he rented her his house for $25.00 a month. We exchange stories of his hapless misadventures. All the years we were together, he made no promises, no declarations, nothing that would hold me down, just the straight every day stuff that love is made of. Unique among my friends, he could voice outrage at the sinister policies of an out-of-control government while his well-behaved Latvian friends still imagined a two-party system was all the glue needed to hold a democracy together. He was a European, as he constantly reminded me. Five years later, he was on his way, back home to Latvia, the country of his birth. In the United States he had nothing to speak of, but with the exchange rate, back in Latvia he discovered he was rich. Generous to a fault, he invited me to spend two weeks to introduce me to his country. It was my first experience flying over the pole.

"I don't know when we'll see each other again," he said to me as he saw me back to my plane. It was the most he could permit himself.

Toward the end, with his friends I sent him medicines and egg-crate bed lining to ease his final illness.

We are survivors, Therese and I. She reminds me how fortunate we are: free to paint or write what we want, go walking when we want; we don't need to answer to anyone. And unlike me, as an artist and citizen of Austria, she benefits from life-long state support. It's a country which can afford generosity to its artists: war is not a foreign policy priority.

On our last morning together, she takes me to the station to catch the train north, and although we hug good-bye, we leave any thought of future reunions unsaid. I'm on the last lap toward my final destination. Past Bressanone the track climbs through the steep, snow lined sweep of the Alps, through Innsbruck, Salzburg and finally to Vienna. But by the time I arrive, given the pain in my hips, any urge to sightsee is a thing of the unimaginable past. Viewing Vienna from the ring streetcar is enough to tell me that its architecture for the most part, is a welter of pompous, baroque, pretentiously ornate buildings, which hold no particular interest, certainly not for me.

The conference itself is an informal affair. I can participate in the routines expected of me, and present an up-beat attitude despite growing discomfort. I accompany my colleagues on the expeditions that the organizers plan, taking pains to disguise my limp. On one such outing we pass Vienna's waste disposal plant with its Lego smoke stack designed by that jokester Hundertwasser, his way of poking a rebellious finger at the pinched-up Vienna skyline, and despite my trouble walking, I'm compelled to make a special detour to the workers' housing complex he cobbled together out of what look like giant toy-chest rejects. For the rest, all stiffness and respectability, still slumbering in the *schlag-mit-gemütlichkeit* of Franz Josef's heyday, Vienna is a city I am happy to leave alone.

I want to head home. The evening before our departure we sit at the outdoor terrace of a decaying hotel watching the sunlight set on the towers of the Votive Church; with two other women colleagues, we order a glass of wine to accompany our simple, but perfectly seasoned meal. Sheltered from the clamor of the streets by a hedge of flowering oleander, we enjoy a feeling of harmony and affection. We don't want anything from one another, we are not looking to impress, academically or otherwise, we are engaged in simple conversation, free of considerations of professional rank, ethnicity, race, or economic situation, of the many ways in which people like to trap each other; no barriers exist, only humor, the freshness of spontaneous talk, the lively meeting of glances as we seek one another out. Each admits to being weary of the road, the churning of wheels, the tramcars, trains, and airport taxis. When the time comes to say good-bye, I feel a twinge of regret: these women have their friends, their family, and their partners. I'm left feeling empty and very much alone.

My 747 flies over the pole. It is a route I first traveled on my way to Latvia and back, some six years ago. Then, from five or six miles up, I discovered that glaciers are rivers of ice, that the parallel crests of crevasses meeting the shoreline at 90 degrees means that these rivers flow toward the sea where they calve so many icebergs it looks like a regatta of tiny white sailboats floating on a white sea. Now, on July 1, 2002—only six years later—Greenland looks like the leeward side of the Sierra in May: brown to purple earth, dusted with remnants of snow on its highest peaks. The great flowing glaciers are no more; what's left of their crevasses stagger toward the sea in rows parallel to the shoreline, the last, exhausted melt. No longer white, the sea can't reflect the sun's heat. Dark wounds yawn, hallucinatory, turquoise, and wide as the Great Salt Lake.

Critical note: When someone asked James Joyce, one of the 20th century's most iconic writers, what he was writing about, he replied he was not writing *about* something. *He was writing something.* That's the difference—a big difference as it turns out.

So far what you read here shows itself to be a writer's memoir, a reportage *about* daily occurrences, intercut with reminiscences, primarily *about* my godmother, and laced through with other associations, some of them writerly, but evoked at the time or place of journaling. Tying it together is the unifying—and suspenseful—theme relating to the onset of a mysterious illness, a theme to be developed in the ensuing section, "Hip, Hip but Not Hurrah." The rubbing together of both elements yields a kind of tension, and lends dimension and some relief to what would otherwise be a flat—and boring—narrative.

Two more journaling sections follow: *about* dancing a devil's minuet with the medical profession; and *about* a love affair, one that ends in an unexpected climax, a turning point where a new kind of writing can begin, in this case a section of oral histories by people who shared them with me. However interesting and poignant they may seem, similarly to everything that came before, it's still pre-writing, preparation for the Real Deal still to come. **But although the eventual climax and what follows is the place where it's still *about* something, it's also the *transition point* where it's no longer entirely *about* anything. It's on the way to *becoming the thing itself. Of becoming an event.***

In the difference lies a huge distinction.

2

Hip, Hip, But Not Hurrah

I come home to the neo-United States, to a one-storey ranch house overlooking a steep canyon, which belongs to the water district. When I buy it—in a misguided moment—I do so with the understanding no other structures can ever be built on the slope below. My view clear down to San Jose will remain wild and undisturbed. A huge pine, my totem, frames the landscape. I ignore more practical matters, such as the roof, which is flat, and poorly designed for drainage. It doesn't help that the realty sales lady swears it's just been re-roofed; I don't have to have it inspected. It will prove to be a thorn in the siding so to speak, requiring re-roofing and re-leveling to provide the drainage its two interior spouts require. As I work in my study, I can hear the rain cascading through the walls.

I had not intended to buy this house—I imagined living in Berkeley—but it was what I could afford. It's a rather ordinary ranch house, with an extraordinary view perched as it is on the highest ridge overlooking the bay. The front door opens to the morning. The light up here is spectacular, with a particular kind of luminosity, especially in the afternoons. The feeling inside is of a country house; the lie comes from seeing it from the frankly suburban street, a *cul-de-sac*, which I share with thirteen neighbors with whom—with one exception—I will always feel as though I don't quite belong.

Now I share it with my younger son who's returned to California following his father's death. I'm fortunate to have two separate bedroom-bathroom suites—room enough to offer him a home and privacy for the time he needs to stay. Its architecture is unremarkable; it's the outdoors that distinguishes it—its 75-foot deck overlooking the canyon, the woods, and the bay beyond, the miracle of light reflecting off the water in the afternoons—a painter's light. When I move in, Algerian ivy and iceplant cover the slope, but the iceplant will soon freeze during an exceptionally cold spell, leaving me with a 100-foot sloped terrain in which to develop a garden, a project I begin after nearly eight years of neglect. I come from a New York City world of public park forsythia and sumac trees. What do I know of gardening, or landscaping? Two years in, it has become a passion that complements my writing, offering the chance to do hard physical work, and to discover the relationship to soil and the miracle of seeing things germinate and grow on a slope which erupts with color from early spring to late fall: the stunning blues of Pride of Madeira; drought tolerant sages, lavenders and yellow artemesia, the gradations of blush to red and purple of penstemon, the sparkle of white daisy-chrysanthemum, candles of white foxglove; groupings of pale daffodils, and rows of purple iris that edge the stairs leading to the stepping stones below.

Critical note: I am using the **transition** in the paragraph above to do the prescribed task of **locating** the reader, establishing time, place and character to allow me to get to the garden slope where I happen to be weeding:

As I stoop on the steep slope weeding, alerted by my groan, my son notices my limp.

"What happened to you?" he wants to know.

"Something bit me. In Spain. I don't know what."

He studies me silently. "You're not the same," he says. "You shouldn't have gone."

The time has come to see a doctor. Although I am among the fortunate 80% of Americans to be enrolled in a health plan, my HMO physician refuses to see me. He prescribes a palliative over the phone. It has no effect. My joint pain intensifies, the tendons in my groin turn hard as rebar. I made another attempt. A substitute examines me, orders a routine screen for Lyme disease. The result is negative. I request another primary care physician, this one supposedly highly recommended. "Something is seriously wrong with me," I tell him. He doesn't seem to assign my complaints much more than routine importance. He insists that my chronic cough indicates acid reflux. He prescribes Tagamet, which I do not take. It's only when I resort to a shameless show of tears that he refers me to a rheumatologist, who opines that at my age, I can hardly expect to have 25-year-old hips. However, he allows that seeing hip cartilage disappear symmetrically and at such a rapid rate does seem rather puzzling. I am referred to an infectious disease specialist who diagnoses Parvo B (normally a dog's disease).

"Show me how you walk," he orders. I oblige down a length of corridor.

"You don't walk like that," he decides. "You're exaggerating."

The tedium of this diagnostic carousel occupies some six months, during which both joint pain and cough show no sign of improvement. The problem is compounded by my sense of futility. The more exhausted I become, the less able I am to advocate on my own behalf. By now I am limping painfully and using a cane. I have even paid the shoemaker to raise one of my soles to compensate for one leg feeling shorter than the other. A neighbor, who happens to be a physician, catches sight of me. She recommends a visit to her own rheumatologist. His report to my primary care HMO physician is fairly explicit: whatever is the matter, it needs to be taken seriously. He refers me to an outside physiotherapist.

I am now in non-HMO-approved territory: the meter has begun to tick. The physiotherapist, who is a marathon runner, identifies my cough. "You have asthma!" she declares. She refers me to her (outside) allergist who makes the diagnosis, and who prescribes asthma drugs. It gives me exquisite pleasure to relieve my primary care HMO physician of responsibility for my care.

I'm walking on the beach with my hiking partner. I've been telling him I have no idea what might have bitten me. It's an autumn day, warm enough to lie down on the sand for a quick nap. I have a dream. I see myself lying face down in the sand. The backs of my legs are covered with welts. On awaking, I tell him my dream.

"Spider bite," he says. "It had to have been a spider."

I discover that the Department of Health has a local vector unit with provision for human, insect, and animal bites. I check "insect." I talk to a Mrs. Hui, who listens to the recital of my symptoms (and who suffers from Lyme disease herself). She agrees that my symptoms suggest Lyme, which normally develops from contact with ticks, but that if nothing else, it should be ruled out—spider or no spider. She provides me with the names of three local physicians who know how to treat it. Overwhelmed with his case load, the first is taking no new patients, the second agrees to put me on the waiting list as number 149. The third is located 50 miles away. He does have time to see me, but beforehand with the lab kits he provides, I need to have blood drawn and samples sent to the only lab in the region which conducts in-depth tests for Lyme—a disease which can be caused by bacterial infection, and/or three possible parasites, or any of the four in combination. The meter is still ticking.

My HMO will not draw blood samples—this testing is unauthorized. I have to find a local unit to draw my blood. The technician is a burly Scotsman with spectacular mustaches.

"If it's a spider-r-r that bit you," he confides, "it's not good news. Spider-r-r-rs like to r-r-r-reduce their pr-r-r-rey to soup, the better-r-r to digest them."

The results are negative. I keep my first appointment 50 miles away. Dr. Davidson takes a look at me. He asks me a few questions. His diagnosis: arthritis and asthma brought on by autoimmune collapse. He puts me on a restricted diet: no wheat, no corn, dairy or citrus. No sugar of any kind. He prescribes enzymes and dietary supplements, and a regimen of daily saunas to sweat the toxins out. Some of my former energy returns, a renewed sense of well being, but the pain continues without let up, day and night. On a subsequent visit, I ask him how he made his diagnosis. He ascribes it to my appearance of complete exhaustion.

He is not alone in his assessment. I am running errands in Berkeley accompanied by my son. We pass a travel agent advertising "Cheap Cruises." I am quite categorical. "That's something I will *never* do." But one should always exercise caution saying "never," particularly when one is slowly turning into soup. Exactly twenty-four hours later, my physician neighbor invites me to join her on a ten-day cruise. She's got a ticket her Alaska-jaded husband doesn't want to use. Now I am faced with a dilemma: do I eat crow or stick to my convictions? "Give me twenty-four hours," I tell her, but the temptation is undeniable. The ticket is mine for the taking, there will be no financial outlay to speak of, and the "fringes" are ten days of being cosseted, fed at whatever hour I may desire. I can even catch some rays on deck, cocooned against Alaska's chill in a deck chair blanket. But the ultimate bonus won't be discovered till we board ship: the sauna is exclusively mine, allowing me to sweat to my heart's content. Although I am friendly with my neighbor, we do not yet know one another as intimates. When I ask her why she thought to invite me along, she says I look exhausted.

In short order I become the darling of the Indonesian dining staff who, convinced that my strength is not adequate to the task of carrying its piled up bounty, insist on hefting my lunch tray to the nearest table. I watch the social rituals of the cruise set, their aging bodies swathed in dress-for-dinner finery. I sample—however briefly—the evening "shows" just long enough to satisfy myself that they're tailored to appeal to couch potato tastes. One evening provides an interesting exception however: a variety show presided over by one of the ship's pursers (British), whose condescending commentary introduces each (Indonesian) act. Where have I experienced something like this before? It comes to me with a rush: a minstrel show. Watch the darkies strut their stuff. And isn't it cute? The folks seem to think so, and the jokes (both the purser's and the Indonesians' who indulge in self-deprecating debasement of their own) are tailored to play to the audience's ethnic snobbery. I am on the verge of walking out but the next act stops me cold. It's a masterful solo performance of a Balinese Legong, normally danced by young girls, but performed now by a deck hand. Not only is the level of execution flawless, it presents a stunning female impersonation as well (received by the self-conscious audience titters one might expect). Paradoxically, it turns out to be the only authentic artistic offering of the entire evening.

However, searching out the performer to congratulate him is no easy project, mainly because several deck hands share the same name. At last I am in the presence of a tall—and very masculine—young man. I complement the grace of his performance. Where, I want to know, did he learn this dance? "In high school," he answers quite matter-of-factly. What if American high schools gave female impersonation instead of ROTC?

And I learn what arctic melt sounds like. Even four storeys up on the observation deck, I can hear the plaintive crackling of the ice, the bubbling which accompanies the final break-up of the smallest particles as they yield up the air they may have trapped for hundreds of millennia. And, trailing us, I notice the dirty brown cloud, which seems never to lift as we plough our course, causing the very glaciers this luxury cruise allows us to admire to dissolve *like snow melting into water* for the very last time.

From the time I accept the probability of my hiking partner's diagnosis, I find myself talking to people about spiders on the assumption that the conversation may prompt useful information from other people who have either been bitten, or who may know of someone who has. One day my on-board lunch companion is a middle-aged woman who somehow doesn't conform to the five-hot-dog lunch culture that seems to prevail around us. When I describe my misadventure, she tells me that six months after being bitten by a brown recluse she was diagnosed with leukemia. Hers is one of two stories, which lead me to realize that spider bites have the potential to maim, and occasionally to kill.

In the evening my cabin-mate and I share a table with an elegant Black gentleman who keeps a garden full of roses. To my delight I discover he's a career entomologist. He is quick to identify the spider I once observed in my garden as an orb weaver. I tell him my story. He describes the two known venomous species found in the United States: black widows, and brown recluses, sometimes called fiddlers for the inverted pattern on their backs. Later I view their images on the internet, including the necrotizing bites of the brown recluse, but my inquiries to Spain produce no additional information. There is no way I can identify my culprit. When people ask me the nature of my nocturnal visitor, I admit we were never introduced.

During the year I learn to dance the HMO cha cha, I see some 15 practitioners to whom I preface my medical history with what I consider to be the precipitating cause of my condition: *I was bitten by an insect.* But curiously, none seems able to hear my claim, although my primary care provider allows that the simultaneous bilateral disintegration of my hip cartilage over the next six-months can't be explained by osteoarthritis alone. But the one very simple idea, name-ly, that I was bitten by an insect somehow eludes these gentlemen; it's not part of their diagnostic reference. I might as well say what I have to say in Greek. Why is this, I wonder? Why are they not able some-how to process this particular piece of the puzzle? Is it that they are indifferent to matters of cause and effect? Or is it very simply that I am perceived as dismissibly female, and what's worse, a superannuated female while they are exclusively male, basking in all the splendor and absolute certainty of their medical authority?

Critical Note: Physical collapse—and collapse of the Ship of State, and of a society—are not exactly laughing matters. Here's where a little comic relief in the guise of wry **humor** helps the medicine go down.

What does it feel like to be turning into soup? It's nine months since the spider bit me. The meter reads four thousand dollars and still climbing. But I have little time or energy to give very much thought to what's happening with my body. I'm much more focused on the grow-ing clamor of war, the barrage of war propaganda in the run-up to the "preemptive" invasion of Iraq, the abrupt shift in the way I see people estrange themselves from themselves and from each other.

A day before the Iraq invasion, we stand on Market Street in a soft rain, my hiking partner and I, holding stretched out between us a soggy 60-foot-long butcher paper banner whose 5-foot-tall letters spelled out the words: "Don't you dare, George..." large enough for the swarm of news copters whirring above Market Street to read. Familiar with history, unlike most Americans, we already know Afghanistan—and now Iraq—to be the "graveyard of Empires."

Next day George dares. Idiot boy king, figurehead of the Pentagon's endless Saturnalia, feet swimming in his father's outsized cowboy boots—boots embossed with the seal of the President of the United States—the son soon outdoes the father who memorialized his own presidency with its signature atrocity: the "highway of death," where convoys of Iraqi troops fleeing the Kuwaiti border were slaughtered by the thousands, incinerated alive in their own vehicles, the same father whose fire-bombing of Baghdad signaled the most expensive—and destructive—munitions commercial in human history.

The Masters of War don't care; it doesn't trouble them that in over 800 cities across the world some 36 million people march to protest the war policies of the United States. Baghdad was slated to be carpet bombed, its museums looted of its 5,000-year-old antiquities, legacy of a civilization that introduced cuneiform writing, that gave the world the first known legal code, the Code of Hammurabi, while the triumphant conquerors stood by. "The best way to revitalize the economy is war," a solicitous George is quoted in "South of the Border" advising then-President Kirchner. In the midst of Argentina's cratering economy, Kirchner received the boy king's confidential tip. "The United States has grown stronger with war."

Even before the Afghan invasion, I was on the lookout for activist groups with the kind of organizing potential to which I could lend my energy. In April of 2002, the alternative media brought news of a massacre in the Palestinian village of Jenin, buildings blown up, some with people still in them, the Israeli "Defense" Forces (the IDF) on a killing rampage, its guns and tanks (fronted by the United States) against Palestinian stones, slingshots, and the occasional home-made rocket.

A demonstration was called, its location the monolithic Oakland Federal Building, a twin-tower knock-off, the five-storey atrium a shuddering pastiche—cold, marble, prison-like functionality—an organ of the State. Along the front walk, young folk, agile as coconut pickers, shinny up the lampposts, lashing banners over the walkway below: NO U.S. ARMS FOR ISRAEL. (In fact, Congress has passed a law that all the arms the U.S. gives to Israel are not to be used against civilians—a law, which doesn't seem to deter the IDF—or the United States.) At the foot of the atrium, locked to its supporting marble-faced pillars, some twenty protesters sit silently. At the conclusion of this exercise, police will appear to saw their lock boxes apart. Above the echoing sound of talk, one single melody hovers in the chill air, amplified by acoustics, which normally are meant to alienate. But these cadences are Arabic. They loop, they arabesque until the air becomes one single cry: Jenin, Jenin, Jenin, over and over—lament for a city destroyed, no stone left upon a stone, a melody as twining as Arabic calligraphy, so beautiful it stabs the heart. I learn the name of the singer, and where the group meets. At my age, I've given up lamp-post shinnying, but my search is over.

I join six months prior to the invasion of Iraq. It's an organization which is as yet without a name, but which meets in the same space from which the lamppost shinniers originate. The people participating have certain things in common. In appearance they are a backpack toting, cyber-savvy crew, well educated, highly articulate. I see them as able to move easily from one place to the next. They are as scruffy as they are mad about the administration's war mongering. Many of them have track records in protest organizing. Present is Starhawk, one of the organizers, who a week earlier organized a shut down of the San Francisco Federal Building, an action which turned into an all-night vigil.

Although my condition is steadily worsening, I attend weekly. My first assignment is to create a 50-foot-long "river of blood" for a demonstration in protest of Chevron and its depredations in Nigeria, at the same time making the connections between oil, America's current resource war, and the hydrocarbon pollution accelerating planetary collapse. I discover a 50-foot-long, 99-cent remnant of red rayon fabric which mimics the properties of the finest silk! My enthusiasm knows no bounds. I sew two channels at opposite ends, thread bamboo battens through them. My "river of blood" can now create waves by two protesters waving it from opposite ends.

As the rush toward the next war intensifies, our group continues to meet; sometimes there might be only four of us, sometimes 15 or 16. At one sparsely attended meeting I am one of three charged with planning a "day after" strategy for shutting down the city the day following any attack on Iraq. We begin drawing maps. What centers of power should we target: Corporations? Government buildings? My suggestion: the "Federal" Reserve (the central bank, and not a part of the federal government despite its misnomer) which determines and manipulates monetary policy and of which we will learn more than we care to know following the crash of 2008.

At one meeting the chair asks me to phone someone who wants to join our as-yet unnamed group, but who is out of e-mail contact. And that is how Ted joins our meetings and sidewinds into my life. Although it's only September, he's wrapped to the eyebrows: watch cap, fleece jacket pulled up above the chin. The effect is of a human pillbox: just his eyes show. Otherwise, he's remarkably unnoticeable. At the very long table where we meet, he always sits at the far end, diagonally from where I grab a seat, usually just inside the door because I manage to slide in just as the meeting's getting underway. Some people are like land mines. They sit quietly in the ground a month, a year, but not a lifetime because they're designed by their maker to explode on contact. But for now, Ted stays quiet as a turtle. There's no way of knowing that we have a Claymore in our midst.

Critical Note: The Claymore 18A1 is a model name for a land mine named after a Scottish sword. I'm using it here to lay in the groundwork for the explosions which are still a long way off. The turtle image mimics the Claymore's shape. In this sense, the mine symbolizes Ted's explosive character, and as such it acts as a **metaphor** for a secretive Ted himself.

I'm really galvanized the day one of our colleagues announces she has permission from the founder/director of the Bread & Puppet Theater, Peter Schumann, to use his designs for the 9-foot-tall puppets his company displayed at a recent demonstration in Washington, D.C. Just prior to the outbreak of the student rebellions of 1969, Peter Schumann touched my own artistic life when the San Francisco Mime Troupe presented The Bread & Puppet Theater as part of a Radical Theater Festival at San Francisco State.

I'm deeply moved to be able to catch this faintest of creative waves as it reverberates back towards me over 30 years' time, through eddies spread world-wide by the genius of Peter Schumann's work. Our puppets will represent Iraqi women bearing their dead children in their arms. We decide on seven to maximize visual impact. We call our affinity group the Mourning Mothers in honor of mothers everywhere whose children have been sacrificed to war. When I revisit the yard goods shop, source of my "river of blood," I discover black remnant yardage 60 inches wide, from which I cut exactly—with not one inch to spare—seven veils and seven chadors with which to costume the giant masks we will collaborate—some 15 or 16 of us—to create. I have scissors, sewing machine and a dining table large enough. True to my way of seeing, the Mourning Mothers are meant to be.

We schedule Mourning Mother work parties. We come up with a pattern for the cardboard armatures on which to build the giant heads. On these armatures we hot glue smaller cardboard pieces to define eyebrows, noses, and the thick mouths, which lend the faces their distinctive iconic aspect. Mask maker Toni Pellegrino, and Lauren Elder and Sydney Carson, as well as many other performer-collaborators work with us. The biggest challenge stumps us at first: what kind of underlying structure will permit someone to wear them? At last one of us, Paul Cotton, offers the solution: inverted tomato cages, which we will bend and pad to allow people to wear the masks more comfortably, but given that once inside, the visual field is narrowed to only what the mouth opening allows, the wearers will need a contingent of handlers to assist them.

All the while, in my own bloodstream a hitherto undetected phenomenon reveals itself: elevated readings of alkaline phosphatase. It's not even clear whether the source is in the liver or in the bone. In hindsight it occurs to me that the mystery of what was going on in my bloodstream mimics the occult activities of the Ship of State because, although we won't know it for some time, in that same September of 2002 George invites all members of the congressional intelligence committee to a secret administration torture briefing in which it became official government policy to be applied in all secret, or black sites, including those located in cooperating eastern European countries, Poland among them, and Egypt and Syria as well. The invitation carries its own poison pill, guaranteeing that the Speaker of the House and all other congressional members accepting it will, by their very attendance, become complicit and incriminate themselves, such that when they are called upon to exercise their function of congressional accountability, they will successfully have been muzzled. From that point on, impeachment of this stale cuckoo presidency would be off the dinner menu. Torture—and all its attendant disgrace—will become national policy. It will fall to the next administration a scant eight years later to up the ante by embracing a policy of targeted assassination, from which not even American citizens will be exempt.

What to do? With my hiking partner and some others we start bannering over the highways. We have access to a vast auditorium where we lay out 60-foot lengths of butcher paper. With sponge mops and paint we lay out our message: NO BLOOD FOR OIL. At first we rely on hand held signage on a traffic overpass. We need some four or five people to stabilize the vertical battens. We confront morning rush hour traffic coming from as far north as Sacramento. Trucks honk, cars honk. Some give us the finger. One driver leans out of his car window to shake a fist. He rams into the car in front. We know it's time to leave—right now!—before the highway patrol shows up.

We rethink our mechanics. We design a more sophisticated system of grommetting-cum-bungie cords, which allows us to hang a banner and take a hike. No one needs to stand for long hours inhaling car exhaust, and if the highway patrol spots the banner, they can't do anything until Caltrans shows up to take it down. With this system, we can't be routed when we've barely gotten there. My cohort takes off leaving me sitting on an inverted caulking tub, minding the banner. By then I can hardly stand and I certainly can't walk.

I'm in pre-surgery mode, half dozing in the soft light of morning. The traffic rumbles under me 60 feet below. In all I think, it's good to be here, the sunlight on my face. There are worse things. I could be in Baghdad or somewhere in Afghanistan being shot at, bombed with depleted uranium ordnance, or detained and tortured. And yet, we are one flesh—all humanity—one flesh held in the fragile amnion of the earth's womb. What wounds one, wounds all. What maims one, maims all. There are choices to make other than killing and being killed. A jovial policeman ambles up.

"Take it down."

"Excuse me?"

"You'll have to take it down."

I smile up at him from where I sit on my caulking tub. "You know what? I can't even stand." My helplessness wins the day. The banner stays through rush hour.

I look forward to these protest outings. There's no way of knowing when we start that we're in for many more years and still counting. The friendships forged this way are every bit as binding as the bonds formed in the course of making theatre, and in a sense it's a performance with some similarities. My partner is a generation younger than I. I love playing Maude to his Harold. And occasionally we reverse roles.

Our best adventure is many years down the line. We pick our overpass, target the evening rush hour. NO BLOOD FOR OIL. We position our grommets. No use waiting here; we go off to have dinner. We linger over dessert, enjoying one another's company. The banner's been up nearly two hours. If our calculations are correct, the transportation folks ought to be showing up about now. We drive the short distance down to the highway, and as we're parking we catch sight of the Caltrans truck pulling up on the other side. We get up onto the overpass just in time to stop the road worker slicing through the first grommet. He helps us take the banner down and neatly roll it up.

In the run up to war, Ted begins allowing us the privilege of seeing more than just his eyes. His silences give way to growing exasperation. He doesn't want to participate in any "day-after stuff." He demands, indignantly, "I thought the idea was to stop the war before it starts. Where are the arrestables?" I take to joshing him with "been arrested yet?" And true to his stated purpose, he does bottom-line a shutdown of the San Francisco recruiting station. Young colleagues half his age, who know tactics better than he does step up to the challenge. Their action is successful. They all get arrested and released; all charges are dismissed.

Spurred on by *New York Times'* dinosaur diva Judith Miller, a sycophantic press claims Saddam Hussein possesses weapons of mass destruction (which he once did: it was the U.S. which supplied them to his Baath regime). By his alleged harboring of Al Q'aeda operatives, he is accused by the administration of responsibility for the fall of the twin towers (and the mysterious collapse of Building 7). Under the Orwellian rubric of "preemptive war," the mounting deluge of media propaganda makes it clear that a U.S. invasion is imminent.

In response, our anti-war meetings expand into ever-larger borrowed spaces to accommodate many more affinity groups besides the Mourning Mothers. One of these meetings is given over to reaching consensus about giving ourselves a name. Lists are drawn up based on membership suggestions. The choice narrows down to two options: Direct Action to Stop the War; or Direct Action to Stop War. It doesn't seem possible, but nearly 200 presumably intelligent people spend over two hours determining the difference between a name which includes a definite article—or not. Eventually we agree by consensus to drop the article. In retrospect, their deliberations appear prescient: we are now in year 14 and still counting, of what appears to have become endless war. Henceforth we are known as Direct Action to Stop War—or by the acronym DASW. Just prior to the invasion our numbers grow to 200, then 300 attendees. In the crowded union hall in which we meet, I try giving up my seat to the only member of a religious order present (whose civil disobedience arrests number in the hundreds) who is very nearly my own age, but happily for my hapless joints, he declines. We are the only two elders present.

We conduct our assemblies as spokes councils. In a structure dating back to the Spanish Civil War, the assembly chamber is organized like wheel spokes. Although there may be hundreds present, such a procedural framework allows decision-making to take place in an orderly and time-efficient way. The meeting is usually chaired by two facilitators at the center of the circle, one who keeps track of the agenda and calls on people to speak, and one who outlines discussion items on a white board. Each affinity group sits in pie-wedge formation with one, and only one, authorized speaker who sits at its apex at the inner circle. Within each group members may caucus with each other and/or with their designated speaker, but none but the speaker is sanctioned to interface with the larger assembly. The "spokes," as we call these meetings, allow the entire body to arrive at consensus either through agreement or, if there is "blocking," discussion may continue until consensus is reached.

As the race to war takes on momentum, we focus our attention on orchestrating the details of what we have always identified as "Day After." Perhaps for this reason, Ted no longer attends DASW meetings although I still do. The rallying time is fixed for 6 AM the day after the invasion begins. The location—an old holdover from our first discussions centering on the Federal Reserve—is to be Justin Herman, the enormous plaza at the foot of San Francisco's Market Street, just above ground from the Embarcadero BART station. Greeters will pass out menus, expressly mapping that day's events. Intersections are designated by letters, buildings by numbers. "Waiter!" they read, "there's a war in my soup!" The menu lists the various "courses" members of the crowd may choose to "order." People may wish to report to an appetizing intersection to block it; they may like the ensalta mista offered by "Knitters for Peace" blocking a designated department store. For a main course, they may wish to express more pointed revulsion for the horrors of war by joining "Pukers for Peace" on the soon-to-be slippery plaza fronting the Federal Building where our pearl-chokered Madam Speaker keeps her headquarters.

Welcoming them will be the brash and sassy Brass Liberation orchestra, known by its acronym BLO, tubas bristling in the sunshine of an Ides of March day. The entire event is designed to be as much an exuberant celebration of the joy of living, of creating art, as it is to be a cry for peace and a condemnation of war and the death culture it represents. There are bikers for peace, and skateboarders for peace, and rollerbladers for peace. Some affinity groups will choose to be stationed in one place, others will prefer to roam from site to site. In the great plaza, greeters will continue to hand out menus throughout the day. It's the downright coolest party any of us ever saw.

Already in January, as part of the huge pre-war demonstrations (one of many) in which millions of people the world over protest the approaching invasion, the seven Mourning Mothers make their debut. Widely photographed, our image is televised throughout the world, garnering more coverage than any of us performers and theatermakers ever enjoyed in the sum total of our performance careers. Spurred on by our success, we develop a ritual. The puppet handlers solemnly lift the dead children from their grieving mothers' arms, and to a funeral drumbeat, we lay them one by one on the burial shroud of the US flag, and sometimes the flags of complicit nations, including the Union Jack, which a zealous police makes sure to prevent us from delivering to the British Consulate. We discover a way to involve the crowd by distributing flowers, which the onlookers are invited to place, stem by stem, over the tiny corpses before we fold them in their winding sheet.

We do not need to carry signs or words of explanation. It is for the people passing silently, pausing for a moment, to confront a reality, which each one sees slightly differently, to react to the scale of these nine-foot tall, black-clad images of mothers cradling the bodies of their dead and mangled children in their arms. Recognition is reflected on the faces of all the thousands of protesters who stop to witness us in the course of the multi-block-long marches. Through their narrow apertures the large mouths of the puppets allow us to see their expressions of undisguised grief.

Our puppets continue to appear on many occasions following the invasion, but as my walking becomes increasingly difficult, my role is limited to acting as a handler. By the time the mothers appear at a rally at the Oakland Federal Building, I am too sick to be able to help at all. When the dead children are laid to the ground for burial, I am no longer present to witness the lone Black woman who places the framed picture of her own son, shot by police in the streets of Oakland, on the burial shroud beside them. Or to witness her tears.

3

Love and War

Although the manipulations of peace activists are seldom as devious as those of governments, on occasion they modify the course of things. One of our colleagues confides to Ted that I'm a "famous Mexican novelist." To me, she allows as how Ted is translating an Aztec pre-contact codex, the *Cantares Mexicanos*, from the Nahuatl. Ted bites. Will I go out with him? At first I am all huff and puff. We run, we stumble, but at last we fall, and despite our shared social backwardness, we manage to go out together. A brief reprieve, all the more poignant for its brevity, the freshness it brings in the midst of darkness, my own, the world's. The fragile closeness of human beings. Momentary consolation for the enduring pain of living. A freak of time called love.

We've been four years without partners. We can't stop talking, spilling four years of stored up silences, all the richer for being long dammed up. He's a poet, living the life of a poet in his narrow sunlit room, like me a Luddite: no television, and in his case, no computer. We discover the pleasure of walking together in the tree-shaded streets of the neighborhood in which he lives. We share the excitement of what we discover, what we read, what we think, and as we travel these streets, our minds range over continents, over centuries of time. We share each other's writings, we haunt bookstores, we read to one another. As he types his translation of the *Cantares Mexicanos* occasionally he shares some of the songs with me. We discover many affinities besides: a love of insects, of the natural world, of poetry, of Blake. We're both given to a kind of secular Buddhist practice; our politics hew to similar lines. Even our true names possess similar sounds to the point where one day he declares quite casually: "I like to think that somewhere when some force in the cosmos first called our names, we both turned our heads."

From the start Ted shows the edgy signs of what I come to recognize as genius. He describes the moment when, not much older than two, as he played with a red truck in the mud, it dawned on him there was no reason for the mud to be there, or the truck, or even for his own small, solitary being. If human beings were required by law to play 15 minutes a day, to romp and skylark like children, he would have no trouble suspending his anarchist beliefs. He collects stones. Sometimes he will pause over a collection of river stones in someone's front yard and take great pains before making his selection. He will carefully place it in his domestic décor. He collects abandoned cell phones, carries one pushed deep in the recess of a pocket. Along the heavily trafficked streets we elbow our way past folks hurrying in and out of stores, cell phones glued to their ears chattering their GPS chatter, declaring where they imagine themselves to be, where they hope to get, and how soon they intend getting there. When we were a great deal younger, we knew for certain that folks like that who babbled in the street had something wrong with them. We still adhere to that quaint notion. Ted whips out a dead cell phone from the recess of his signature cargo pants, flips it open with a flourish.

"Hello? Hello? Jennifer? Is that you? The WHAT? The dog did what? Are you telling me...? Oh, your mother is going to be very, very upset, Jennifer. No, this isn't the first time.... Jennifer, you know you're not supposed to.... You didn't tell me that. Jennifer. I don't know what I am going to tell your mom..."

I play along, the disapproving mother, the disillusioned house-holder. We don't miss a beat.

Of all his qualities, most of all I'm captivated by his ability to play. It will save my life quite literally although there's no way I can know it yet. For now, what dispensation to embrace and to be embraced! In love, one rediscovers the beauty of the world-made-fresh. The scales that blind one drop away to be replaced by other scales. But while it lasts, the ravishing perfection of every leaf, every flower reveals itself. Despite the war and its horrors, at home spring flowers pay no heed. Everywhere the streets seem to explode with color. Our footsteps fall more and more lightly as our walks take on the enchantment of paradise. Words become caress. But for Ted and me, there's only one—one very precious—season. By now I'm walking bone on bone, doubled over, leaning on two canes, my nearly two inches of hip cartilage having all but disappeared. In the park, a small girl stares at me, horrified. "What happened to you!?" she gasps.

"You never saw a lady with four legs?" I laugh. "I got old and my legs got funny."

She knows she won't ever get old, but all the same she turns her head to stare long after we pass each other on the grass.

"We have been unable to save your hips." Following my primary care physician's verdict, at last I gain access to appropriate treatment—from a woman physician who knows how to listen and who feels comfortable saying, "I don't know." Later I will learn that the magisterial procession of specialists to whom I've originally been referred are top of the HMO list for expertise in arrogance. But after all, I'm one of the lucky 80% of Americans who have health insurance, and there's no reason to quarrel with it. Not even when one is slowly turning into soup.

Ted accompanies me on my visits to the physiotherapist. We discuss hip replacement. "What are you waiting for?" my physiotherapist wants to know. At last I am referred for surgery. The problem is which hip to replace first. Originally, the left is scheduled, but as the intervening days pass, the right degenerates even more rapidly, and the plan gets reversed. To strengthen my compromised muscles, an intensive exercise regime is prescribed. A ski champ in his early life, Ted is still very much the athlete. Now, less than a year after we meet, he volunteers to become my trainer. During the six-month pre-op period, he walks with me every day over the hills and sand traps of the local golf course—a low impact surface. He spends hours and days coaching me, encouraging. Low-impact water walking is prescribed. Ted takes me to the neighborhood pool. He gets himself rubber swim shoes to walk alongside me. He times me: five, ten, fifteen minutes. Up to one half-hour daily.

When we're not training, we're reading to each other. He introduces me to poets I have yet to discover: Cornford, Espriu. We sit on a bench, reading Llamazares' novel, *The Yellow Rain,* the author's lament for a dying village not unlike his own. A *New York Times* review calls it "a bitter, poetic elegy for a lost Spanish town.... Though he lives in Madrid, Julio Llamazares was born in the now-vanished town of Vegemian, a heritage that probably spawned the intense emotion that pours from *The Yellow Rain.* In this profoundly somber but moving elegy he explores the last days of a ruined, deserted village high in the Spanish Pyrenees."

We alternate. Ted reads in English. I read the Spanish. We uncover the liberties the translator takes to honor fidelity to the rhythms and feeling of the Spanish turns of phrase. I discover a novel whose tragic reverberations will come to be reflected later in my own play, "Like Snow Melting in Water," which I will set in contemporary agrarian Japan.

No matter how harmonious, our idyll can't defend against reality. On March 19, the U.S. invades Iraq. It's very clear to us that the government has embarked on a disastrous course. We know enough of the history of that part of the world to know that the tribes of Iraq and Afghanistan have never suffered military defeat. We recognize the stress lines, drawn over centuries between the Islamic and Christian worlds, lines evoked once again by the administration's deliberate framing of this invasion as a "crusade." The "day after" has arrived. Much as I want to roam the entire San Francisco downtown area to partake of the liberating chaos, I am in no condition to contemplate walking any great distances in my present state. Slowly and patiently at best, I manage to accompany the Mourning Mothers as a handler. We station ourselves behind the front lines where people who have locked down blocking the intersections will eventually be sawed apart and hauled off in the paddy wagons. After a time, we move in slow procession to another location. Our calmness and silence provide a welcome counterpoint to all the wild animation of the streets. At a certain point, when wearing the heavy masks becomes too exhausting, we pause in the shelter of a commercial entryway to exchange wearer for handler roles. To our happy surprise, some of the firm's employees welcome us inside to refresh ourselves. Then it's back out in the street once more. We move uptown as far as the Tenderloin where, before exhaustion overcomes us and we finally break up, a speeding fire truck deliberately attempts to run us down. I discover that, despite the pain that has reduced my gait to a hobble, I still remember how to run.

With all the millions in nations throughout the world marching in solidarity as early as February 15 a new force is born; humanity shows itself worthy of the company of poets. To be among one's fellows, part of the great chorus of humanity turning out in the millions in places as far away as Kuala Lampur, Jakarta, London, Paris, Rome, Madrid, Berlin—as Saint-John Perse writes: *"One great wave throughout the world...one great wave throughout the world,"*—that raises its great collective voice for justice, for peace, for love and reverence for all living things, is perhaps as close as any of us may ever come to the joy of seeing paradise on earth. But the glory—like all glory—is short lived. With each new presidential signing statement, constitutional violations proliferate unchecked, either by a complaisant congress or the outrage of popular resistance.

During this time of war and rumors of war, my Alaska cruise neighbor receives a couple of visits, the first by someone in plain clothes, who rings her bell, and failing to identify himself, asks about me by name. The second from a person identifying himself as a member of the Oakland Police Department, who, despite the recent proclamation that the City of Oakland would refuse to cooperate with any program of surveillance by the Department of Homeland Security, asks her what she knows about the people living in our cul-de-sac. On both occasions, before closing the door on them, she lets them know she's not in the habit of talking about her neighbors.

Regardless of any chilling effect her report may have, I continue leafleting and bannering over the highways for as long as I can walk. My last two outings are to support two days of protest outside the offices of the INS where persons of Middle and Far Eastern extraction are being swept up off the streets, some of them to be disappeared: Iranians, Palestinians, Iraqis, Jordanians, Hindus, Sikhs, Arabic speakers, Farsi speakers, Pashto speakers, much as generations earlier, my husband's friends and all the Jews of Paris were rounded up to report to the Conciergerie. But the seven-block walk from the Montgomery BART station to Washington Street takes me more than half an hour. Soon my condition and my upcoming surgery will force me to join the twilight of my sleepwalking fellow citizens who conduct business as usual, whether we shop, talk on our cell phones, listen to our iPods, brainwash our heads with our planet-polluting plasma TVs. Whatever noise we fill our days with, it will not be protest. It will not be resistance. And by default, we will be sanctioning whatever horrors are done in our name. It will take the Crash of 2008 to wake us up, but not all of us, not even then. Despite Congressman Phil Sherman's 2008 claim that to pass the "bailout," Congress had to be threatened with martial law, most of us won't even realize the government has made us and the economy victims of a monumental heist.

In the course of many years of street activism, I have encountered the repeated skepticism of disaffected people who argue that protest is a futile exercise. "What good is it?" they ask. "What difference does it make?" I have come to think that, although outcomes can never be predicted, in the great karmic soup, nothing is ever lost. I am not among those born to remain silent; I feel an obligation to myself and to all beings to advocate for their dignity. As the great historian A.J. Muste said as he held a protest sign outside the Pentagon: "I'm not under the illusion I can change my government. I just don't want my government to change me!"

But if my ideological principles are non-negotiable, my body is quite another matter. I've always imagined that somehow it would maintain itself in its original condition without ever having to undergo invasive surgery of any kind. My unwillingness to consult a doctor, at least during my time in Europe, stemmed not just from a false sense of invulnerability, but from what I saw as the futility of such an exercise. I couldn't imagine that a Western-trained doctor would know what to do for a venomous insect bite. Ironically, it was not until several months following the onset of my illness that a friend put me on to a book titled *Energy Medicine* by Donna Eden in which the preface reads:

> By my early thirties, my health was extremely precarious. I retreated to Fiji to live a very basic life. Early in my stay, I was bitten by a poisonous insect. Because my immune system was already badly impaired, I had no resistance to the bite. I became very sick and went in and out of coma. It seemed I might die.... But the shamans of Vatukarasa, a nearby [Fiji] village, learning of my plight, came with a treatment for the bite. They buried me up to my neck in the sand and left me there for long stretches several times each day over a forty-eight-hour period. They believed that the toxins would be drained into the sand. I recovered....

I am way past wishing that my misadventure had occurred in Fiji. My two hips are to be replaced, four months apart. There will be long and difficult weeks of recovery. Although I know I'll need help, I have no sense of where it may be coming from until the day Ted announces: "I'm moving up there with you." He's helped me "train" for the half-year preceding surgery. Now he's offering to nurse me.

My house is in a remote neighborhood, unserved by public transportation. Located in a *cul-de-sac*, it is one of fourteen overlooking a steep canyon, vulnerable to updrafts in the event of fire. I've tried organizing it for disaster preparedness, but despite its diversity, people don't set much stock in neighborliness. Two years ago a Vietnamese family moved in. In short order they terraced the hillside, planted fruit trees, established flower and vegetable gardens. One day, Dr. Pham sees me hobbling—leaning on two canes. He wants to know what's wrong. I tell him I'm shortly going in for surgery, the victim of an insect bite. Within minutes, Thu, his wife, is at my door. What do we need she wants to know. For the ten weeks following my return home from my surgeries, Thu and her niece will bring hot meals for Ted, my son and me on Saturdays and Sundays, and not ordinary meals, either, but the most delicious and artfully presented Vietnamese cuisine. This is the same Thu who, before her family even moved in, confided in me her worry that the neighborhood might not accept her family; now more than all the others living in our *cul-de-sac*, she sets the bar for neighborliness.

My first surgery is scheduled for April. I sign a release, which, among other things, says that surgical consequences and/or complications may ensue, resulting possibly in death. It is not something I sign lightly. Now much of my inner time is spent meditating, reviewing my past, allowing it to tell me where I must go, where I must place my energy. I am not concerned so much with outcome as I am with developing a sense of calm equal to the test I must shortly undergo, seeing to it that my state of mind is in the most focused condition to support my will to live and my strength to heal.

For the past ten years I've shared my house with my German shepherd, Elke. I notice a curious relationship between our bodies. If, for example, I have a physical problem in a part of my body, often she shows a problem in the same part of her body, although the cause is usually not the same. I am not surprised to see that now she seems to have increasing trouble walking. The change in her is a gradual one, but we begin noticing that like me, she begins showing signs of lameness, as though by taking it on, she's trying to cure me.

As my legs weaken, I am no longer able to take her for her daily walk, and eventually she's no longer able to walk without painfully dragging her lifeless hindquarters behind her. She's always been fastidious about her hygiene; her physical state causes her grief as well as pain when from time to time she tears her hind nails to the quick as her paws drag along the concrete sidewalk. My son is able to do for her what he can; but on the subject of putting her down, he is adamant. He pushes for hip surgery for her as well. We arrange for a vet home visit. But the diagnosis is not arthritis as we have surmised; it's spinal myelopathy. In other words, her neurological disconnect makes her forget she still has hindquarters. We put her down. Sobbing, I hold her as we watch her go. My son carries her body to the vet's waiting car while Ted stays behind to comfort me.

Two weeks later, my first surgery takes place. Although I don't suggest it, my elder son offers to take time off from work to fly up from Los Angeles to be with me. The pre-surgery call is for 6 A.M. We drive to the hospital, my two sons and I, while Ted catches a 5 A.M. bus in time to meet us there. We are assigned a small individual room where all of us will wait. Finally at 8:30 the long wait ends. An attendant straps me to a gurney and wheels me upstairs. Under the bright O.R. lights I recognize my surgeon and his assistants behind their masks. With dispatch I clamber unassisted aboard the narrowest table I could ever have imagined. I am ready. "Good morning, gentlemen!" I say. Then I'm out.

On emerging from anesthesia, the first thing that strikes me is that the nearly unendurable level of pain in my right hip has disappeared. I am also aware that my legs have been anchored to an immobilizer, and that compression stockings pulse away, stimulating lower extremity circulation to prevent blood clotting which, along with infection, is a serious consequence of much hip replacement surgery. The first 24 hours I am placed in a ward with two other women; one of them insists on blaring the television at full throttle through the night. Allergic to TV as I am, I experience the torture not only of a sleepless night, but the anguish of being forced to listen to the jackass braying of canned laughter, the smarminess of talking heads, and the trashy kitsch that goes for music behind the endless string of ads.

I expect to go home on discharge, but because my un-operated side feels too rubbery to bear my weight, for the first two weeks post-op, my HMO sends me to a rehabilitation facility far removed from the city. I share a room with a 90-year-old stroke victim who seems to sleep most of the day. But throughout the night she lies awake, softly calling "Argonne." It turns out it's her husband's name. They have been together for some 70 years. She calls for him only at night because during the day he spends long hours at her bedside, quietly sitting, holding her hand. Sometimes he holds open house at her bedside for his more flamboyant friends, one of whom, nearly 80 himself, shamelessly flirts with me, to my great amusement, especially when I discover I can call up enough energy to flirt back.

If I experience any disappointment at being assigned here, it quickly gives way to my discovery of a whole new world, a world, which I might not otherwise have known. One day his friend tells me Argonne's story. He is the son of the first "Negro" (as people were called in those earlier days of American "diversity") commissioned officer in the United States army, a veteran of the World War I Battle of Meuse-Argonne in France. He named his son for that battle. Inheriting his father's *métier*, Argonne became one of the Tuskeegee airmen who fought for the United States in World War II as the 332nd Fighter Group of the US Army Air Corps, the first all-"Negro" battle group. They ran interference for bomber squadrons so successfully they never lost a single bomber to enemy fire. After much delay, they were awarded a 2007 congressional gold medal for their extraordinary bravery, an award I hope Argonne and all the others of his fighter group may have lived long enough to enjoy.

Ted makes the trip by train to visit me. In the long summer afternoons, to the vast amusement of our convalescing audience, his daredevil wheelchair maneuvers whip me around the patio walkways and around the intervening palms accompanied by his very own, Gerald McBoing-Boing-inspired automotive grumbles and screeches. But wild as they appear, his clowning is a pale foretaste of what lies in store following my discharge home into his care. At last the day arrives. I receive instructions how to use a walker, how to enter and leave a car while keeping my operated leg immobilized. My nurse brings me the small departing gift of a palm leaf fan from the Philippines to cool me through the last sweltering days of summer.

During the first few days of my titanium-assisted life, all the lowliest aspects of human existence normally taken for granted require strategic maneuvering and long range planning: bathing, toileting, eating, all normal patterns are called into question. Even sleeping. For the first few days, Ted helps me navigate. On one of these excursions, my supporting leg gives out, but in the very nick of time, he rushes forward to interrupt my fall mid-way to the floor. This scare prompts him to arrange for a bedside visit from venerable 90-year-old Dr. Kussy, the world-famous, pre-historic medical authority. Dr. Kussy specializes in pre-historic trepanation, namely drilling open the skull to perform a maneuver known as a cerebral re-calibration for which he has received numerous citations and awards.

Elaborate preparations are required. Ted draws on his abandoned cell phone collection to phone Dr. Kussy, wheedling and dealing for him to make one of his almost unheard of home visits. But because the real Dr. Kussy almost always seems to be preoccupied attending patients in up-scale Marin County where he still holds a lucrative practice, Ted himself decides to substitute. As faux Dr. Kussy he's ready to drop everything, ignoring all his other patients to arrive— immediately!—by private helicopter if necessary. Whirring helicopter noises give way to rapping at the door.

Despite his great age, faux-Kussy hoists himself aboard my bed. Carefully he lays hammer, saw, and screwdriver on the covers.

"Now, Cecile, relax. That's all you have to do. I know you're a very excitable patient. Just place yourself in the hands of The Power to Recalibrate. It takes less than a minute. It won't hurt a bit and you'll feel better right away. See this saw? All I have to do...Oh! Excuse me, excuse me. I have to take this call! It's from my wife, Mildred. She gets awfully upset with me." Faux-Kussy pulls out his signature cell phone.

"Yes, Mildred? Yes, I'm visiting Cecile. Yes. I'm about to perform a procedure. Yes. A cerebral re-calibration. Anesthesia? No, no, she's resting quietly; she won't need anesthesia.... Well, Mildred, I can't help it. I'm busy. Just tell them they'll have to wait. I'm helping Cecile. Mildred, Mildred, I just can't go on like this. You know how over-worked I am. Just tell them they can wait...."

"Now, Cecile, you've seen this saw before. You know it only removes a little tiny piece of bone, just enough to get at all that nasty grey matter that's causing *soooo* much trouble..."

"I don't know what's keeping my assistant... Cecile, would you mind just holding onto this screwdriver for a moment?"

"Oh, there's my phone again." Dr. Kussy teeters wildly on my bed, saw and hammer in hand. "Mildred, Mildred...I'm in the middle of a procedure. You can't keep interrupting like this. Just cancel the other appointments. He what? He *what???*"

"Oh, Cecile, I'm terribly sorry. A patient just couldn't contain himself. He's drowned himself in the toilet bowl. I have to leave at once. And just as we were getting started..."

Faux-Dr. Kussy tumbles off my bed and hobbles out the door.

Despite the operative let-down, Ted can't help raving about Dr. Kussy's pre-historic surgical technique—although he's left all his rusting instruments behind.

From the age of seven when I got a dressing down in second grade from the good nun who imagined she could civilize my laugh, it's gotten me into trouble. Even so, I can hardly recognize the untamed howls coming from somewhere inside a body I never knew I had.

"It's time we heard some laughter in this house," observes my son.

But there are frictions. The first day Sarah, my hired helper, comes in to prepare lunch for us, she feels called upon to take Ted on. She is not at all happy that he's—in her words—bossing me about; I just wonder what she'll say if she and Dr. Kussy ever have a run in. But in this hotbed of growing domestic disarray I am in no shape to run interference from my bed.

Despite Ted's reluctance to add to anyone's carbon footprint, he drives me to my post-op appointments with hunky Dr. Phil who gives me the OK to go out, first in a wheel chair, later graduating to a walker. I'm eager to give up nightclothes for daytime wear. Sweats are the most comfortable outfit for someone in recovery. From my Alaska cruise I retain a particularly egregious cherry red set, but they're warm and they cover the essentials. Their color doesn't appeal to Ted's conservative tastes, especially when I enhance the effect with a gold, red, and purple scarf. Off we go to the redwood trail, Ted driving, my wheel chair in tow.

The whole business of extracting me safely from the car, still favoring the healing side, and lowering me into the wheelchair is at best a tiresome maneuver, one not calculated to encourage anyone's good humor. But Ted doesn't complain. He pushes me off the parking lot and onto the paved portion of the trailhead. The day is unseasonably warm; the sun beats down. I rejoice at being outdoors. Without warning, a cloud of butterflies surrounds me. Monarchs, tiger swallowtails, and fritillaries, all alight on my neon red sweats, to probe the juiciest flower they've ever encountered. Slowly they dip, folding and unfolding their wings until we reach the dirt track and the shade of the great trees.

I've no way of realizing that my feelings of enchantment may not be shared by Ted. In the Nahautl mythology in which he's steeped himself the past thirty years, butterflies signify death. And death, for Ted, has always been too proud to argue with. But for now, spring is already in full bloom. When we find the time, we still enjoy our outings. The wheelchair gives way to the walker. To cushion its bare feet, Sarah hacks away at two tennis balls with my best Sabatier. Ted accompanies me on short loops in the nearby parks. The ritual of lowering me into the car is now somewhat less mechanically challenging, and the walker is more easily collapsed than the wheel chair, or it was before Ted accidentally drives over it.

Although our dormitory arrangement stays put in anticipation of my second surgery scarcely two months from now, when the time comes, Ted is showing signs of strain. He decides to return to his apartment in senior housing to resume the preparation of the *Cantares* for anonymous publication, a project he wants to attack with renewed energy. Much as I thrive in his company, I will see less of him than I might like.

I'm hurrying to bathe and dress for a close friend's fiftieth wedding anniversary party. I happen to glance at my bare legs. With its astonishing rainbow of purple and orange my leg could sub for a Phillips 76 sign. I recognize the signs of blood clot. Unfortunately I'm home alone, there's no one to drive me to the hospital. I can't yet drive myself, and even if I could, there's no car in the garage. As a last resort, I phone my Alaska-cruise neighbor who lives down in the *cul-de-sac*. He has just enough time before his next scheduled meeting to take me to emergency. Once again, I am confined to bed.

I remember how I felt once before as I was becoming prey to pain and impaired mobility. There were days when I really thought I might be dying. Norman Cousin's cure of watching Groucho Marx movies day after day isn't available to me but on one of the rare occasions Ted pays me a visit, I plead for another bedside call from Dr. Kussy. Obligingly Ted retrieves the good doctor's rusty surgical tools from the garage, but it's no longer quite the same. Ted's heart is not in it, my laughter feels forced. I recognize the sadness I feel.

Ted sits on the edge of my bed, preparing to leave. "Whatever happens to us," I say, "No matter what, I will never forget what you've done for me. I think you saved my life."

After a silence, he turns to me. "I think I did it for myself," he says.

How do I feel about his reply? This ability of his to get to the truth—no matter what effect it may have on me, or what the cost to him—has won my respect. I ponder his answer. Now I'm getting well, he's taking his gift back. And although he may have been quite happy to impersonate a grotesque Charon to my wilting wraith, now he's returned me to the nearer shore, I know I'll not be seeing Dr. Kussy ever again.

Critical Note: Pain. It's hard to recognize pain as a gift—at first. But there it is. Again.

For the writer, pain needs to speak in **metaphor** sometimes, under the cover of another story, one that seems not to be about what it's really about. It was the wound that propelled the writing of my debut novel, *Face*, still attracting critical notice 30 years after publication:

> He tries to get up. It is night now. A cold fluorescent light pulses in the corridor. In the obscurity of the room, he can make out the night stand and the darkened entrance to the toilet.
>
> His legs are made of lead. He slides them over the cool of the bed sheets till his feet hang over the edge. He lowers

his weight onto them carefully. Supporting himself, first on the guard rail, then the dresser's edge, he propels himself forward into the darkness. The door jamb is within his grasp. He shifts his weight, regains his balance.

He runs his free hand over the cold tile of the wall, fumbling for the light switch.

In the sudden light, someone stands weaving before him on unsteady legs, something without nose or mouth, eyes dark purple splotches, sealed almost shut, particles tattooed onto the skin.

His groin goes hot.

Not me! Not me! His voice gargles in his throat. No sound comes, no sound at all.

He would remember distinctly switching on the light. He would remember sensing that something had changed. He would remember the sound of the light switch. He would remember seeing a mirror in the sudden light. He would remember the first instant of seeing something. He would remember feeling nothing, nothing at all.

He would remember them lifting him from the tiled floor where he must have fallen. Being unaware of any lapse at all. It was that absence which frightened him the most.

I remember taking a question from a woman attending one of the many public readings I gave after *Face* was published.

"Why did you choose a man as your protagonist?"

In a way I put her off. "What makes you think I did?" Although she had no way of knowing it, I had also told the truth.

There's no way I could have foreseen that help would appear on my doorstep. Some six years ago, when the memory loss of one of my favorite friends made her unable to continue living independently, I found a home for her in a locked facility. For a year I continued to visit her every week until such time as Jerry, her daughter, could steel herself to take over her mother's care, but by then her mother's savings had run out. "It's either Ireland or the streets for her," her daughter remarked, and determined it should not be the latter, she took her mother back to Ireland to die. I had always promised Jerry that, were she ever to return to the States, she had a place to stay until she could make her own arrangements. And now, just when my own need is great, she pulls up in a rental car. To her surprise, she finds me confined to bed with a blood clot.

"My," she says to me, "it's a shame you don't have a third bedroom. You need help."

I spend a wakeful night re-imagining the space this house puts at our disposal. My son uses the former dining room as his music studio. Accommodation is in order. Jerry and my son take charge, a good thing, too, given that my own strength is now so limited. They install me and my one-ton bed in the small bedroom normally occupied by my son who trades it for the master bedroom, which is large enough to contain him and his music studio as well; the formal dining room at the opposite end of the house will become Jerry's private quarters. The lengths of fine Brahmin wedding homespun I've stored since my return from India will serve for curtains to insure her privacy. So it comes about that Jerry finds a temporary home with us. She will stay from the time her referee job begins in the fall basketball season through spring.

Our first order of business is to find a second car, one she can make use of to meet her far-flung assignments, one which will become mine when once again I'm OK'd to drive. We borrow my son's station wagon to answer three Craig's List ads. We buy the third car we check out, an '89 Honda civic with only 30,000 miles on it. Jerry gives me car rental money up front against the cash purchase price, and the car is mine—and hers to use.

She's not much of a cook, but she more than makes up for this deficiency in the garden. Her great physical strength allows her to clear the tangle of overgrown cypress to the north side of the house and to create an arbor in which she transplants three clumps of Japanese butterfly iris before they take over the front yard. At the same time she pulls up all the blue Nile lilies, favorite fodder of the local deer, transplanting them to the pool enclosure where she creates a border running alongside the fence's entire length. She hacks away at my overgrown backyard to clear the area for planting. And she puts our under-used TV to use all day and half the night.

The rains have come, ushering in winter. Curled in the comfort of my bed in the very small and snug bedroom, which I now call home, I listen to the drops battering the windowpanes. Soon the solstice will be upon us, the time when, in healthier days, I invited friends from different epochs of my life to come celebrate the returning of the light. But this one will go uncelebrated: these days I keep in touch by e-mail. But my computer guru fries my hard-drive. He offers to replace it with another computer in which he installs two hard drives, one for backup. Sometime thereafter the second hard drive icon disappears from my desktop monitor, but since I haven't yet learned how to make use of it, it fails to cause me much alarm. At the time, I am still unaware, as most U.S. citizens are unaware, that warrantless surveillance is being carried out by the NSA and has been since before 2002. Or that I have a thief in my house, someone to whom, unknowingly, I have entrusted the key.

Come spring, I'm back to eating my broccoli, although Jerry, being a meat and potatoes person, doesn't care to share it. I've restored some sprightliness to my walk, my appetite is ravenous, and I'm well enough when the time comes to drive Jerry to the airport to see her off to Ireland. It's a touching good-bye, but she's all bluster to the end. I watch her waving jauntily through the airport windows. And although my son and I recognize how much she's been of help, we're relieved to re-install him in his studio and turn the television off.

Back in my own room once more, I stand before the mirror, examining my scars, two still raw symmetrical lines, following the axis where, within, hip ball socket meets pelvis. I'm twisting my torso trying for a better look as if in the twisting I can somehow erase these lines. I run my index over the slight ridge. As if I'm examining them for the first time I'm still surprised to see them there. As I bend for a closer look, my father's hand flashes at me from a buried past. My mother holds me down to help him zero in. Down comes his open palm—in the place where a lifetime of cell memory is stored.

I return to my garden, but in Jerry's absence, there's little I can do myself. Stoop work is beyond me. I watch helplessly, unable even to join my son weeding. I begin to wonder what I'll do when the time comes for him to want to move on, as surely he someday must. How will I keep up these gardens, all five of them, as I have in the past, or prune my trees? Now I can't even manage to spread deer control netting to discourage them from munching on my front yard landscaping. And how will I keep up such a huge house and garage? It's clear to me that from here on in, I'll have to depend on help.

Ted and I call each other every day. Fiercely principled, he trudges the mile up hill from where the bus deposits him. Once I return to driving, we take to meeting half way between "base camp" and my place, he on his bike, I in my antique Honda. We take short walks along the redwood trails. He's in the home stretch now, taken up with proofing the *Cantares Mexicanos*. The typing's nearly done. Normally such a work would be issued by a university press, but because he's been out of the scholarly loop too long, he's dreamed up plans to self publish anonymously. He'll have the manuscript reproduced in two volumes, footnotes and text, both bound by a copy shop. He'll transport the 200 copies by dolly back to his apartment where he'll store them in the only place available—under his bed. Some he'll deliver to a list of private readers accompanied by miniature ears of corn, the rest he'll smuggle into bookstores one set at a time, placing them in an appropriate location (under anthropology perhaps, or pre-Columbian cultures) and leave as inconspicuously as possible. His rationale is that the work has no monetary value, and as such it should be accessible to all; culture should be part of the commons. He agrees to include a P.O. Box number should there be feedback or occasion for any scholarly exchange.

Ever since Abbie Hoffman published *Steal This Book,* and probably long before, booksellers, leery of shoplifters, have resorted to convex mirrors, video cameras, and electronic gates. But in all probability the dangers of reverse stealing have never occurred to them. I recognize how deeply writers yearn for our work to see the light of day, for others to share it. My sense of Ted's outlandish plan is tempered by the realization that it represents thirty years of dogged determination, of mastering Nahuatl, used still by native speakers living in the mountains of central Mexico.

The day comes early in August when he makes the trip to deliver my very own two-volume bound copy of the *Cantares Mexicanos*, which he inscribes to me. The poems themselves I leave for last. Ted has shared enough of them for me to recognize how arcane they seem. In a way, they remind me of the so-called "Dansantes," incised in the Monte Alban stone, which, anything but dancers, on closer examination, reveal themselves to be torture victims writhing in post-castration agony. The *Cantares* are expressions of an art-valuing culture, which displayed warlike qualities and practiced human sacrifice, numbering its own children among its victims. How to encounter, let alone explain such a cultural enigma? It is this contradiction that Ted finds so compelling.

I begin reading the footnotes, embarking on the fateful path that I can't yet foresee. I'm still reading them as I prepare for my own public reading that will mark the anniversary of my last surgery, a reading I'll be sharing with my publisher, who's up from San Antonio and staying with me overnight. Before dinner, he catches sight of volume one—Ted's translation of the poems—lying on my desk. He asks to have a copy, a message I pass on to Ted, but when Ted fails to show up at the reading, I know something is amiss. Next day, just after my publisher takes off, there's a knocking at my door. It's Ted's birthday, August 29, but it's clear from his expression he's not got birthdays on his mind.

"Where's the book?" He sweeps me aside. "The *Cantares Mexicanos?*"

"Where you left it. On my desk."

He plows into my study. I pick up the two volumes in their bright red covers to hand them to him. He yanks them from my hands. He makes it clear to me what a calamity it is that I've linked him to a work whose authorship he intended must remain strictly anonymous. He storms out the door. I follow him, trying to placate him in whatever way I can, but there's no way to reason with him or to calm him down. I retreat at last, leaving him in the front yard shredding the pages of the *Cantares Mexicanos*, tearing them to bits. It's August 29, Ted's birthday. The day Katrina strikes.

Critical Note: The climax, the place where the story "turns," works best when rather than relying on something predictable, it turns on an unforeseen event.

4

Summing Up

At this writing, war has occupied nine years of my life, years that in other circumstances I might have used to make theater, write poetry, paint, travel perhaps, instead of diverting my small energies, protesting Goliath. We live in a country that was promised a "peace dividend" following the end of the Cold War. We could have seen to the "happiness index" (like Bhutan) of our citizens, to nutrition for all, to wiping out hunger, to the improvement of our decaying roads and bridges, to the universal health care that would have allowed our country not to rank 44th on the mortality scale—just next to Albania. We could have rejoiced in the cultural ferment of ideas, of music, of the arts. Instead, greed was chosen for us.

I live in an occupied country with all the benchmarks of an occupied country: population control through warrantless wiretapping of telephone and internet communication. Our newspapers—what shreds remain—have become organs of the state, censoring, or delaying at the government's request publication of information necessary if we are to remain a participatory democracy. Our minds have been colonized by advertising, by TV and the internet, and by a "public" (mis)education system designed to test but not to think. Our bodies have been poisoned with proprietary chemicals and nuclear waste, and colonized with corn syrup so that a rapidly growing proportion of our children are diabetic. Our screens and newspapers have been swept clean of all images of carnage associated with war; universal conscription has been replaced by the deployment of mercenaries euphemistically called contractors—both lessons learned from our failed excursions in Vietnam. Minorities, Black, Latino and Muslim are subject to unrelenting racial profiling and arrest; both documented and undocumented immigrants are held indefinitely, denied habeas corpus—the cornerstone of jurisprudence since the Magna Carta—and deported on trivial or trumped-up evidence. Legitimate protest, guaranteed by the first amendment, is restricted to "free speech zones;" non-violent demonstrators are beaten, pepper sprayed and routinely placed under arrest and prosecuted. Public universities are a thing of the past. Tainted mortgages have allowed banks to repossess the homes of millions of mostly very poor people. The government no longer publishes M-1, the measure of money in circulation, allowing the mint to print money day and night, robbing workers of their retirement savings. Altogether it adds up to an economic pincer movement that has gutted the middle class, and thrown 40% of the population into poverty and what's called "food insecurity" now that words like hunger and starvation are no longer politically correct. Throughout the land, cities have passed "no sit" ordinances. Benches are spiked so that the homeless can't sleep; cops harass them, forcing them to keep moving through the night.

Workers' wages have stagnated since 1975 when credit companies began offering a substitute, the new means of keeping up with rising living costs. Increased debt has caused increasing bankruptcy while bankruptcy laws have been re-written to tighten the noose. Under the effects of globalization, jobs have been exported to sweat-shop countries; foreign workers, willing to work for less and better equipped by their educations to occupy highly technical jobs, have replaced American workers, who show the effects of declining educational opportunity. Is this onslaught warfare? Or simply the normal *reductio ad absurdum* of Gothic-stage capitalism?

Three men hang in Guantanamo, "suicided," yet with their feet bound, their hands tied behind their backs. My brain has become Guantanamo: each lobe is a cage. Seven hundred seventy-five cages; in each cage a man squats, hooded, chained to the floor; at the end of row upon row of cages, at the end of the long corridor, there is daylight; the sky is blue; birds sing; there is the suffocating heat of Cuba. I am looking for the end of that corridor, night after sleepless night.

Like Brecht's *Good Woman of Setzuan*, I want to cry, "Help!" But there are no Confucian gods to hear me.

II.
Gathering

OUT OF THE
WHIRLWIND

And God spoke to Job out of the whirlwind: where were you...when I watched over the birth of the sea when it burst in flood from the womb, when I established its bounds and fixed its bars in place, saying, "Thus far shall you come and no further?"

—Job: 38: 4-11

I

Coming Home

Floodwaters stagnate over New Orleans' Ninth Ward. Bodies, bloated in the heat, float in the petroleum and alligator-infested waters of a city which, more than any other, is the heart and musical soul of a country in the process of being gutted, and left to die while its ruling elites cut birthday cake in celebration of a war troubadour who, with his boozy croaks of "bomb, bomb Iran," will attempt a presidential run some three years hence. Crude signs spell out "God have mercy on us" and "Here lies..." over a makeshift grave. We see pictures of people waving from their rooftops, women, children, men, old people, these abandoned great grand children of slaves who built this country's wealth, spreading their American flags on their pitiful rooftops, waiting for a rescue, signaling to the helicopters which pass overhead day and night, night and day, their rotors flinging dust in people's eyes, promising help that never comes. They will be left to drown, discarded as so many others have been discarded, their work stolen, their homes foreclosed. The ruling "president" doesn't consider the obliteration of a major city, port of entry of 40 percent of the nation's goods, to be worth his imperial notice until fully five days later.

Kanye West makes a statement: "George Bush doesn't care about Black people." In fact, in his great exalted majesty our own sclerotic monarch doesn't much care for the entire human race. We are all colored people now, although many of us don't yet seem to know it.

Ray Nagin, wheeler-dealer mayor of New Orleans, makes a statement. "Get your goddamn asses down here." It is Day Four of his government's criminal dereliction.

In conversation with Governor Blanco, Karl Rove makes a statement "We need to get this as close to martial law as possible." (Peter Dale Scott, quoted in a Pacific News Report.)

Bush golfs while New Orleans drowns. To the Arabian horse-rearing head of FEMA he crows, "Great job, Brownie." And indeed it *is* a great job. The government has been waiting to bring "urban renewal" to New Orleans, as it did to San Francisco's old Fillmore District. In the exultant words of Republican Congressman Richard Baker, overheard telling lobbyists shortly after Katrina destroyed the low lying districts of the city: "We finally cleaned up public housing in New Orleans. We couldn't do it, but God did." (*Washington Post*, September 10, 2005.)

I've donated half my wardrobe to Congresswoman Barbara Lee's New Orleans caravan—the trucks are already on their way—but up on the hill, far removed from sea level and poverty, my neighbors know I must be good for at least another run. They turn my car trunk into a used clothes depot. Others, like my late friend Kali, drop everything to volunteer at the Broadway headquarters of the American Red Cross. Through her I learn the story of a client, a man of some 30 years or so who applies to the Red Cross for aid, but they won't help him because evidently when he swam to safety, he forgot to take his ID with him: no proof of his existence, no utility bill addressed to him, no driver's license. The Red Cross directs him to FAX the Louisiana DMV, who will—in their own good time—FAX him back a temporary license. Without food, or carfare, or map of a city unfamiliar to him, they send him to the DMV on a day, which just happens to be Sunday. There is no more time to waste. I have to see this "operation" for myself.

What greets my eyes in the entryway of the Oakland headquarters of the American Red Cross is not like anything I could have imagined: a young Black woman stands outside howling with grief. Two women, also Black, one of whom has a small child in a stroller, try to calm her. From the two women I learn she's a survivor of the flood. In the mass evacuation, she's been separated from her twelve-year-old who's somewhere back in Houston. Yesterday the Red Cross promised her they'd try to help her find him, but today, when she's come back from Antioch, over 50 miles away, they've told her they can't do anything to help her. I put my arms around her.

"How do you want to get to Houston?" I ask her, "by bus, by train, or plane?" She stops screaming.

"Come on," I take her arm, "let's go back inside and see what we can do. Let's see if they can't help you find your son. What's your name?"

"Jamiya," she says. "Jamiya Singleton."

We approach the reception desk.

"Clear the lobby. Clear the lobby," we are told. "If you don't clear the lobby, we'll call the police."

And that is our reception from the American Red Cross.

"Never mind," I tell Jamiya, "We're going to have an adventure anyway, but you need to let me hold onto you because after that kind of welcome I'm pretty shook up myself. Let's see about that airline ticket before we get you back to where you're staying."

But I'm thinking: first things first. "And let's get you a map of Houston. And a map of Antioch for me." The distance from the Red Cross to California Triple A is not far. I notice Jamiya's very cautious about getting in my car. Before sitting down, she places some paper on the seat. Without toiletries, she's soiled her clothes until someone at the Red Cross recognized her predicament and offered her a sanitary pad. Not only is she cautious, she's freezing.

"Is it always winter up here? Don't you get any summer?" I have to laugh. Summer is San Francisco's winter. "Can you use a coat?" I raise my trunk lid. "Take your pick." There are three coats to choose from. She picks the one that matches her jeans. It's the perfect fit.

"Now let's see to that plane ticket." She stops me now. Her cooler self is beginning to take over. It turns out she's come north with a friend of a friend who has family in Antioch, some 50 miles away. They're minding her infant daughter for her while she tries to patch her life together. She thinks she'd best call them first. We pull into a gas station. I give her telephone change. I wait. Presently she returns. "They want to buy me a ticket," she says. "They're coming back to pick me up. They'll be here in an hour."

"At least we can share a lady's lunch while we wait."

The nearest place is the basement cafeteria of Kaiser hospital, a place with which I have reluctantly become acquainted, but the food is fairly adequate. We sit at a table sharing time, eating lunch together. She tells me her story. She's 28 years old. She worked in the French Quarter as a chambermaid. She prides herself that she's never asked anybody for anything. She describes being in the New Orleans Superdome with her children. She tells me what it was like. The Dome already had a reputation before the storm of being really disgusting. She was crowded in with families and many children, but in an area that was relatively safe. Along with a number of other people, she assigned herself to take care of the children, to distract them by playing games with them, at least as much as possible in such closely confined quarters. She watched people taking turns carrying old people who became separated from their wheelchairs. She watched a mother of a two-week-old infant crying of hunger, who had no milk to give it. Over and over she saw people helping one another, sharing what they had, sharing water for the crying baby until they ran out of water. She saw people with guns helping other people get supplies for themselves and their kids.

After four days, accompanied by her children, she was allowed to board a bus for Houston. There she was made to wait with other evacuees in an empty parking lot until it could be decided where to put all of them. Eventually, they were transported to the Houston astrodome where she became separated from her son whom she hopes will have connected with his grandparents who happen to live there.

She tried through the Red Cross to have information posted in the Houston Astrodome about her whereabouts for her son to find out where she is, but they were unable or unwilling to help. She has no photographs, no baby pictures. All has been swept away, including the place where she lived. She tells me her tiny girl is just two months old. I ponder this, put myself in her shoes. I wonder if I would be as long on courage.

"Is her father with you?"

"No," she says simply. "But we're friends. She was a surprise, but you don't know how much that little girl has taught me already. I love kids. That's my weakness. Some day I want to start a nursery school. What do you do in life?" she wants to know.

"I write books. It's nothing special really. It's just what I do."

"I like the way you said that," she says.

I'm deeply moved by the strength in this very young woman who's been so traumatized. I scrape the bottom of my purse. I find a lipstick and a hairbrush. I give these to her. She accepts them thankfully. In my wallet I have exactly $18.63 left. "For your journey," I tell her. "To help you find your son. I'm going to start a fund for all the Katrina folks who need help, and I'm going to name it after you—the Jamiya Singleton Fund."

We return to the entryway of the American Red Cross. She prefers to wait outside for her ride. I can see how traumatized she feels, anxious that her ride somehow may not materialize or her friends may not find her inside. She starts to cry again. "Sometimes I get so scared," she says. "I feel bad: those two women I was with...the ones trying to help me...they're both homeless. They came all the way here for help but the Red Cross said unless they were hurricane victims, they couldn't do anything to help."

Not all my future encounters with Katrina survivors end so easily. Each day, whenever I enter the Red Cross lobby, it's a challenge to know which person to help first. Usually it's the first person I encounter. Today it's a family of five: the matriarch, Mary White, her daughter Janice, and a stepladder of small children. This family needs everything: clothing, food, toys for the children. They've been referred to Glad Tidings Church, some eight miles away—but they have no way of getting there. They pile into my car. Mary's the one to tell me their story. They lived in the Adelphia District of New Orleans, close by the hospital where 45 patients drowned. They were asleep, unaware of how rapidly the water would rise. Mary was the first to wake. She was the one to rouse her family. But by the time the children were dressed and ready to go, the water had risen to the second floor. They were able to escape only by passing through a second storey window. They were marooned on their roof for nearly five days waiting for rescue along with all the other people on their street who were stranded on their rooftops calling for help, screaming in horror as they watched the corpses of drowned people, drowned pets, all manner of jetsam floating by in the rapidly rising waters. She watched her neighbor's son drown. "We all seen it. His mama seen it, too, " she says. "He didn't know how to swim. He just jumped in. They was nothing she could do. In all we seen," she says, "in all we seen, the worst was not being able to help people who needed to be helped. O, Lord!" she exclaims, slapping her hands on her generous thighs.

At last a boat owner came by, saw them and took them aboard along with as many other people as he could. He took them all to the bridge where they waited three hours in the sun with no food, no water, and no diapers for the little children, no money and no identification. A van came by, loaded them up along with other folks and drove them to Baton Rouge. At this point, Mary lost sight of her man and has not seen him since. "I don't know where he's at," she says, "but they say God don't send nothing your way that you weren't meant to handle."

Deposited in Baton Rouge by the side of the highway, they waited, still without food, or water, and with nowhere to go. Someone picked them up, all five of them—a man with a van who was heading west to California, where he had a place in Oakland. It took them four days to get to the Bay Area. When they got there, this same man took them in.

At Glad Tidings a massive volunteer effort is underway. In the church hall, a banquet table is set up; refreshments are laid out: salads, sandwiches, hot dogs, and all kinds of drinks, including milk for the kids. The five-year-old takes charge of her brothers, sees they all have something to eat while the two women check in with the in-take counselor. I keep a discrete distance, my eye on the children, but I can hear Mary sobbing bitterly. Janice remains quiet and withdrawn. The two women are invited into the storage area. It's the size of a small department shore. There are shoes to choose from, clothing, strollers, and household appliances. While Mary and Janice begin picking things out, I take advantage of my temporary freedom to chat with the church ladies who coordinate this amazing operation, hoping to bring more Katrina survivors their way. When I return, Mary's loading a shopping cart. Janice takes the kids outside for me to mind before returning to pick out clothes and shoes for them.

In the churchyard, hundreds of pallets are lined up, all shrink wrapped, ready to ship. Through the plastic I read some of the labels: diapers, toilet paper, disposable paper plates; some contain cartons labeled clothes, or shoes, or toys. The kids run about ecstatically, hiding between them, chasing each other, skylarking. They're really excited by all the animation going on around them in the yard.

A church lady emerges from inside to caution me not to let them play between the pallets: she's concerned for their safety. I shepherd them outside the gates to play on the front lawn. At last the women emerge. Janice pushes a stroller filled with kids clothes and shoes; Mary hauls two shopping carts. The challenge will be cramming all this stuff and five passengers into my tiny Honda sedan. It takes some doing and re-doing till everything fits. Janice takes one child on her lap. The oldest takes her brother. My concern is to return them home safely without the highway patrol pulling us over because we don't have car seats for the kids.

Once home, the process of unloading takes some time. While Janice minds the kids, Mary takes over, making several trips upstairs where the family occupies one small room. I'm concerned for her. She's overweight and clearly out of breath. But in the family this role appears to be her established one.

The afternoon is still oppressively hot, but we have no time to lose. Another errand is still ahead of us. Everyone piles back in the car. Located in the industrial area of Hayward, just beyond the freeway, the food pantry is hard to find. The volunteers there serve the many below-poverty-level residents of Hayward. Once again I mind the kids while the women go inside. The people working there show themselves to be more than sensitive to this family's particular plight. They even come out to the car to greet the children where I'm doing all I can to keep them entertained. Tayari, the youngest, rides my lap, busy working the steering wheel. At last we're ready to load: milk, cereal, bananas, and cakes, cakes, and more cakes. The kids are all excited. "It's a birthday party," squeals the eldest.

We return to the Fruitvale district. This time I run into the man who's taken them in—a White man—with a dour, hardscrabble look to him, the kind of man whose forebears might have figured in the photographs of Walker Evans or Dorothea Lange. I try expressing my appreciation for what he's done, but he's not much given to ceremony one way or another.

I will revisit this family several times to take them shopping or to bring art supplies for the children. Mary disappears for some days, leaving Janice alone with the kids. One day I find them playing on the second-floor deck with only the skimpiest railing between them and the concrete driveway below. The oldest is only five. When she sees me, she runs inside to try to rouse her mother. "Momma!" She seems alarmed that she cannot wake her. But is it any wonder that someone as traumatized by Katrina's horrendous aftermath might never want to wake?

In the next few days I make frequent trips to Red Cross head-quarters. The waiting area's filled to overflowing with folks from New Orleans, from Mississippi and other affected areas of the Gulf. I'm helping a very young man from Hattiesburg who cradles a small baby in his arms. He's trying to reach the Mississippi DMV to obtain temporary ID, which will allow him—and his child—to eat. I work the desk phones, but no matter how hard I try, Mississippi state agencies keep providing me with dead-end numbers. It turns 5 PM Central time. The offices are closed. I feel impelled to apologize to him, not just for my failure to help, or for his fatigue at the end of what must have been for him more than two weeks of hopeless days, or for the infant he holds in his arms, but for a history going back to Jamestown which has washed both of us up on such cruelly indifferent shores. But words fail. If nothing else, I have listened to him—which may count for even more than the small bill I press into his hand.

So far the Jamiya Singleton Rescue Fund has been financed from the annual withdrawal from my IRA retirement account. It's cash I don't really need. When opportunity presents itself, I sit down with folks to talk with them. In this way I acquire a growing list of resources: clothes closets, food pantries, helping agencies. And I take down phone numbers—if they have any phone at all—to make appointments later to help them get the basics of what they minimally need, clothing, food, and a place to stay. But sometimes, as I wait passively while they try on yesterday's jeans, I am reminded that folks with so few options are not always thrilled when it comes to wearing someone else's clothes.

My mom and pop philanthropy lasts a very few more days before the Red Cross authorities are on to me. "What are you doing here?"

"Same thing you're doing. Doing it differently is all."

I hope my cheek buys me some time but, fresh from appealing to the higher command, my interlocutor wastes no time throwing me out. I am now Banished from the Garden, which has sent so many of its clients out into the streets armed with not a whole lot more than toothpaste and brush.

Although it's dwindling fast (and I've been working just as hard as I can to dwindle it), the Jamiya Singleton Rescue Fund still shows a positive cash balance, but I need to find another way to disburse the funds. I take to parking on the curb outside the Red Cross entrance, waiting for folks to come out. I resort to an inelegant *psst* to attract their attention.

"Where you from?"

"New Orleans."

"You got kids?"

"A whole family of 'em."

"Could you use a twenty?" The first man to whom I pass a bill announces to anyone on the street who might care to share his amazement, "that's twenty more than I had before!" So I pass him another.

"What's your name?"

"Cameron."

Shortly following this encounter, Just Cause, Oakland, an organization working for tenants' rights, calls a meeting of Katrina evacuees. The meeting is facilitated by Van Jones, whose visionary and recently published *The Green Economy* proposes a tandem effort to combat socioeconomic and environmental ills. I attend with Kali, my Red Cross volunteering friend. Mr. Cameron and members of his family are also in attendance and I discover his name is not the same as the one he's given me. I can't fault him for his caution. It's not every day someone parked curbside calls you over with a *psst* without having questionable intentions.

The "Cameron" family consists of some six adults and ten children. Jamika, his wife, tells their story. They lived in a large apartment complex on an upper floor with enough room for everyone to crowd in, some thirteen in all, six adults, the rest children. Before the storm struck, the family got together to decide what to do. They pooled their resources laying in necessities for everyone, food, drink, and some emergency supplies. They hoped to wait the storm out, but when they saw the waters rising, they realized they needed to evacuate. They'd had the foresight to garage their cars on an upper level, but the problem was that with so many people, in addition to one car, they needed their van, and the van was low on gas. Their first effort was to siphon gas out of another car to transfer to the van.

Unlike many folks, they were able to get out of New Orleans successfully. They had heard of a place where they could take shelter farther along the way, only to be turned away because it was already filled to overflowing. Their journey continued north through Louisiana into Mississippi. There they began running short on gas. They tried obtaining cash with a credit card, but without power, none of the teller machines worked. The gas pumps were down as well, but a kindly station attendant siphoned gas out of his vehicle to send them on their way. Their journey, which took them nearly as far as North Carolina before they decided to turn west, was laced with extraordinary encounters between people—perfect strangers—who, under the pressure of catastrophe, showed them exemplary generosity.

That evening others told their stories, old people, young people, all had amazing stories to tell of resilience, courage, and above all kindness. But we were listening to the fortunate ones, the ones who had some resources—a car for example, or relatives in less severely affected areas, and something set aside for the proverbial rainy day. None had experienced what we learned later of the horrors either of the New Orleans Convention Center or of the Superdome. That night it became clear to me that this event—so far the greatest catastrophe the United States had experienced in my lifetime—had the scope of history. The plight of its victims should be heard and recorded. Their histories should become part of the national narrative. This was the 21st century's chapter of the story that began even earlier than Jamestown—and like any holocaust, none of it should ever be forgotten or denied.

At this same meeting, I learn that Catholic Charities of the East Bay is offering people help finding food, clothing, rent, and transportation money, even jobs. I think if my friend can volunteer, I can, too, but with an organization doing effective work. Despite my closing the door on official religion some fifty years ago, any agency that extends substantive help to folks who have been so severely traumatized is good enough for me. At the same time, an office with a desk will offer me a more reliable base from which to continue making small disbursements from the Jamiya Singleton Fund, although by now the fund is running low. The time has come to organize a benefit, something I know about ever since with Bill Graham, we bailed out the San Francisco Mime Troupe on charges of obscenity by producing one of the first public rock concerts ever in what subsequently became known as San Francisco's Fillmore Auditorium.

They keep coming, the Katrina folk, in pairs, with children, some come alone, from the Ninth Ward, from the Sixth Ward, from Chantilly, from outlying parishes, all of them Black folk, crowding the Catholic Charities conference rooms, spilling into the corridors. Eugenia Cecil, still a young woman, tells me her story. Although she hasn't lived in New Orleans for many years, she's continued visiting. Her father—"may he rest in peace"—died in jail a year ago. "Blessed," she says, because if he hadn't died, like all the other inmates he would have been left to drown, locked up in his cell. Now she's applying for assistance for her three grandchildren whose mother has sent them up by bus for Eugenia to raise. As we talk, one of the clients I've met earlier passes by in the hall. Through the open door Eugenia catches sight of her. "I *know* you!" she exclaims, jumping up. The two women embrace, overjoyed at finding one another. It begins to dawn on me that even more than displacement, even more than the loss of their homes, it is the rupture of their communal ties that extracts the highest toll.

The war hammers on, piling up new atrocities. The news reports the attempted rape and murder of Abeer Hauza, a fifteen-year-old Iraqi girl, the murder of her mother, father and brother, and the setting of their house on fire to conceal the crime by three American G.I.s. Had she been from my culture, she would have had her *quinceañera* today. A modest memorial is held for her at sundown in a Berkeley Park. Some forty of us huddle in the chill of early evening, among us the Japanese-American parents of Lt. Ehren Watada, the first American commissioned officer to refuse combat orders to Iraq. Candles are lit, prayers are said. Presiding is Samina Sundas, the Pakistani executive director of American Muslim Voice, who reports that during her recent FOX news interview call after call came in demanding that she "leave," "go home," evidence of a country convulsed by the racism and xenophobia characteristic of wartime from which no country is ever exempt.

The weather is turning. The long shadows of November's wintry afternoons give way to December's mist and drizzle. The day dawns chill, misty, with promise of rain. It's just after nine o'clock. Normally full to overflowing, this morning the lobby is empty, the kitchen deserted. People already at work have left the remains of breakfast lying about: donuts, a half pot of coffee, creamer. I register all this as I pass through to the area behind closed doors where I've been assigned a desk and phone. It rings as I enter. My initial bafflement yields to surprise: a woman is speaking to me from Atlanta. She's been flown there from New Orleans without knowing till the plane doors closed exactly where she's going. Now she's holed up in a hotel room; separated from whatever family she has with no way of knowing where they are. She's the sole Katrina survivor lodged in her hotel.

"It's very hard," she says, "I wake up to another day. I start wondering why I'm here. Then I get flashes of the water rising. All they give me is a roll and coffee, but I can't eat breakfast after that."

"Breathe," I tell her. "Try taking some deep breaths. Does that feel better?"

"Yes," she says, "It does."

"When was the last time you had a good soak? Why don't you draw the water and just sit in the tub and soak? Let the water help you to relax. Do you know any people in Atlanta? People who know you from New Orleans?"

And it turns out that maybe Atlanta does hold some links for her if she'll just leave the hotel room she's holed herself up in for a week.

"I don't know what else I can do from here to help you. I'm on the West Coast, in Oakland, California. I'm not sure how you got our number..."

"You helped me already," she says. "I so badly needed to talk to someone." I take her phone number. Later I pass it on to a client who's got relatives in Atlanta, encouraging them to contact her.

I go out to check the lobby. A lone man is sitting there. He's come in out of the drizzle. He's hunched over trying to get warm. I ask him if he's had breakfast yet.

"No, I haven't." I invite him to be seated at a table in an empty conference room.

"What do you take with your coffee?"

In the kitchen I even find an apple. I prepare a tray to bring him breakfast. We begin our conversation. I fill in the required intake form with the usual name, address and other identifiers.

He tells me his story. He's come by bus, all the way from Houston. He's used the money the Red Cross doled out for food to pay the astronomic—for him—bus fare of over $200 to get here. He's here with no prospects, no money, and no job. He's used to New Orleans weather and he's freezing. He has on only the sweater he's wearing and a shirt.

While we talk I'm drawing a mental image of the clothing in my car trunk. There's a size "small" man's fleece sweater, one I recently salvaged on one of my morning hikes. It's washed and ready for its next owner. And indeed, bright red though it is, it fits perfectly, although he prefers wearing his sweater over it to tone down the effect. I give him a list of agencies and addresses and a map of Oakland to help him find his way around. And a collapsible umbrella from my umbrella archives.

"And last, but not least..." I extract a bill from the newly revitalized Jamiya Singleton Fund. And that is my first acquaintance with Lou Victor who comes from New Orleans. This memory will return with every future meeting that reunites us, but for now, neither of us can take the measure of the future's gifts. A shirt, an umbrella, and a map, each talismanic, in much the same way the gifts I remember my adopted grandmother giving me—miniature wooden shoes—to walk my path; an inkwell—to point out my direction; and a sweet-smelling Russian turned wooden box—empty, wellspring for me of the dreams to come my way.

The following morning the sun is out. Even before 9 o'clock the Catholic Charities lobby is full to overflowing. My supervisor asks me to interview a couple, Jack and Jamie Johnson (not their real names), but every conference room, every office is already occupied. I rearrange three lobby chairs to give us some measure of privacy. I make sure there's a box of tissue near at hand. Jack is a large, very quiet man somewhere in his 50s. Already he is a candidate for diabetes. He speaks barely above a whisper, but I get the sense that he must be a very angry man. His companion, Jamie, begins speaking for them both. She helps me fill the first two pages of the intake questionnaire, but when we get to the page that lists clients' needs, Jack finds his voice. "They left us there to die," he growls. He comes from the Ninth Ward, the neighborhood most devastated by the flood.

"We've seen so much," he says. "Six days we were without food or water unless we got it ourselves. We were left to die." He saw houses in his neighborhood destroyed. His own house was entirely under water. On Sunday morning he heard three booms (sounds of the levees being deliberately blown up)—a story I will hear repeated many times over by other folks I interview.

"Oh, yes," he says, "this has been going on for a very long time. We were left to die," he says. Jamie nods solemnly. She is crying softly.

I pass her the tissue box.

"I'm still missing my son. There's no word of him. We've been searching for him, listed him as missing. I am very angry," he says. "Counseling, yes, I need counseling. I am very, very angry. It was like a war out there. Helicopters kept circling overhead, but they did nothing to help us. We lost everything. All my clothes. That's one thing I love is good clothes. I always like to dress good, you know what I mean?"

I am touched by this glimmer of pride amidst the story of so much devastation. Briefly I take note of the gold rings, some of them diamond studded, on his every finger.

Jamie interjects, "We come from good folks. My father served in the military in World War II. His father served in World War I..."

"And to call us refugees," Jack spits out his indignation. "This our country. We live here. We're not refugees."

Jamie shows me her blue plastic wristband. "It's from the Dome," she says. "We both got one."

"You couldn't get in or go out without it," Jack adds.

"We're keeping them," Jamie says, "We're not taking them off." And as she speaks, I am reminded of the Holocaust survivor's numbers I once glimpsed on a friend's arm.

She shrugs in resignation. "Everything I'm wearing is not mine. Even this scarf I got me from a free box."

There's no way to miss seeing how traumatized these people are. No intake questionnaire can come close to encountering the way they really feel. "Let's pray," I say—I, the non-believer. I hope these two have prayer enough in them for three. I clasp their hands to either side of me. I bow my head.

I hear Jamie's whispered prayers. When at last she becomes still, I release their hands.

I have listened by now to enough folks to recognize that this event is a story that must be told. And told in the voices of the folks whose lives have been forever changed by it. And I'm thinking: what better way to dignify the experience of these folks who've passed through the whirlwind and come out the other side.

"I wonder," I say to them, "if you might be willing to let me interview you? I'd like to ask you to tell your stories. And would you be comfortable if I brought along a tape recorder?"

The business of transcribing Katrina oral histories takes up my time day after day. Whether transcribing or composing, I tend to indulge my restlessness from hours at the keyboard with the kinds of distractions that wipe the slate clean, allowing me to return to the task with renewed energy. Now it's no different, except that instead of gardening or preparing dinner, I find myself gravitating to those neglected corners of the house.

Like the nautilus whose shell is described by Bachelard, inhabiting a place requires the slow build up of chambers to accommodate growth. But for humankind, time marks its rings of accumulation at the corners of the house, in the margins of basements, and attics, places where children indulge their imaginations in the ambience of a world turned upside down: old trunks, rocking chairs, old clothes to dress up in, mysterious letters and musty photographs.

During sixteen years of living here, not consistently—there have been periods of itinerant teaching—but over time, I've built up my shell: boxes of craft materials; art supplies; shelves crammed with remnants of vacated obsessions; drawers of antique napery, fabrics left over from years of making my own clothes, of fabricating costumes, bedspreads, recycled window curtains.

And books, of course, from the very first purchases financed by a starter job at Harper & Row: A Merriam Webster dictionary; a UNESCO folio edition of Persian miniatures, a full collection of Horizon magazine, from its inception to its final issue; a 1964 edition of *Encyclopædia Britannica*. There are vinyl records from the early '50s, of Georges Brassens, and Yvette Montero; a full row of Glenn Gould. And all the rehearsal logs and press releases, posters, and photographs from my theater days packed helter-skelter in a basement vast as a freight car, big enough to play host to any number of nomadic friends who've needed space to store possessions before taking to the road.

Behind its discreet screening our old formal dining room conceals rows of shelves; three columns of drawers, and display shelves for china and crockery inherited from my godmother's legacy and from my first trip to Mexico. For some reason—I don't yet know why—all this stuff starts to bother me. Some of it I've never even begun to use, and most of it I'm not planning ever to use again. What's it doing here? I begin attacking the most obvious: all those anthologies and fiction manuals will have to go. I box them and trundle them to Oakland's McClymonds High School where they'll be put to better use. And all that craft stuff inherited from my godmother—did I ever imagine I'd take willingly to needlework? Off to the auction gallery. I look for ever more excuses not to have to enter another word, at least not today, not to have to reverse the tape to listen, then reverse again, to make sure that not one word is lost, that no meaning is distorted or betrayed. Because these voices belong to other folks, not me, folks who've been through a drowning and come out with their lives and not much else besides.

But spring cleaning is in order—even if it is November with winter closing in. I need to shed my godmother's bobbins and her lace, her boxes of cotton and silk thread, and her embroidery frames and patterns, some of them already started but put aside because her ever-inquiring mind probably found other, more compelling things to do. And the unstrung zither, the dulcimer, and a guitar built by my late husband, and his legacy of heavy Indian turquoise necklaces, the heavier ones designed by native silversmiths for pawn, and the laces, the antique set of place settings, and the cobalt saltcellars too precious to part with until now. And all that material, fabric remnants—did I imagine I'd take up quilting in my old age? My hobbyist boss at Catholic Charities can put them to better use. And all those leftovers from my floral designing days? My favorite Katrina survivor will be glad to have them now his design warehouse lies drowned under Lake Pontchartrain. I breathe in the smell of the empty raw wood shelves, savor the satisfying click as I close the empty cupboard doors.

The transcripts have to wait. I attack my bedroom closets next, and once they're empty, there's the basement, and last and most dis-organized of all, there's the garage with all the tools and hardware to sort, and the stale paint cans, two whole shelves of them, waiting for me to cart them to the toxic dump, plenty to do to tide me through the next transcript, and then...and then...will I still be putting things in boxes once I'm done? All this giving away, getting rid of, selling off of stuff, what's this about? It's not just diversion-seeking. Something's happening to me, maybe something that started way back when I first laid my wardrobe out and picked out all the things I'd not worn in over a year, and those adornments given me so long ago that I never wore, and the coral snake-skin shoes, and the sun hat, and the visor, and the embossed and studded Polish leather belt, and the metal-lic leather shoes that were always a bit too small, all this goes back to the day in early September when I parted with half my stuff and watched it being loaded onto Barbara Lee's truck caravan bound for New Orleans.

By now I've just about completed some six or so oral histories of Katrina evacuees. I know all my subjects are still homeless, parked in dismal hotel and motel rooms, separated from one another—fish out of water deprived of their communal bonds. Thanksgiving is shortly coming up. Why not make a celebration exclusively for them? And why not complete the transcripts in time to give each one of them a copy? Some few folks have already migrated to other areas of the country, but those I manage to contact come with their families: wives and relatives bearing ham hocks and greens to complement the turkey and sweet potato pie, and an arrangement of American Beauty roses which, in all its Victorian opulence, has to be relegated to the sideboard so that everyone can see everyone else. No sooner are they removed, someone sitting at one end of the table speaks up: "I know you. Weren't you working in the fish store...?" And gathered round my Oakland table we celebrate a re-knitting by people so cruelly displaced of a community they shared to such a remarkable degree that when I ask one of them: "How many folks did you know in New Orleans?" I get (for me) the staggering answer: "At least five hundred—but only two hundred of them are my best friends."

Although I have no way of knowing it yet, this Thanksgiving will be the last we celebrate in this house.

Shortly afterwards, I talk to a client whose subsequent interview contains a depth of detail that lends context to all the others. In the process, we strike up an acquaintance so that, when I start planning my solstice celebration for late December—which happens to fall on the night of the winter's fiercest storm—she offers to cater for our many guests and with her daughter's help, to serve, even though my son, who's vacationing in Los Angeles, won't be here to share it.

Catholic Charities calls a meeting for January 3. All the directors and staff of a coalition of city and private agencies are deeply troubled by FEMA's latest eviction order. There is no question that the New Orleans evacuees must not be returned to shelters after experiencing nightmare confinement in the Superdome. The housing coalition agrees that all member organizations need to get a census of how many of their clients still remain in the Bay Area, find out how they're faring and re-assess their needs. I am assigned a list numbering over 200 names. I'm not even past the C's when I contact Jimmy Connor (not his real name). "How are you doing?" I ask him.

"Not so good," he says. "I got no ID. I got no money, I got no job, and I don't have anything to eat."

Why I jot his response down next to his name, and hang up, ready to move on to client number 16 I can't imagine, perhaps because the afternoon's getting on and I have 184 clients left to go. But almost immediately I remember the Jamiya Singleton fund. Borrowing from the New Orleans vernacular I call Mr. Connor back. "Where you at?" He has a truck. He's parked close to the Oakland airport approach. I make a quick calculation. "I'll meet you there in 17 minutes. I have something for you."

Just past the intersection, I pull into a parking lot. I scan the street. At first I see no one who might remotely resemble Mr. Connor. But a little to the north of the intersection on a raised grass median, I notice a Black man of somewhat stocky build. I approach him. I extend my hand.

"I'm Jimmy," he says.

I shake hands. I invite him to talk to me in the privacy of my car. "First things, first," I say. I pull out $140 from the Jamiya Singleton Fund. I do this so that he doesn't feel he needs to sing for the kind of supper that might never come.

"Now I'll be able to pay the $80 dollar parking ticket I got!" he exclaims. A quick calculation tells me that leaves him $60.00.

All he has is his truck, which he drove all the way to the Bay Area from New Orleans. He doesn't know a soul up here. He's nearly out of gas money, and he hasn't eaten today. He says that everyday he drives down to the bay. "I just sit there and watch the water," he says.

"There's a food pantry just down the street here." I give him the address. "But they serve only the first ten people who show up each day, so it's best to get there before they open in the morning." I refer him to another agency, a private one, which I know is very effective in getting help for folks who are without any ID. Our short visit ends. He is about to close my car door. "Lots of love," I say. It's a parting I use so habitually, I hardly give it any thought.

"I feel it," he says.

Evidently word has made the rounds. Early one morning, I receive a call from a man who's hungry. He has no job, no money, and no place to go. I assume at first he is another Katrina evacuee. "No," he says, "I'm a released felon on parole."

"Can you get food stamps? Social security?"

"No, Ma'am," he informs me, "people out of jail, we can't get anything like that."

I don't understand at first. "What do you mean, aren't you eligible for any kind of help?"

"No, Ma'am," he tells me. "None of us are."

On the sixth of January—the Feast of the Magi—my son comes back from L.A. I am unprepared for what he has to say. "Mom," he says, "I think I'm moving to L.A."

"I'm selling the house!" The words leap out of my mouth, without my even thinking.

So *that's* what all this has been about, all this business of putting things in boxes, giving them to people who have better use for them than I. I'm moving out! I'm selling this house! A feeling of relief, of elation takes over. I'm free! I'm free at last!!!

Emptying a seven-room house, basement and garage is no work for sissies. I draw up lists of what gets shipped where. I scotch tape these to the walls where with my son's help we stack boxes as they get taped shut. We tag all the furniture that neither of us will be needing. I invite my Katrina interviewees to take my linens and my queen size bed. Catholic Charities sends Francisco, their volunteer with a pick-up to haul the rest. As it happens he's a real estate agent. "What you need here is a bamboo floor," a thought I've been entertaining myself especially since, once emptied of furniture, the existing carpet bears the historic record of generations of house pets who've ever passed through.

Francisco's truck is already stacked full to overflowing. He piles on my bed and dresser. "I have a guy who'll be glad to get a hold of these. He drove his truck up here all the way from New Orleans." His story rings a bell.

"Jimmy Connor?"

Francisco registers surprise, but, given my experiences of New Orleans' close-knit community, by now such synchronicities seem quite natural to me.

On the appointed day, the Tibetan-speaking movers storm through like some fierce pillagers from Genghis' army, stripping every scrap until at last the house lies bare. A friend from my early teaching days drops by. She seems to have this unflagging instinct, always there for me in those moments of my greatest need. My house gapes empty, my son is gone. Our voices echo in the empty rooms. We go outside to watch the sunlight glinting on the bay as the afternoon begins to wane. There's nothing left to sit on but the garden stairs.

In all, I met over 100 families who migrated to the Bay Area in Katrina's aftermath, some of whom lost relatives, lost homes and all their possessions, all the things, which bound them to their former lives—all but their cultural identity. Could it be that, in the long view, "home" for me had to do not so much with the piece of ground to which I found myself attached but with those vestigial cultural emblems, which I imagine make me who I am? What do I really need to lend pattern and meaning to my life? Can I redefine myself by what I peel away?

"Why should one man feast while another man starves?" These words are usually attributed to Tom Paine, although they may first have been spoken during a British Parliamentary session. It would take quite a few more years till I recognized how Katrina changed my life. How I had been privileged to glimpse through its shattered window what real poverty in the richest country in the world looks like. I didn't need an "establishment" anymore to help me compose *The Love Queen of the Amazon*, with its interchangeable parade of politicians and prostitutes. From now on home would be where I am.

2

Katrina Survivors in Their Own Words
(excerpts collected and edited, 2005-2006)

In an article dated February 8, 2006, writing for Pacific News Service, Peter Dale Scott states: "It is clear that the Bush administration is thinking seriously about martial law.... In response to Hurricane Katrina in Sept. 2005, according to the *Washington Post*, White House senior adviser Karl Rove told the governor of Louisiana, Kathleen Blanco, that she should explore legal options to impose martial law 'or as close as we can get.' The White House tried vigorously, but ultimately failed, to compel Gov. Blanco to yield control of the state National Guard."

Themes, such as population concentration, which first became familiar to the world when the criminality of the Third Reich was exposed, are repeated here (notably the separation of families, men to the left, women and children to the right), together with techniques of occupation and torture refined in the Iraq War of 2003 and the 2009 Israel-Palestine War. Among the latter are withholding of food and water, and the subjection of internees to loud and unpleasant noises.

Interview with W.W.
Conducted December 14, 2005
433 Jefferson Street, Oakland, California

[I was born] in Calcasieu Parish, Lake Charles, in south-western Louisiana. I was first generation American. My father was born [on] the Island of Antigua. His parents were from Egypt and Morocco respectively, and my grandmother was a German immigrant from Russia.... My maternal grandfather was also a Russian citizen; [his family] immigrated to Argentina where they had a large German population. They lived there for several years, and in 2005 they entered California through Mexico.

I lived in the Eighth Ward...about ten blocks from the French Quarter.... Over the years I kept in touch with a lot of people in New Orleans that grew up with me...my neighbors, and my friends, and people that were my neighbors as well as my friends in my neighborhood.... We had two or three older people that...we as a community and neighborhood collectively took care of. The lady next door to me [Miss Connie] is wheelchair bound...and I knew that she was there alone.

Where I live in the 8th Ward we had the storm surge of course. A big part of it came when they broke the 17th Street Canal. I talked to one man in particular.... After the storm, he heard that the 17th Street Canal levee was breached; the water was starting to rise in his neighborhood—he lived over there in Carrollton, very close to the 17th Street Canal. He said that he had his grandchildren in the house. [When] he saw the water start rising, he got a ladder out; he went up to the roof to make sure [it] was secure and while he was up there... he saw them blow up the canal. Basically what they are doing is trying to save everything uptown where all the more affluent people [live], guarding the French Quarter and all those places, and so they let the water into the poorer neighborhoods.

Someone who did an independent study of the rock and debris, they were able to get into that 17th street canal, and they took the rock samples of the levee breach and all of that to an independent forensic laboratory in Atlanta and there were indications of explosives that were used on the levee.

We had anywhere from 3 to 5 feet of water in my house. Everybody had evacuated, or they went to the Superdome when the water started coming in. [But] we stayed in the house for about two and a half days...because I didn't want to leave Miss Connie.

A day and a half after the storm, the water got real black.... I went over to talk with Miss Connie. I finally got her out. When we were walking to the freeway, every store was open in my neighborhood, looted open I should say, so of course we went in there and got more food, and I was very glad that we did because there were so many on the interstate that didn't have anything. So we had more than enough not only to sustain ourselves but to help the elderly people and the very young children.

[As] we walk[ed] up the exit ramp onto the bridge, [we] could see down the corner of Claiborne and Orleans, two men had just gotten out of a boat. They were getting ready to walk up the Orleans ramp...[towards] that same freeway overhead. I saw them get eaten by alligators. Two 'gators came out of the water and took 'em.

On the bridge...there were at least a couple of hundred [dead] people there; there were tens and hundreds of thousands of pedestrians lying down, sitting down, and crying hysterically at any given time. There were several people that were dying [or] that were already dead. People were camping, eating, sleeping, and resting amongst dead people because there was literally no where to put [them].... When I got [up] on that bridge, I found a grown woman I had to rock like a baby because she left her mom on that bridge dead, she left one of her brothers that had health problems, on that bridge dead, she left one of her children on that bridge dead. As soon as the wind died down..., the Coast Guard and the Army [helicopters] were above us... four and a half days, not dropping one bottle of water, not airlifting any of the elderly or the infirm people that were suffering, they just...watched us from the air...; they flew down as low as they could...and all it did was stir dust around...; it terrified the old people and the children.... We were on the bridge an hour or two [when] we saw...a convoy of about 30 plus U.S. Army trucks, bringing White people out of minimally hit areas—and bear in mind that the interstates had no motor traffic.... People started hollering because they thought it was help [coming] until they saw all the able-bodied, healthy White people grinning and waving.... They stepped on the gas..., speeding through that area where the people were all sitting on the freeway. The whole time we're on the freeway, the state troopers and the New Orleans Police Department were racing up and down the freeway amongst all of those pedestrians, not carrying people out, [only] one person in the car, the same

officer up and down the freeway all day and all night. We saw them...
for two days.

We already knew what's been going on in the Superdome—they had been broadcasting it on the air waves before I left my house—and no one would go in there. Once people were in the Superdome, they weren't [allowed] out. So we walked back up on the freeway. We parked [ourselves]...directly behind the Superdome. We met a lot of people that said they were breaking out of [there]. They got [up] on that bridge with us.

We were there for not even an hour when this huge contingent of buses starts rolling up, parking out there on the interstate. We just all figured we're ready to go. We're asking them [but] the police don't tell us anything.

We spent the night on the freeway.... There were no lights. It was pitch black. People were alone, old people, adults; people were crying, people were hysterical.... They didn't know the status of their loved ones, their homes. When was somebody coming to get us? Were we going to see medical [help]? I couldn't even sleep. I walked the whole freeway all night [long], talking to people....Two men stopped me. They were all out of place, two young White men...speaking French. That's when I found out that they were reporters from Norway...! That's when I got the first word from the outside. They told me that the whole world's eyes are on New Orleans right now.... "You guys have had a storm of such magnitude, they are actually saying this is the worst natural disaster your country has ever had...." The roads were impassable and the railroads were all washed away, no one could get in New Orleans to help us....

Everybody heard a big explosion and nobody knew what it was. We only saw the smoke.... [But] my daughter...was down...on that [other] end of the freeway. She [and some other] people saw helicopters throw some type of fiery objects on that building and blow it up. They said it was a chemical plant, so we were exposed to some type of toxic fumes beyond what was coming out of New Orleans.

It's been amazing to me how Fox News, how CNN and all these news entities could get in and question people while they're literally dying, and chronicle their misery, [but] they couldn't put a nurse or a doctor, and they couldn't put medical supplies, or at least three or four of the main types of insulin or any type of blood pressure medication, or heart medication on [their] damn plane.

To reach the trauma center that they set up at the New Orleans Arena which is right next to the Superdome, you had to come off the freeway [and] walk through four feet of water.... We went in that clinic [because my friend was injured]. I wouldn't even have a dog treated there. Feces all over the floor, everywhere. The toilets were overflowing [to twice the height of the seat] with feces. One of the buildings that was adjacent to the Arena and the Superdome was some type of storage facility. One of the young men came up to me and told me, "They got bodies stacked in there all the way to the roof." I didn't believe him, so I went by and looked. I saw 500 to 700 hundred bodies [there].

Toward the evening of Friday, we started seeing vehicles appear on the freeway. We saw Dade County, Kentucky, Texas, different counties in Florida, New York. I started seeing Orange County, I saw L.A. County, I saw San Francisco County, and Alameda County and when I saw the Oakland rescue unit, I stepped in front of the truck.... He stopped for me. He start[ed] throwing bundles of food out of the [cab] and signaling to people to come get it, feed[ing]...people that didn't have anything.

This guy from Oakland gave me some insight about how to get out. "You see those ambulances sitting down there? They're all open. Once you get in, they can't put you off." I didn't say anything to any-body else because we would have had a stampede. [We] just start[ed] picking up [our] stuff and...walking down there.... Don't look around, and don't say anything out loud.... [We] just walked up to the door... opened it, and [got] on...! The driver...looks at all of us, and...he closed the door..., got back in the driver's side..., turned on the sirens, and we were out of there, just like that.

He took us to the airport around the long way, all through Jefferson Parish.... They had a lot more help over there.... People were still driving along the streets, it was nothing like New Orleans [Parish,] not to mention people that were trying to leave Jefferson Parish across the city connection. The National Guard had guns drawn on them, they wouldn't allow them to go over to the west bank. The High Sheriff of Jefferson Parish, Harry Lee, [who happens to be] Asian..., is an extreme racist. He's been the High Sheriff for almost thirty years. In the same position.

[At] the airport...people [were] trying to save their pets, people everywhere, water, feces, everything. They have a whole area of the airport that was just a morgue about five feet high with dead bodies. People that they couldn't do anything for, they were just wheeling them over there to where the morgue was and allowing them to die.

We got flown out by the federal sky marshals, we were taken out on a cargo plane...to San Antonio. From what I understand once I got to Texas, most people who left after we did...were put on buses or planes, and not even told where they were going until the doors were closed. Literally hundreds of people I've talked to said that to me.

I talked to a big contingent of Black men at the Astrodome in Houston who told me when the buses finally did come—for the people that were leaving on buses—they were dividing their families...and the first thing they did was take all the men out of their families, sent them to the side.... *They purposely separated the men from their families!* They would take [people] and two of [their] kids and then put [their] other two kids on the next bus. This is how a lot of people got separated. People...had been purposely separated from their children, the men were purposely separated from their households.

There are people out here in California right now [whose] wives are in one place, [but] the husband's out here 'cause he had family out here. They are just now finding each other. And this holds up their FEMA [disbursement].... They can't apply either place because they have to wait until they reunite. [From] the way [FEMA is] not distributing the money...we know that...they're trying to make it financially [impossible] for them...to come back.... They have huge developers [with the backing of] the New Orleans tourism board... waiting in the wings to buy up that property in blocks. 'Cause they're developing all the area where I lived. To give you an example...on the west side of Claiborne—we're on the same street—the houses are selling for two or three thousand; on the other side of the street for twenty to thirty to forty thousand dollars. Another thing people are not talking about: there's over 300 Black children missing out of Orleans Parish. No one's talking about that.

I talked to people that were in Orleans Parish Jail, and people who lived by the jail where the water was about 20 feet deep.... A month after the storm, that water was still up to four stories on Tulane. I talked to some people that did get out of there and were able to swim to the interstate. They told me that they left them...in the jail for three days, the women's jail and the men's jail, with no food or water, or electricity. The police actually abandoned the jail and left the people in there. About 50 women drowned in New Orleans Parish Prison. They never did let the women out....

But 98% of all these deaths were preventable.... People's conception of Hurricane Katrina['s toll] is all those people were killed by a hurricane. *Be real clear, most of us survived the hurricane.... All the death as a result of Hurricane Katrina was from lack of medical attention, no emergency medical response, no rescue. It was all a lot of unnecessary death and dying and all of it was preventable.* Who got rescued [was] drawn down racial lines. For all those naysayers who don't want to believe any of that, I don't know what to tell them. When you seeing able-bodied, White people being trucked out and people dying all around you, it don't take a rocket scientist to figure that shit out. Even a Black person could figure that out.

As a Black woman in America, I don't deceive myself to think that the system has any care or concern for me. I'm Black and a woman, so I'm shit to the government and the powers that be and extremely expendable. Don't think that I don't know it.... The hatred [in] this country under...institutionalized racism makes it a factor of who lives and who dies. [But] I did witness one thing that I never thought I would see.... I saw a big wave of international humanity, not just from this country, but from all over the world. [To] the people that helped and did all they could for us I am extremely grateful.

Interview with L.V.
Conducted November 21, 2005
Best Western, Jack London Square, Oakland, California

What strikes me about this interview is the cohesive picture the informant paints of New Orleans society. It provides a clear accounting, not only of this exquisitely rich cultural—and musical—background, but a detailed narrative of his week spent in the New Orleans Superdome, and of an aftermath marked by the insurmountable obstacles faced by survivors trying to regain their footing in a life which, for all intents and purposes, no longer exists.

I was born and raised in New Orleans. We grew up in the Sixth Ward.... The Lafittte Project* I lived in was in the heart of town. We were the only Black[s]...in our neighborhood. In order to get an apartment in the Lafitte, you had to have a job. You were screened four times before you got the apartment. We were middle class Blacks, from families with parents, a mother, a father, and you couldn't find a home where a parent wasn't an adult when they had you. Nobody was a child of a child. Our neighborhood was not a welfare recipient neighborhood. Everybody worked. It didn't have that stereotype that people have of projects now. We lived in a project, but we didn't live *like* a project.... We were well groomed, hair cut. We did not go to school looking like hoochies and thugs and convicts. And we dressed very well no matter where we were going.

---

*For some months after the hurricane, although it was undamaged, the Lafitte Project stayed boarded up. Despite the desperate need for housing by people who tried returning, it was raised.

We had all shades of Black. You had Spanish Creole Blacks, beautiful people. Some parts of the project you had Blacks who didn't have Creole ancestry. They were beautiful people, too, in their own right. Very good dressers, [too]. The side of the project I stayed on was the west side of Lafitte. We had French Creole Blacks. Beautiful people.

We all loved each other, and we all got along. There were some German people who had ballrooms. Across the street we had the Italians whom we affectionately called Dagos. And they loved us, too. And we had the Chinese, we had the Japanese, and the Koreans and...a couple of blocks down the street, the White folks lived.... We had true French people.... They had gold curly hair, and we had true Spanish people from Madrid, Spain, brown skin with black curly hair. And we had Native Americans. They were red skinned people with high cheekbones and big noses. During that time, growing up in New Orleans, we had...every culture there was. That's what made our neighborhood beautiful.

In Lafitte everybody was family. If you lived in the Sixth Ward, you had it going on: treat you like family. It was beautiful.... We gave each other food. We could sleep with our doors open, nobody would break in. If [I] didn't have no sugar, I went next door by Miss Eileen and got sugar. If you were hungry, we would swap meals. "Check this out, girl, this is what I cooked today." Every Friday we'd have a waist line party. We measured your waist, that's what you paid. Every Friday! It was fun. It was a full house every week.... We played Motown, and the Beatles. I was a kid then, 7, 8, 9, ten years old. [W]e were big on the Beatles. You heard every Motown song, and you heard every Beatles song.

In New Orleans, everybody stay with each other. In the fifties or sixties or seventies, it was all for one, and one for all. Grandma, the daughter and her husband. Everybody was family. The Black family then was the [traditional] Black family. I'd say in the early '80s it changed. We became Americanized. Everybody go on their own. The Black woman started getting more from White America. They didn't need the Black man any more. They got independent, they left their husbands, they could do things on their own now. They broke away from grandma. The family atmosphere broke up. The more they got, the more they want. It was like how America wanted it: dispersing us.... By the mid '80s the Black family as we knew it in the 50s, 60s and '70s was no more. Everybody had to fend for himself. Let me give you an example. When a kid gets 18, he's kicked out. It wasn't like that before in the Black family. You could stay home as long as you want. You was family. There was no such thing as "you're eighteen, you gotta go." We became so Americanized, when a kid got 18 he was kicked out on his own. Just because he's 18 doesn't mean he's ready to face the world.

Cause you gotta remember, we only be free [since] 1862. You're talking about 120 years. That's nothing. That's still nothing, as far as time go. People got a misconception. New Orleans didn't have slaves like Louisiana and other places. Blacks lived in New Orleans as far back as 1510, when they came with French and Spanish explorers before Iberville named it New Orleans. Louisiana Purchase, 1803, that's when the slave trade came. We were in the south but slavery was mostly in the bayous and Northern Louisiana. You might have some people in New Orleans who did have slaves, but it was a very small percentage.... Louisiana...[was] Union, all the way.

That's why our roots [run] so deep in us. In the United States..., the only Blacks have culture or roots or heritage is New Orleans Blacks. [Elsewhere] Blacks don't have anything to identify with. They have...no heritage, nothing to connect to.... [In New Orleans] from Navy Day to December 31st [t]here's a jazz funeral all year around when anybody dies. Second Line every week. Even the animals, if you have a dog and he dies, we Second Line behind a dog. If you have a cat, she dies, we Second Line behind a cat. Anything we love, it dies, we have a jazz funeral for.... See, for instance, I love music. You would bury me with all my record albums and all my tapes. That's how you would bury me. You like movies, they would bury you with all your videos in the casket. All Miss C's movies, man, put all Miss C's movies in the casket with her....

I had a collection of 5,000 albums before the hurricane. I had rock and roll, jazz, Black music. I started collecting them when I was in seventh grade. I had every Beatles album, every Rolling Stone album, every Chicago album, Doobie Brothers album, everybody, a whole library, Motown, history of Motown. Everything the Supremes made, the Temptations made, I had everything that Billie Holiday made, I had everything Dorothy Dandridge made.... I had bookshelves that went around the room.... Every day I would play four albums. A female vocalist, rock, jazz, blues, every day. Sundays, I play live music. Always live music on Sunday.... If I was planning to have a party, I would plan a month in advance. When I come home, I would record music for the party. I would play reel to reel, play the whole night.

The hurricane was about to hit the Gulf. We'd been watching the news all week 'cause we knew the hurricane was out there. We haven't had hurricanes in so long...only...Betsy.... We were lulled into complacency mode. Friday, August 26, my last day of work was at Lusher Elementary School where I worked as a teacher's aid and custodian. Saturday the mayor...tell everybody to evacuate. Naturally everybody said, no, we gone ride it out. They opened the Superdome the night of the 28th. I went [there] Sunday morning.... At 8 AM there's [already] lines on the street as if they're going to a Saint's game. By 12 o'clock Sunday afternoon, you got about 20,000 in the Superdome. Sunday evening about 6 o'clock you got about 40,000 people. The hurricane struck 11 PM Sunday night. It vanished Monday morning 9 AM.... People still be coming to the Superdome as of Monday, Tuesday, and Wednesday, and Thursday so by Friday after the hurricane you had about 80,000 people in the Superdome. The water stopped running Tuesday, and the air conditioning goes out. And lights went out in the city, but the Superdome have generators, so we were still able to have light....

I spent six nights, five days in the Superdome. Horrifying. The [National Guard] came from everywhere. They all had uniforms on, they had military uniforms on. They had this old lady 85 years old had a heart attack. [One] shoved an M-16 in her face and told her get out of his face and sit down. The woman's daughter—I know her because I went to school with her—tells the National Guard, "My mother's having a heart attack. She needs help." "I don't give a damn what you need, go sit down." [People] assaulted every National Guard they could when they refused that lady services.... And from that point, they were shooting National Guardsmen in the Superdome right and left because they weren't treating us right. They treated us like dogs. You had women having babies in there. Some woman died in childbirth because she couldn't have a C-section. Some girls and women died in childbirth. Some people couldn't get medicine, they had seizures and died. I saw three women die. I saw one guy dying of a seizure. They tried to rape this girl. They bust her on the head but she got away. They raped this little boy, bust his rectum. He couldn't even get stitched up. I don't know what became of him. Three men in the bathroom. With no lights.

They fed you twice a day. Seven o'clock in the morning, seven o'clock in the evening. The brown bag stuff. Water, one bottle of water per meal per day. You are constipated..., you got locked bowels.... You didn't get anything [until] seven o'clock in the morning, you not gonna get anything until seven o'clock that night. I probably slept but one hour the whole six nights because of the riots, the mayhem, the brutal mishandling by the National Guard. It was a war zone.

In the beginning, they ask you to throw all your drugs in the garbage can the Sunday when you was going in. By Wednesday, they didn't care. There were so many people who were very stressed out, so you had people getting them drugs to get high to alleviate the stress. "Smoke this weed, man, ease the tension. Drink as much beer and as much liquor as possible to help you go to sleep." They broke in the suites in the Superdome and got liquor and beer. We actually had a party in the Superdome while we were being held hostage like animals and criminals.... It got to a point where National Guard didn't care if you was getting high in front of them or not.... They had some kids with crack, crack-cocaine. They didn't even care anymore.

There's a freeway by the Superdome. The helicopter[s] passed over fifty times, wouldn't stop to help. You're in the Superdome with 80,000 people, and let's say a thousand of them were White. So that was a horror movie for them.... Some brothers who had rifles and guns shooting at the helicopters in retaliation for them passing people up on their roofs. "They gone pass them by, we're going to show them." Ratatattattat. And people round the world want to know, why they shooting the helicopters? Because they're not helping us. They're overlooking us, passing us by on our roofs. Or on the freeway.

The water around the Superdome was 15-20 feet high.... We were in the Superdome for a week, before the water subside so the buses could come. They sent buses Friday and the National Guard sent the buses back to wherever they come from. Why? That was our question. They had another convoy of buses and they started loading on them. So we wound up in Tyler, Texas..., and for the first time in a week, everybody had a shower.... You took off your clothes, your clothes stood up. We had to throw our clothes away.... They brought us to Green Acres Baptist church..., 280 people. Those folks were great. Gave us some clothes, gave us shelter.

[But] Green Acres [closed]. Red Cross put us out. I had nowhere to go when I was evicted. We were on the street, at the bus depot, sleeping upright, sleeping under the freeway, sleeping wherever we can get. I've been arrested off the street for loitering.... Here in Oakland, I'm about to get evicted and I'm going to stay under the freeway by the police. And in the morning, I'm going to knock on the door and ask them if I can wash up?

Red Cross refused to pay for [you to reach] your destination, so the debit money they gave you, the $360, which you're supposed to use to get something to eat or whatever, I used that to come here to Oakland. I came by bus, two and a half days.... Family friends, they took me in....

We weathered the disaster, we're still alive. The exile part is worse because you can't get help, they don't want to help. All the money Red

Cross got from all over the universe—you have 300 million people in the US. The whole Gulf Coast, let's say about 5 million were disaster victims. Why can't we get anything? "Oh, we got to support the war in Iraq. Oh, we still rebuilding Afghanistan...." And on the 21st of November [they'll evict] my people again. They don't give a damn what happens to us.

They want to know your grandfather's past history, your great granddad's past history.... Do you pay income tax? For what? We don't have any tax forms. I can't get rental assistance. If you're a renter from a property owner, or if you live with someone and you don't rent, you can forget it.... You may as well shoot yourself in the head, cause you're not going to get a damn thing. You're not entitled to nothing. Nothing at all....

My question is..., Japan gave 500 million dollars to the Katrina fund..., Great Britain gave 700 million..., Canada gave 400 million dollars.... It was still baseball season. Every major league baseball game donated money from each game—this is before the playoffs and the World Series now—*every* baseball game, *every* N.C.A.A. game, the opening game in college football, in all the stadiums across this ugly country—and that's what it is right now—they gave the proceeds for every game, one particular game raised $20,000. If every college game donated money, you're talking about zillions of college games. You're speaking about inconceivable numbers here. *Where's the money gone? Where's it going? We don't got it and we're not getting it.*

Like the FEMA representatives. They not really FEMA people, they given a shirt and a blazer. They go to a class for one hour.... And you under the impression they're from Washington D.C. or Bethesda, MD. But the people you talk to [here] are volunteers. They call Bethesda, MD. They tell you dial the number: "Here!" they give the phone to you.... There are separate entities for assistance. The rental assistance is a whole other outfit that a lot of us don't know about. Then they say give you a loan. I don't want a loan. I want assistance, if I wanted a loan, I'd have gone to a bank or credit union. We need assistance. We don't need loans, because how we gonna pay if we not working?

And then they cut you loose. Go find a job. Out here you don't know where you're going. You don't know where nothing's at. You don't know how to get around. They talk to you like you been living here for years. *They want you to act like nothing never happened. Just be cool. How can you get on with your life when you don't have any?* Like everything is normal. It's horrifying for me, and I'm a 49-year-old man!

You know they detonated the levees.... BOOM. One of the evacuees heard the explosion. She stayed near the 17th street canal. If they detonated one levee, they detonated the four other levees. We had a hurricane in 1965. In March '66 New Orleans asked Washington, from March 1966 to 2004, New Orleans asked Washington for money to rebuild levees. For 40 years, 40 years, Washington, D.C. has denied New Orleans money to build a proper levee. Forty years, OK.... As late as last year Mary Landrieu went there and didn't get it.... That's 40 years of requests that been pushed out the window and swept under the carpet.... It's blatant criminal neglect. If you stop rebuilding Afghanistan and [Baghdad] to the tune of so many billions of dollars, you can do this.

We were on the verge inadvertently to becoming the first city in America...to be totally Black. Because at the time [of Katrina] we were 75-80% Black. The more Black we became, the less money the government...sent. So when the levees were detonated, and the flood waters came, of course we evacuated. And [Michael] Brown said, "Well, fellahs, we settled the housing problem in New Orleans, didn't we?" I guess they did. He was doing a real good job.

At the function [last night] at the Washington Inn some of the evacuees spoke about them being on their own..., but I spoke about the atrocities of the U.S. Government and that just blew them away. Because they never heard an evacuee speak with such bitterness and hatred for the government right now. I spoke from the heart, and that's the way I felt. Until they do better for all of us—not just myself, but all of us—I won't never be comfortable or speak favorably of my government.

Interview with B.M.
Conducted November 9, 2005
Jack London Inn, Oakland, California

To the sounds of the New Orleans Hot-8 Brass Funeral Band—and thanks to the following informant—I joined over a hundred dancers in West Oakland's streets to form a small but gyrating part of this historical occasion, West Oakland's first ever Second Line.

I love to dance since [I was] a child.... We lived in one of the best parts of the city, which is uptown.... I was always around my grandmother's house, and I can remember hearing the music outside, so when I ran to the front door and saw all the people, I went and got my aunt. My great aunt...was the first person to bring me to a Second Line when I was two years old.... She was just as excited as I. We ended up walking for miles, following it. I've never forgotten that.

When you think New Orleans, you think marching to jazz music in the streets. It's...a funeral tradition that dates back to Indians, and Haiti, and to the rich culture that's embedded in New Orleans. The first line is for the deceased person and the immediate family and close relatives. The Second Line is for whomsoever might come, the folk. They used to pass through the neighborhoods of uptown and downtown New Orleans. If you don't have a Second Line when you die, you weren't nobody, honey.... I love the Second Lines. It's the best free party in the world, [something] you could just stumble on, be it a birthday celebration, or a funeral, or an annual celebration for a club... it's a big to-do as we say in New Orleans, a big, big production. If you come with jeans it's fine, if you come with your finest garments—it's a fashion show of course—that's fine. If you run out there with your housecoat on, your pajamas, nobody would say anything, no second looks. Just "get in line, come on let's go."

I'm the oldest of all the grandchildren and great grand children. Actually my dad was a rolling stone, just to cut to the chase. There's approximately 12 of us, 12 or 13. By different mothers, by maybe four if not five different mothers—that we know of! And I'm not sure there's not somebody else out there...! My mother has four kids. I had a little brother that drowned at six years of age and my dad just couldn't handle it, and that's where the separation came.... My dad's previous [wife] has four kids, and outside of those two marriages he's got offspring, maybe three or four other kids. Whenever they came to town, they came to our home. That's New Orleans! It's...family just like it is in Oakland....

I have a grandmother who's 90, a grandfather who's 90. My mom lives with my grandparents. They all live together. My sister and one of my aunts have three houses that we own on the block. My aunt has multiple sclerosis (my mom's sister) and my great aunt who is my grandfather's sister had a stroke in May.... We were kind of jammed in [together] because they were kind of resistant about going. [Although] my brother wanted to provide a way out, they...decided to stick it out. Most people from New Orleans, especially the elderly, didn't want to leave. We...got stuck in my sister's house. But we were kind of prepared 'cause she's a Wal-Mart queen.... She prepared all sorts of stuff for them [anticipating] that they would not leave.... We ended up being in the house maybe three or four days, and on the second day I...decided to pop a hole in the roof. Because you could hear the helicopters and see the helicopters pass us. So my nephew and I took turns alternating on the roof. Fear set in. My aunt with multiple sclerosis [said], "I don't want to put anything on you because you guys have been phenomenal just keeping everybody calm and providing this and providing that, but we gotta get out of here." So I decided to swim until I ran into somebody with a boat that could come back and get help. And when I say swim—'cause the water was 12, 15, maybe 20 feet in my area of uptown New Orleans—I decided to swim to one of the local hospitals which is maybe a mile away.

It took me maybe an hour, an hour and a half to swim there which is normally a ten minute walk.... But I got there and there were firemen from Texas.... One was 18 years old, the other was a veteran, he might have been maybe 40 years, close to my age actually rescuing folk.... They were leaving, but one of the boats was damaged, so the guy promised me, "If you just stay here till tomorrow...I promise you I will rescue your family...." So I decided...to spend the night because it was dark, and the water was so dirty, and it was really scary...[not knowing] what was under water—I stepped on a dead body—[so] I waited for them and...they did come back like they promised..., but when we went to get my family, they were gone. The night I left, the helicopters came [and rescued them.] So we were separated. My sister, my grandparents and my aunt and my little nieces (my sister's two kids) were all evacuated to the airport.

[Later I heard from my sister] the airport was one of the [most] chaotic scenes in New Orleans—like the Convention Center and the Superdome. [She] kept pushing and pushing [for the family to] stay together, but the military was very, very abusive to say the least. To have guns pointed at you in the midst of this was traumatizing enough—and we are dealing with people 90 years old who have been in the house three days....

A gentleman overheard the conversation [between] my sister and one of the military guys, and he told her just to calm down and sit in a corner and keep everybody together. Little did she know he worked for Al Gore. Al Gore's...personal jet was at New Orleans airport— just to help. He flew my family from New Orleans International to Tennessee, but *when he tried returning to rescue others, the authorities wouldn't let him land.*

The helicopter [pilot] promised he would come back [for my aunt].... They didn't take my aunt because [she'd] had a stroke [and] she can't walk or talk. My nephew and my thirteen-year-old niece were there with [her]. I took my niece with me, and...my nephew stayed with my aunt till [the coast guard]...came back with the cage.... [After that]...we rowed through the neighborhood, [rescuing] as many people as we could. We convinced them to get out.... I came across Miss Paine, one of my mom's neighbors and friends, an elderly lady who had been sick a couple of months ago. [Larry,] her nephew, provided care for her, but he had had cancer surgery three weeks prior to the hurricane and had lost his colostomy bag. In turn she had had to become his care giver. She was sitting on the porch. She told me, "I prayed to God to deliver us today [but] I didn't know it would be you...." Larry was sitting inside in a chair with water up to his knees, and the whole living room was flooded. We rescued [them] and maybe 30 other folk in my neighborhood and the neighborhood between there and the drop off point.

[By then I knew my family was safe] so I [decided] to stick with Miss Paine and her nephew Larry because she's an old lady.... We got shipped by ambulance to Baton Rouge, Larry, Miss Paine, my niece, myself and two paramedics. LSU's assembly center was a triage center and mine was the first party to receive medical...assistance, and food.... From there we went to another shelter which was on Airline Highway. It was a K Mart store which they haphazardly threw together just to expedite people out of the triage center. It was not the most pleasing place to live for the two days we were there. So I talked to some social worker there about Miss Paine and Larry receiving medical attention, especially Larry because he's a cancer patient and he hadn't had medicine. He didn't even have a colostomy bag. I stayed with them as their caregiver until they found facilities for them in Baton Rouge and when they got comfortable in their rooms, I went back to LSU and started all over.

I was at LSU two days, still not knowing [exactly] where my family was. After I put my name on the Red Cross register..., I got a 3 AM call from a gentleman in Tennessee.... I didn't know anybody in Tennessee, but it was the gentleman from the shelter where my family was. I talked to my mother. "Everybody's been worried to death about you. If you want to come here, you're welcome to come," [she said, but...she] convinced me they were all fine. "Whatever you want to do, you need to air out and get yourself together right now."

There's been a lot of bad publicity but the good stuff's got to get out too 'cause there's been a lot, a lot of love. People [in Oakland] have been just phenomenal. [The Jack London Inn] has provided transportation, food every morning, there's a church that comes on

Sundays, provides a Sunday dinner as well as services. I don't know if they're interdenominational [under] normal [circumstances], but for this situation there's no barriers. There's a worship service just to gear you up and give you the motivation that you need. This hotel has provided FEMA workshops, they have provided medical attention. Red Cross has been here. Alameda Social Services has been very helpful. They have been here almost every day....

There were...families [here] with gobs of kids, when we first arrived. Someone anonymously contributed Xboxes for all the kids. Since then it's gotten kind of quiet. The kids have either been settled in school, or most of them have moved on to permanent residence or temporary residence in the neighborhoods, or apartments that have been provided either by the private sector or through the Red Cross....

We had about fifty families, some of them with kids. Sunday mornings they got together. Breakfast in the morning. The hotel also provided a toy room...and people donated toys, and clothing, and computers for the kids. Actually most of these clothes I have came from people just donating to the hotel. So I don't know who was responsible. The hotel provides a continental breakfast, but the transportation guy has been...going out, to whomever it is...providing hot meals for us, be it breakfast, be it lunch. It's not really a scheduled thing, but when he gets it, he and one of housekeeping guys...they pretty much know everybody that's an evacuee and they'd just come and knock. So many people want to help.... [They] want to help, but [things] are just not set up to facilitate [helping] for a long period of time. We're going to need long term assistance and long-term care. This approach worked, probably because it's small, it's not government, it's not an agency, it's a few people with imagination and heart....

The restaurant directly behind us...Everett and Jones...provided anything you want off the menu for almost a month.... No charge.... Whatever you wanted off the menu, from a meal, drink, desert, an appetizer, anything you wanted, heart and soul...!

For a lot of people from New Orleans it's hard to receive. We are so used to just doing for each other.... It's kinda hard for some of the people...now...to be receivers actually to receive wholeheartedly and without resistance.... And that's partially due to...the way things were...in New Orleans.... The culture is very, very rich, and they're very, very proud people. In New Orleans, when you walk past anybody, you speak. And [people] respond. Here in California it's not like that. In Atlanta they tell me the same thing. Houston is kinda iffy, but it's just not a hospitable community atmosphere like we're accustomed to, [one that] goes back to a tradition of respect.... But it's really interesting to see just walking down the street [here] if I have eye contact, I'll say "hi" or "what's up?" or just anything, and sometimes the response is "hi" or people just keep going. New Orleans was just New Orleans. Don't get me wrong. There were strong racial lines, very strong, but if you had love for the city and love for each other, it kind of dropped by the wayside. It was a blessed place. A very special place.

Kids adjust well.... I'm concerned...about the things that they saw, and the losses they encountered. But I am so excited especially about the educational aspect, with the chance that these kids that were from New Orleans who would never see anything other than New Orleans, are now going to be exposed to...an education that will provide them with a chance to be a part of this world. Because the education system in New Orleans was just deplorable.... I am also concerned about the emotional aspect. New Orleans was such a family- and community-oriented place.... Everybody knows each other and everybody interacts. So with the holidays approaching, I'm kind of concerned about how its going to hit.... [I'm concerned] as well [about] the rebuilding of New Orleans, because with everyone displaced, our influence is not going to be respected; we're not there to vote, or to go to city planning meetings, or discussions or just to voice an opinion, so its really, really scary to think about what could happen. I don't want to see New Orleans turn into a glorified Disney World, or Las Vegas with lights....Because I love New Orleans. There's no other city like it in the world. And there's no way really to put it back together.

Interview with M. N.
Conducted October 21, 2005
Woodfin Suites, Emeryville, California

I was born in New Orleans in 1957. I was mostly raised by my grandmother because my mother had seven other kids besides myself: I had six sisters, and for a long time I was the only boy. When my daddy used to get behind me, I used to run to her because when I got to her, he wasn't going to touch me. She saw how my daddy was an abuser. She took me from my daddy and my mother and raised me. She's all I had in my life [although] I had my mother, I had my sisters, I had my baby brother. [But] I was about 15 years old when he was born, so I didn't have a chance to grow with him because when he became a teenager, I was [already] a man.

We lived in Carrollton section. Ward 17. It's [for] low income Blacks. It was beautiful to live there.... My grandmother...looked [after everyone] because she always did. Everybody in the neighborhood knew about Mama Nelly. I could name everyone from one end to the other, [the whole] six blocks. Even the pets. I can name 'em all, from the left side and the right, from the even and the odd side. 'Cause we were like one big family. Everyone enjoy everybody. People always said, "Mama Nelly's my mom...." Her name was Penelope. But they called her Nelly for short. When she made dinner [if] she [saw] people sitting out on the [porch], she called them.... "Want something to eat?" [For] all the kids she used to make zips, icebergs, praline candy and popcorn balls. She used to sell all these things for...a nickel, whatever a kid had.... If you didn't have nothing..., she just give it away. She had all special recipes. She...always say I won't tell nobody my recipe. I take it with me till the day I die. She had a kind heart. That's why she lived to be 95 years old. She watched me grow...into a man, she watched me leave the household, come back [home], leave again, [go] to the service, come back [home again].... I just couldn't live without her.

She would never move. She was in heaven where she was at. She didn't want to make all the big money like everybody else want to make. She always said, "a penny a day is a penny earned...." When families gradually started moving out, other families come in their place and they grew to be close knit like we had in the old neighborhood along the six blocks.... Three generations of neighbors that came in and left. A lot of them died off of old age, a lot of them moved out, a lot of kids grew up and married. They moved out, to different towns, different states but God just kept us remaining there.... My grandmother wasn't going to move away, and the house was kinda falling down on us, the roof was leaking, you know, it was cold, we had holes in the ceiling, the heat couldn't stay in, but she was in her house and she didn't want nobody to do nothing to her house. When I say, "Grandmother you need to fix your house, want me to repair this?"

"No," she say, "this is my house I'm going to take care of my own house, God will take care of me in this house." That's the way she lived. She was still active, from the age of 90 to 95. She would get up in the morning, she would fix me breakfast, she would wash my clothes, if I dared to touch her stove or her washing machine—"Boy, you know I don't want you to touch my stuff. I do my own work in my house. This is a woman's job to do her work in her house."

She [used to say] she wanted everybody to be happy. She [had] six guitars, two pianos, two organs, and one banjo. And she played them all. She wouldn't play for a church, but she would teach the kids in the neighborhood lessons on the piano.... As far as I can remember there was always someone in there that she was teaching music to. She said it was a...gift God gave her just to pick up music and just to hear and play it on an instrument. She lived for her music. She used to play Count Basie's music and all the hymns they had in the hymn book in church, she could sit down and play them on the piano. All day long she would play her music. If it wasn't the piano she was on, she was on the guitar or one of her organs. She learned to play by listening. She used to tell me she played by ear. [But] way back I think it was in [her] early [50s] she used to go a place they called World Lines. World Lines was a music store with a music school. They charged her money to teach her...five dollars per lesson. She used to pack her guitar up and catch the bus, she'd go to World Lines and they...teach her the notes and stuff where she could start reading music and when she learned the chords and notes on the guitar, like she say, the piano was similar to the guitar. And she picked up the guitar, and she picked up the banjo. She already had the instinct on the piano anyway because that's what she learned from. But most of the time, she just used to pick up music on her own. She was a jolly old thing always with her music. It used to keep her happy. If you didn't sit down and try to get her to do something for you, she would sit there and play music all day long.

She used to tell me her father had bought her a ticket to Chicago to play music. She was sixteen, going on seventeen. When she got to the window to give the man her ticket a White guy came up and took her seat on the train so she couldn't go. I guess it broke her heart. But my grandfather came along, and he tried to change her mind about leaving [so] she decided to stay. "See if that man wouldn't have took my seat, you wouldn't be here today. That's the only reason why I be with you all today because if that man wouldn't have took my seat on the train, you wouldn't be here today. I would have been gone to Chicago to play music.

[When I was young] I fell in with the wrong crowd. And that came from me being abused as a child and I didn't have where to turn. [So] I turned to the streets, and drank alcohol, but all that time ...my grandmother...was always there for me no matter what. I have been to prison for fifteen years, nine months and 22 days for a crime I didn't commit. I was in a car with the wrong people at the wrong time. And I couldn't tell people that I didn't do nothing because the guy that was in the car with me said, "Yeah, he with us." and I had to stay in Angola for—oh!—fifteen years, nine months and 22 days before I got released.... I went back to court and the judge said, "I don't know how you got in here, I don't know why you did all this time. Only God knows." And he cut me free. I just had all this time knocked out my life.

When I went to prison..., every month for fifteen years [my grandmother] came to see me without fail. One hundred some miles. The first of the month when she got her check she was there at the prison gate to see me. And she would make that trip every month.

She stuck with me all the way through it. I learned first hand from [her] how to live good and how to treat others good in order to be good yourself.

At the time of the storm it was just me and my grandmother left in New Orleans. Every time there was a storm she would ask me "What we going to do?" I say "Well, we going to ride this one out. I don't think it's going to be that bad." But this one came up and all of my kin folks was calling her telling her she gotta get out now because the house got old now, it was real old. We couldn't stand a category three or four hurricane. And this was supposed to be a category five when it hit and everybody start talking about leaving.... And...she say "What you think, you going to stay?" And I said, "Well, I don't think we should stay for this one." She say, "Where you goin' at?" I say "I don't know." And she told me "Well, your sister want me to come with her and they going home to Memphis." And I told her, I say "Well my cousin stayin' in California. She had asked me if I could come up that way...." My sister got her kids and my grandmother and my [other] sister's kids and they was so many people [and] they all was going. The household wasn't big enough to hold all of us. So I said "Well if my cousin send me bus fare I'll go to California." So the day of the 28th I boarded the bus to go to California and she got in the car that day and she went to Memphis with my sister Laura. Laura told me at one point she thought she passed over because it was a silence in her body. Her whole body low by travelling so much. But she said she prayed to God. "God please I don't want to die here. I want to die around my family."

As the storm quieted down, the next day the levee broke. That's what sent all the water through the 17th ward and [my grandmother] couldn't come home, so she went to Hammond where my mother and a couple of my sisters and my brother stays.... She stayed in Hammond for about three weeks, and each time it was time for her to go home, something would come up. The threat of another hurricane, or the water was still so high, there was no one in the city. [She said,] "something don't want me to go back to my house. Well I'm going to my new house because you all don't want to take me to my [old] house." [Then] when the water did come down, she got sick and she went into the hospital in Hammond and that's where she died. She died the next day.

She loved me. She loved the world. The morning she passed, I called her on the telephone. And she asked me, she said, "You all right?" And I said "Yes." "Well, I'm all right," she said, "take care of yourself." And she died. She just wanted to hear my voice to know that I was all right. And she passed. Right after she talked to me on the phone. Almost as though she decided that she was about to leave. "Well. I can't go back home and there's no where to go."

After the hurricane, our house was the only house demolished. Of all the whole six blocks, ours was the only one totally demolished because it was the oldest one. The storm took it away. The mayor from New Orleans say from Canal Street to Claibourne there's going to be a baby Las Vegas. All these families that lost their houses, they're going to buy them out and they're going to run casinos for miles. And in the New Orleans Ninth Ward area, there's going to be a Disney World and a brand new football stadium for the New Orleans Saints. They had plans for all of these things that happened. Maybe before it happened. They just needed the things that happened to happen. Now the way I look at it, it could have been because all the places in New Orleans where they had high crime areas, all those places was wiped out, the dams broke at certain spots and those spots were the Sixth Ward, the Ninth Ward, Carrollton Section.... It could be the will of God. That God came in there and wiped it out like that but I don't believe God wanted [to] bring gambling and entertainments like that, strip entertainments and stuff in that area. [Take] all these people out and...corrupted it again? Why not build low income houses out here? And put all these people that lost everything back. They giving them $2000 dollars when they gone make two...million dollars off of their property and the average poor person with $2000 dollars gone spend them $2000 and not gone have nothing [left]. They gave their whole life away for $2000! Something not right, something not fair..., but see, the Ninth Ward, the Seventeenth Ward, the Sixth Ward, the Third Ward, all these places where they had bad crime..., is gone. All the people that was in them areas are gone. And...then you gone turn right around after they [gone] not quite 30 days, and... build casinos all across their land where their places was. You going to build a football stadium and Disney World in their place and make money? Come on, something not right.

I have a copy of my grandmother's will that she says I should always have a say so, a stake in that land and all the materials that was in the house is mine. All her possessions she left is mine. But my mother never really owned anything in her life before neither, so ...she says, this my daughter's land, but her son have a place to stay. This was her dying will that I should always have somewhere to live. [But] everything in the house, all them pianos, guitars and stuff was destroyed. The salt water ate it all up. Big ol' grand piano just breaks up in my hands.

I really want to go back home. Carrollton Section. Ward 17. But there's no home anymore. No one else is there.

Interview with W.J. Jr.
Conducted October 15, 2005
Civic Center Lodge, Oakland, California

I'm fifty years old. I was born in New Orleans, Louisiana. I was raised up in the Third Ward. My family was living in the Ninth Ward, so I moved into the Ninth Ward. [I used to] clean ships. I loved it, I loved every bit of it. Climbing on the ladders, and stuff like that. Sometimes I'd get a cushy job, sit down, tell some people what to do if they didn't know what to do. It went like that for about 19 years. Live with my mother, my father, my uncles, my cousins and some friends, and it was beautiful.

I played the alto sax..., from 4 or 5 all the way up to the age of 16.... My father asked me what I wanted to do. Wanted to play music.

I pointed out to him...I want to play sax. First I learn how to play by ear until I started learning how to read sheet music.

For a long time we went to a teacher.... [As] I was getting older, I got a little better at it, and in school playing music too. Then we got a little band together. I used to love to travel. From Baton Rouge and different places. Make a few dollars. Oh, it was beautiful! But me and another friend of mine...was playing with a gun.... I thought—least I thought—he took...all [the bullets] out. I clicked it, the gun went off. Ricocheted off the project wall, and caught me right here in the head. And I thank the lord I am still here. I'm blessed 'cause I'm here. I am kind of blind on one side, so...every time I would blow, I would have a great big old headache. And I had to stop.

[After some] time, things got a little better for me, [but] I found out that my daddy had sold the horn. I think about it, what I used to do. My sister used to sing in the band. We used to have a name. Before the accident happened. "The Incredible Mob." It was beautiful, though. We used to go over...Claiborne Street. I played different bands over there.... We had a manager who used to get gigs for us. It was beautiful. I miss it. It's a beautiful world.

To me, the way things is today, if you don't teach children the right way, they gone wind up in jail, they gone wind up dead. Always had to say "yes, ma'am, yes, sir." That's the way I was brought up. One thing I praise myself: I'm a good father.

I had six [kids]. I lost my oldest son. [He] died at the age of 17. He was shot in the east, by the skating ring. I have one son I haven't seen since the age of one. His mother said he wasn't mine, so I kinda left it like that, but my sister tell me he looks just like me. Then I have another son that's seventeen. That's the one I had to go to the social security office to try to find, to see if he was still living, but they told me they could not tell me where he was living at, but I could write the letter, and bring it to them, and they would mail it to see if it would be all right, if he want to see me. I take care of all of my children.

My little son is in jail. I haven't heard from him because every time he would call, they said "press one," and it would click off. I tell him, it's not me, it's the phone. I just talked to my brother, so I know he's OK. He has four more years to serve. Another son.... He about 26 now.... [He] has nine children. He's a busy man, too busy for me! When I was in Texas I seen him and my grandchildren. Some of them. I didn't see all of them—I talked with them when I left to come to California—and my daughter. I have a girl—she's in Texas, married, finished college, she's doing well.... I talk to her every now and then. She'll call me, I'll call her.... I try to stay close to all of them, because they're my children. Just to call and say "hello."

On Friday [before the storm] me and my [lady]...decided to work things out. I called her. I say with the storm coming, I'm coming by you, because she have three levels, so if the water was going to come that high, I would have a better chance being over there with them. So I left and went over there and stayed with [her] that Friday and that Saturday. [T]here was about 13 or 14 people in the house, mostly [her] family, aunties, cousin, grandchildren. About 13. [On] Sunday when the storm hit, the lights went out.

We had food and we had water.... We had a grill out on the porch. We did a lot of cooking on the grill. We were looking at the helicopters flying over us that Monday. We kept on talking about what we gone do. Because...we were running short of water, running short of food.... At least 100 to 200 people were still in that area. We saw these guys jumping off the balcony, swimming a little distance. Jumping off and swimming, and we seen another guy jump off, start screaming he can't swim, and I see another guy jump in try to save him. And...he went down and the other guy went down [so] he had to let him go.... So we watched him drown. Sixteen or seventeen years old. And his mama saw it too. Yes, yes, oh, yes. We didn't see no more of him till next morning and we listened to someone tell how the body was [caught] against a railing....

My daddy have a boat and we had a lot of people. So [my buddy] asked me if he thinks I can make it swimming...cause I'm a diabetic. I didn't know I could make that long of a trip swimming..., but I said, "I think I can." So...Tuesday morning, we went and start stroking, swimming and stroking, trying to rest, trying to keep going until we turned the corner. And we rest against one step and we kept on going on, until we got to where the posts was. About seven blocks, we went from one post to the next post all the way till we got to my father's house. It's a nice little distance. The Good Lord was with me. So me and [my buddy] got in my father's boat. We didn't know anything about the motor, but we see a friend of mine. So I called him [over] cause normally he would go fishing with my father when he was home. We cut the [lines]. We went to get food, we wound up not just getting food but helping other people that needed food or water. We...went all the way to Broad and Louisa. There was a store there..., a Walgreens or something.... The mayor said you can go in these stores and get whatever you need. Because he say it was gonna get bad anyway.... So we went in the store and we loaded the boat up with water, beer, canned goods, anything we could eat. Because everybody was terrified. I never drink but we was getting [it for] people who needed it.... We got charcoal for the grill. We went down to other houses and gave them food. And liquor and beer.... We would go out in the morning..., go back out in the evening. Two trips a day. Sometimes I would let someone else go in my place, so they could feed their family.... I would stay behind. Next day I would go out, we would alternate. It was [three of us] and another neighbor....

[One time we saw] this guy—he was on top of the Florida Bridge.... He was a truck driver—he had a rig up there. He got bit by an alligator. And my lady's sister, [who] was a nurse, she told us tie his leg tight as he can be. We told him we'd come get him next morning. Because we couldn't see at night. Next morning [when] we went to the Florida Bridge [we saw] he was bit to the bone. We brought him to [my lady's] house so her sister can try to take care of him. She poured peroxide [but] we had to put him back in the boat because his leg was swollen. We brought him to St. Mary's but nobody there could help him. So we took him all the way to San Carlos Street. We seen some guy with a bus that they had stole. We asked him please to stop and bring this man on [his] bus and take him to the Superdome. Because that's what he was trying to do, bring people to the Superdome.

You know what was the hurting part was that nobody came to get us. [Not even] by the third day. I can understand the first day, I can understand the second day. Because at nighttime we would put flash lights, or we'd be waving our hands. But you're looking at helicopters flying over you.... One of them did stop and say we're coming for you all [but] he never came back. That was the fourth day....

We kept going back and forth to different stores...trying to get what we can get. Filled the boat up again with everything we could think of. Water, food, canned goods, liquor, beer...because we felt nobody care about us, period. I mean you're talking about the fourth day or the fifth day. The water got to about 23 feet. Just to see the helicopters flying over you, they're not stopping, just flying over.... Nobody cared. I think it was the fifth day we went out to get some more food... one guy was so angry he fired his pistol at one of them. He just fired because no one would stop.

Army and coast guard helicopters flying on, all day, all night, like we was nobody. They just flew over. They never picked us up. We seen an explosion. We seen some things burning out of control. Close to the bridge. We seen the people in cars on the bridge. They was looking at the water. The cars wasn't moving. At night about 50 of us hold a flashlight or a match so they can see something shining. They seen us, they saw us in the daytime. *They left us there to die.* They're looking at us. At night time too. Yes, at night time too. Then the sixth day came.... We was going back out to get food until we heard helicopters. And we looking at the area that they was in. It was right around the same area.... [So] we stopped and we turned around.

They was picking people off [the roof at] St. Mary.... We made three or four trips taking people to St. Mary's. About six boats were tied up there. That evening when we got everybody out, we went on the roof at St. Mary's so when the helicopters fly over us at night time, we hope they were going to pick us up but they...[just] shine their light down on us, and circle again and shine the light. It was cold. We broke in the closets and got sheets for the old people because we had a lot of old people and children that was cold. They broke into the cold drink machine. It was bad, a mess. I guess they did what they had to do to survive.

[Next] morning here come the helicopters.... All the stuff [from the rotors] got in our eyes. He picked the first group up. "Well, look," he say, "what we gonna do is keep all y'all together." Because me and [my lady] was together. [So] he hoist [us] up and...about four or five people and he flew us away. We went to the Causeway. We got a [cardboard] box and lay down and go to sleep. About 200,000 people under the Causeway. So we lay there. And next day we was seeing the bus pull up and pull out. School bus, taking only people that had physical problems. Older people, and my lady's sister and her husband, he was in a wheelchair. So they got on, and me and [my lady] got on because I have seizures, but they couldn't take the others. Then we went on to Texas in another bus that didn't have any air conditioning, and no bathroom. It was a school bus. All the way to Houston on that bus, four to six hours. No air conditioning, no nothing. When we got to Houston we went to the Astrodome, where they were tagging us. Once they put it on, you take it off, they not going to let you back in. So we stay there and [my lady's] sister's friend lived there, so her sister called. That's how we got to stay...with them. We was there in Houston about three weeks. I didn't feel right by living there with them [anymore] so I [told] [my lady] I have a sister live in California. So we went to California.

We been living here ever since. We were lucky to get this motel here [but] personally I want to go back home.... What I'm angry about: these people, you know, that little change that you given, it just to buy food, trying to put something on yourself. You got to stay on the phone hours and hours to try to get these people to do something for you. You supposed to receive three checks, two for $2000 and one for $2300. I'm going to be honest with you. I can prove that I did not receive $2300. Guess what, I'm not going to struggle. 'Cause you know what? *Always have been a working man. And I'm not going let no money destroy me....*

I lost everything. I had brand new clothes, brand new shoes, brand new.... People that know me would tell you I love to dress. The money they send me couldn't buy [what] I spent on my house, they clothes, they shoes.... I'm a picky man, I'm sorry. What they give me ain't shoe.... They don't know how I feel, or all the other people feel when they left us there to die! I'm looking at people thrown in the water, full up, looking at children drown, and you ask yourself how could this happen!

You imagine you are there. The first day no one. But you still fine. The second day, the third, the fourth day.... Where the troops at, where the national guard at? Where these people at? The fifth day. You got a hundred thousand people that need your help. I wish you could have really seen the water we had that day.... If I'd a stayed in my house where I lived...I be dead. I being honest with you, I be dead! Mine was under water. And everything I had was in that house. It took me years to get what I had. I had dress clothes, cause I love to dress. It means a lot to me because I came a long way. I can't write that well, I can read as far as that goes, but I'm not going to let no one handle me in any kind of way and before I do something crazy I'm going to walk away—if I could. Maybe that's what's keeping me alive. I don't know.

I'm angry with our supposed-to-be-government, with our supposed-to-be-president. I'm angry with FEMA. What was holding them back from coming get us? Did it need the president to say it's OK? That's my question. You got 100,000 people that need your help. But sure, sure. He was on vacation and he couldn't be bothered. I know what they did do. They got—you know—they got the rifles out first. I'm tell you why. When I went over there and slept under that bridge, I could count the White folks on my fingers. Couldn't have been more than a hundred. So they got the rich out first—200,000 people!—they in homes, they in hotels, they in campers. Where are the rest of the people? What about me? I'm a human being. What about me? I don't have nothing either. Where are they sending [people] at? Oregon? Kentucky? You know, I kept on saying to myself: where the White folks at? Aren't we supposed to be together?

3

What She Heard

Katrina had every mark of a natural disaster, with this exception, that for nearly 40 years, New Orleans—and the State of Louisiana—had been appealing to the federal government of the United States for funds to maintain and strengthen the system of levees which hold at bay the waters of Lake Pontchartrain, the Mississippi River, and the Gulf of Mexico. Repeated studies showed that New Orleans, with its many areas lying below sea level, was a disaster waiting to happen. On August 29th, it waited no longer. Subsequent studies seem to indicate that there was an unforeseen weakening of the levees because their footings were sunk in peat and too shallow at ten feet to contain the onslaught. Notwithstanding, it is moot to speculate what the consequences of the storm might have been had the levee system been properly engineered and maintained in a structurally responsible way, if, for example, the footings had been sunk to a depth of 17 feet, and if the federal government, acting as landlord, had fiscally underwritten the upkeep and protection of the real estate—not to mention the people—in its charge. But in the low lying districts, the residents were Black and poor, the tax base lower in proportion to the real estate value of the land. Two years later (August 29, 2007) although nothing had been done to construct a levee system able to withstand increasing storm severity guaranteed by future global warming, the national treasury continued to be looted to underwrite a war industry with no-bid contracts and kickbacks running into the billions, in favor of a Pentagon, which at this count cannot account for the disappearance of $8.5 trillion dollars.

Recording oral histories is painstaking work, winding and rewinding the audio tape, respecting accuracy, and recapturing the music of regional speech and colloquial expression wherever possible. It required determination prompted by the deep feelings I acquired over time for so many people who had been so cruelly and traumatically displaced. At the time, I had no idea that such a process, as well as the reverberations left by reading Llamazares' novel, *The Yellow Rain* were preparing me for something, something that would emerge nearly three years later as a work for the theater, but one set thousands of miles distant from New Orleans and its Creole culture, one that would take me to a village in contemporary agrarian Japan.

Patricia Hampl, writing in *I Could Tell You Stories*, makes a strong case that memoir is not complete until it pulls the public world into the realm of the private. "Out of the dread ruin and disintegration [of the world] emerges a protest which becomes history when it is written from the choral voice of a nation, and memoir when it is written from a personal voice."

Abridged as they are here, when I transcribed them these oral histories were originally intended for publication in full because, more than anything, I understood that in the words of my informants—as the original preface points out—I recognized the voice of a drowning nation.

What exactly did I hear? I heard a chorus of voices, what Hampl refers to as "antiphonal texts," phrases, overheard conversations, sound clouds, acoustic chambers echoing with sorrow and with loss.

The cut-up technique helps shake the mind clear of linear thinking (this happened, and then that happened); it loosens the bowels of the imagination, sometimes with explosive results. Thematically arranged, the cut-ups which follow are meant to provide readers with a visual idea of what I heard.

Critical Note: William Burroughs picked up the technique of "cut-ups" from his friend, Brion Gysin. Wikipedia defines it as an aleatory (meaning random) literary technique by which a text is cut up, only to be rearranged to make a new text. What's ironic here is that Gysin re-discovered what had first been a Dadaist technique. He had protected a table by spreading newspaper in order to be able to cut through papers with a razor blade. As he sliced through the layers, he discovered fascinating juxtapositions of words and image. From the start of my writing life, I, too, have made use of newspapers in much of my work. My debut novel *Face,* was triggered by an article I read way back in 1977, which I never forgot.

MORE BLACK WE BECAME

just doing for each other

six guitars, two pianos, two organs, and one banjo

ALL GOT ALONG.

ROOTS [RUN] DEEP

I love to dance

love to dress

WE THE ONLY BLACK[s]...

bought her a ticket to Chicago

maybe four if not five different mothers

5,000 ALBUMS

BLUES, EVERY DAY.

called her Nelly for short

EVERYBODY FAMILY

Ain't we sposed to be together?

brand new shoes

EVERYBODY STAY WITH EACH OTHER

been gone to Chicago to play music

when you die you weren't nobody, honey....

SECOND LINE BEHIND A CAT.

best free party in the world

EVERYBODY WORK

ANYBODY DIE: SECOND LINE

been a working man

If you don't have a Second Line

came to see me without fail One hundred some miles

ONLY BE FREE [SINCE] 1862

fifteen years, nine months and 22 days

time knocked out my life in jail

ALL MISS C'S MOVIES, MAN

if you didn't have nothing

MEASURED YOUR WAIST,

left us there to die

What we going do

take all the men from their families

getting out of here

What you think, you going to stay

guns drawn on them

nice little distance

we gonna keep all y'all together

All the way to Houston on that bus

gonna get bad anyway..

didn't want to leave Miss Connie

WOULDN'T STOP TO HELP.

lost his colostomy bag

watched him drown

his mama saw it too. yes, oh, yes

nobody come get us

not even told where they going

50 women drowned

Never did let the women out

I being honest with you, I be dead!

no one would stop.

ride this one out.

A WAR ZONE

bodies stacked

You imagine you are there,

all the way

to the roof

FIVE DAYS IN THE SUPERDOME

got a ladder out

stepped on a dead body

water got real black...

water up to his knees

saw them...for two days

night time too.

Two 'gators came and took 'em

TREATED US LIKE DOGS

no lights

BUST HIS RECTUM

Toward the evening of Friday

Just wheeling them over

they got the rifles out first

first day no one

wouldn't let him land

all day, all night

Then the sixth day came

four and a half days

HOW WE GONNA PAY

I want to go back home

Calcasieu Parish

going to buy them out

Carrollton Section. Ward 17

All these families lost their houses

LIKE EVERYTHING IS NORMAL

What about me? I don't have nothing either.

No one else is there.

Big ol' grand piano just breaks up in my hands

Where they sending [people] at?

HOW CAN YOU GET ON WITH YOUR LIFE WHEN

didn't have nothing

NO WHERE TO GO

selling for forty thousand llars

ACT LIKE NOTHING NEVER HAPPENED

NO HERITAGE, NOTHING TO CONNECT

YOU DON'T HAVE ANY?

gave their whole life away for $2000!

They had plans

just needed the things that happened to happen.

Something not right

no way to put it back together.

WHERE'S THE MONEY GONE?

no one there to vote

run casinos for miles

no home anymore

III.
Making Something

LIKE SNOW MELTING IN WATER:

Song for a Lost Village

An Elegy for the Theater

For Anna Goins

1

Spring Awakening

By now, although most of my Katrina informants have returned to New Orleans, a few have settled here; I am overjoyed whenever I meet one of them in the street, or hear from the happy ones who've made the journey home, but I feel a sense of loss that the oral history project itself has come to its natural close. As with any creative effort, its energy was fueled by momentum, but now it's been lost, I'm not inclined to fight it.

Something new has captured my attention, a clip I keep mislaying since I first came across it, from the Sunday, April 30, 2006 *New York Times*. "A Village Writes Its Epitaph: Victim of a Graying Japan" was a full-page feature about a contemporary agrarian rice-growing village on the Sea of Japan, whose elders determine that to survive in their old age, they must sell their village to the highest corporate bidder. I tack it to my bulletin board where it can migrate no longer. The story itself resonates not only with the present stage of my life, and with having given up my home, but with the planet—dying of exhaustion, no longer able to sustain itself.

After years of writing novels and mononovels centered around solitary protagonists, I've fallen under the spell of Katrina folks telling me their stories, of hearing the clamor of their laments: *Something ain't right.... They left us there to die.... I got nothing, no food, no job, nowhere to go.... We all seen it; his mama seen it, too.* Now I begin listening for the voices of far-away Japanese villagers, people who inhabit a landscape and a culture far removed from my own. But more than voices, I see pictures. And the *Times* article provides just enough imagery to give me a solid sense of the landscape, the look of the village people and their tumbling down houses, windows and doors out of plumb. I imagine a world contained by the cast of light, season to season, hour to hour; I hear the sounds of such a village as they pass through varying densities of air from season to season. I imagine elements down to the finest details: the rice husk raincoats the peasants wear; the sensation of tamping down rice shoots in the muddy paddy; the still water acting as a mirror of the sky, especially for people who all their lives are bent over water growing rice; the earth folding over itself, creating waves of soil as the plow cuts through the dirt. I draw on sense memories etched during the first 24 years of my life, lived in a climate given to harsh winters, snow drifts many feet high, a frozen Hudson River, its ice floes groaning and squealing with the current. I remember the smell of wet wool scarves wrapped around my face. I see snow melting in water.

I bring my experience as a theater-maker, directing a company over a twelve-year period in works based on collective creation; I know the feel of a performance space (not a stage)—a space with all the endowments that the word "space" implies: light quality; color, or its absence; the prop requirements reflective of a specific world, in the case of such an old village, one of messiness, entropy. I allow myself to dream.

From the beginning, I know the tone I want to create in the concluding section where we hear the isolated voices of the villagers one last time—the night scene before they blow out the lanterns, their reveries before sleep. And from that understanding, my sense of structure will emerge: five parts, call them Morning, Noon, Afternoon, Evening, and Night, and the epilogue—the triumphant corporate voice, the final "thank you very much."

And then, one morning, I begin to write. I date each day's production. The first, May 25, 2006: "Winters are bleak here in the mountains. We are used to it. I watch the road. My breath makes clouds in the frozen air. Below I can see past the three rooftops where the road terraces the mountain. One twist, then the long curve. This house is the highest. Up here the wind is fierce."

It's three months after the violent disruption of my move, only one month after discovering the article in *The New York Times,* although it feels to me as though I had been incubating ideas about this article for two or three years, and perhaps in emotional years—if there can be said to be such a thing—I had.

Without a sense of place, no story can begin. I take long solitary hikes in the woods, into the steep watershed where a creek runs through. I'm getting a visceral sense of the landscape where *Like Snow Melting in Water* takes place. In the revision, the passage above goes like this:

> I wasn't born here. I was born in Kanazawa. I came to Ogama as a bride. I've lived here now for fifty years. No! Fifty-one. A long time. I never thought I'd be forced to leave. I was a farmer's wife. I was smart, but you know how it is: I wasn't very pretty. I raised a family, worked with my husband in the fields. Kept house. Pickled and preserved for the winter, gathered firewood when I was stronger. But now...*(Pause.)*

When my two Japanese neighbors find out I'm writing about a real village, Ogama by name, near the Sea of Japan, they begin volunteering insights into a culture, which I (and probably most Westerners) find hopelessly opaque. Fumi, who spent the war years in a United States detention camp like so many of her fellow Japanese, is particularly helpful. Originally her hopes were to become a poet, but her concentration camp experience diverted her to a lifetime of political activism. She lived in Japan after the war. A samurai herself, nonetheless she declares her deep respect for the hardships of the peasant life, that is, except for one aspect: she can never accept the idea of infanticide. It is she who is the source of this astonishing revelation: that in a culture bound by such harsh life conditions, there is no provision—and no infrastructure—to care for any infant born with a handicap, which might exclude it as an adult from the backbreaking labor of working in the rice fields.

Sadako is a Japanese graphic artist who survived World War II in Osaka. She shows me her high school graduation picture. It looks like any other graduation picture: rows of smiling students nearly indistinguishable in their uniforms, instructors lined up to one side posing before their school building—until one notices, almost incidentally, that behind all this order, every single window pane is blown out. It is she who tells me about the *tanuki*, the burlesque, mythical and very real animal found nowhere else but in Japan. She shares articles with me about naming customs and rituals accompanying the birth of Japanese children, and about the meaning of names. As we become more familiar, we begin playing practical jokes on one another, indulging in droll little pratfalls—a touch of kyogen* in the hallway.

Next door, a neighbor takes a rusty kitchen knife to both wrists. I visit her in the hospital where I watch her get stitched up. Self-dissection, no matter how determined, does not pretty results make, but my debt to her is a steep one. My character Hiroko is preparing to trudge up the mountain where she will lie down in the snow and close her eyes for the last time:

> "Time. It must be time now. The bath has turned cold. Wipe my old body dry—wipe it dry. Between old legs, under old arms where the skin shrivels like a stale vegetable, like a withered leaf. Old knees, old back, old breasts and belly. See how they droop and sag, poor things—growing tired, exhausted, falling to earth where they must rest at last....
>
> In my mind...I try to think what I will need. Ah, Hiroko, I say to myself, Hiroko you will need nothing. You have everything you need: old hands, old eyes, old legs—just quick enough to feel the path. And no one left to bother you! They will be sleeping, the ones down below—the fortunate ones...!
>
> Put on the shirt, the sweaters, the foot coverings, the boots. Put these ridiculous things on one last time. Enough living. Enough...."

---

*A style of Japanese low-life comic theater.

This passage was composed early on, long before my neighbor made her suicide attempt, but, although at the time I was not yet aware, on some level I must have been picking up her energy before she made it obvious.

Over the nearly two-year period in which I continue working on *Snow*, the work decides it wants to become not a novel, but a work for the theater. And then, one day, they're all there, my villagers, the headman and his wife, and the village simpleton, and the woman determined not to lose her thirteenth child as she's lost all the others in childbirth, and the midwife: they're all assembled, telling me how little I know about things like growing rice and thatching roofs, and mushroom hunting in the forest, and about savage love that goes howling through the woods, always hungry, never satisfied. They tell me about things about which I know nothing—or very little. They tell me what snow feels like when it's melting into water.

2

Like Snow Melting in Water: Song for a Lost Village

Without rice, nothing happens: no life,
no food, nothing that is beautiful.

—Cecile Pineda, *Frieze*

The paddy fields save the world.

—*Popular saying*

Inquiries regarding dramatic rights for Like Snow Melting in Water *should be directed to Wings Press.*

I. MORNING

II. NOON

III. AFTERNOON

IV. EVENING

V. NIGHT

VI. EPILOGUE

"Like Snow Melting in Water" is an elegy for a dying village. It takes place in Ogama, a contemporary, remote farming village near the Sea of Japan. The characters for the most part are elderly former rice farmers. They have been born in this village (except for the two widows who were born in distant cities and came as picture brides) but they cannot die in this village. The play presents the reasons for their displacement.

Characters:

With the exception of CEO Yamashita-san, all 15 characters inhabit Ogama. The 16th character, Yamashita-san, who speaks the Epilogue of the play, is the CEO of a toxic waste disposal company.

Cast in order of speaking:

Sadako: A sensible, realistic widow of 85.
Hiroko (Hiro for short): A widow of uncertain age, either 79 or 80.
Harunobu (Haru for short): The village headman, still vigorous at 68.
Budo: A shrewd, irascible farmer. The village gadfly.
Toshi: An old farmer, something of a poet.
Ishio: An aged farmer who thinks of leaving.

Kazuo: An old farmer.

Goto: A simple man.

Yuki: Budo's wife.

Eiko: A farmer's wife.

Ayaka: When she was young, Kazuo's wife.

Chieko: Toshi's wife. (Her name means blessings.)

Ichiro: When he was young, Hiroko's husband.

Eno: When he was young, Eiko's husband.

Yumi: Harunobu's wife.

Yamashita-san: CEO of the Tashima Corporation.

Two silent salarymen who accompany Yamashita-san.

In the course of the play some characters will return to remembered moments earlier in their lives. This is true of Harunobu, Ishio, Budo, Hiroko. And Yuki. Some roles can be doubled at the director's discretion.

At the conclusion of the play, only eight villagers remain: Harunobu, Budo, Toshi, and their respective wives Yumi, Yuki, and Chieko, and the two widows: Hiroko, and Sadako.

Time and Place:

Ogama, a farming village near the Sea of Japan. The play consists of five movements to suggest the rhythmic passage of the seasons and the times of day: morning, noon, afternoon, evening, and night, followed by a short epilogue. Each section is distinct in feeling.

The Set:

The piece can be performed in many effective configurations. Or it may be contained in a proscenium, in which case the cyclorama is black, the legs black. The stage is bare but for a series of small, low, battered-looking tables, or possibly wooden cubes, which can double as stools, and actor-operated lights such as hurricane lamps, incandescent lamps, candles, lanterns, and flashlights. If it is not too difficult, the actors may sit on their haunches, Japanese style. If low stools are used, they may vary in design, but they must not be new or uniform, and they should not call attention to themselves. In some sections, all actors are illuminated at once, in others, some actors sit in darkness while others are briefly illuminated as they speak. Primarily the work depends on sound, i.e. text and sound design rather than on any elaborate scenery or props to create the feeling of place. If musical instruments are used, they should be limited to Shakuhachi, Koto, and Samisen.

Lighting and Sound Design:

Lighting and sound design should support rhythmic structure suggested by the passage of the times of day (and season) when appropriate.

Choreography:

From time to time a scene may lend itself to episodes of stylized movement punctuated by sharply visualized freeze-frames. Such a device must not be overused. Rather the tone must remain honest and authentic throughout.

Production values:

In the larger sense, the work represents the dying out of a sustainable way of life the world over. The protagonist of "Like Snow Melting in Water" is the village itself. Production values should reflect this in the use of monochrome costume design; monochrome backgrounds, and monochrome make-up, even extending to the possible use of masks.

Iconic to villages the world over are humble objects (none of them made of plastic), such as stools, buckets, rope, hammers, spades, shovels, rakes, and so on. Such elements should be used, not to "dress" the space, but to furnish it.

Between scenes, time cards might appear placed by a black-clad stage assistant in a display area, or on a music stand reading

MORNING, NOON, AFTERNOON, EVENING, and NIGHT. These scenic interludes might function as integral performance elements, perhaps accompanied by a sound design making use of some of the very same humble items of village utility as those used to furnish the space.

The use of the sound of water (perhaps visibly poured by a black-clad stage assistant) should be used sparingly to punctuate highly charged moments.

A note about the *tanuki*: The *tanuki* is an animal native to Japan (and unknown anywhere else). It resembles a small fox or dog, with a tawny coat, and black extremities. I have ascribed to it mythic properties in keeping with the ancient folk culture of Japan.

Critical Note: *Like Snow Melting in Water* braids three **plot** strands. The central one occurs in **linear time**: it tracks the economic forces working to displace the eight remaining characters from the village. The strand of infanticide, infant mortality, and mental retardation, which raises the **theme** of toxic pollution (and foreshadows the play's final **resolution**), occurs in **modular** form, that is, the progression of time moves backwards and forwards. Its resolution is linked to the central plot strand as well as to the third.

The third strand involves the through line of Hiroko's life—and death, also represented in modular time. At the same time as we are introduced to her, the **intimations** of her death are laid in. In a certain way, her fate, although a **private** one, **emblemizes** a **public** one: that of survival of the rice-based culture itself.

The **climax** with its determining scene occurs in the Evening section. It serves to resolve the three plot strands at once: it determines Hiroko's fate; it determines the fate of the village; and it points to the threat of a contaminated world.

MORNING

The feeling in this movement is the most frankly presentational. The actors sit facing the audience. They speak directly to the audience as if the audience were an interviewer, or perhaps a tape recorder.

SADAKO:

I wasn't born here (*Pause*). I was born in Kanazawa (*Pause*). I came to Ogama as a bride (*Pause*). I've lived here now for fifty years. No! Fifty-one. (*She laughs.*) A long time. I never thought I'd be forced to leave. I was a farmer's wife. I was smart, but you know how it is: I wasn't very pretty (*Pause*). I worked with my husband in the fields. Raised a family. Kept house. Pickled and preserved for the winter, gathered firewood when I was stronger. But now... (*Pause*).

It's like this every year. Snow; snow everywhere. Drifts all over where the wind raises the powder. It doesn't stop. You can see the flurries—past the rooftops down there, where the road terraces the mountain. The road always snowed under. From up here you can see the pines down below, their boughs drooping under their weight of snow, the birds, poor things, pecking at the suet hanging from the eaves. Smoke rising from the three houses further down: they must be trying to keep warm.

I've got no one to help me. When he could still climb the ladder, Koji could keep the thatch from getting blown away. When it blows up here the wind is fierce. Cold seeps through the cracks and now there's no one left to help me caulk. No one to give us widows a hand. Two of us. I'm eighty-five, and Hiroko, seventy-nine. She doesn't quite remember. "Maybe eighty," she says and she laughs and laughs. A picture bride like me. Poor thing, only 16 when she came here! She comes up every time she needs something. (*She mimics Hiroko's high-class accent.*)

"Sadako, help me untie this." Or "Sadako, thread this needle, will you?"

She doesn't want to leave here either. "Where will I live?" she says. I don't say anything. Just make a kind of noise—in my throat—to let her know I hear. But I don't talk about my son or his wife in the city. Because when it's over, when we have to leave Ogama, he'll be up here with a cart to haul my stuff away. But where will she go? She has no one left. No kids, no husband. Five kids, poor thing, all dead in infancy.

Me, I'll go back to the city where I came from. I'm young, I can do things in the house: cook, sew. My hands are horrible! Like skeletons. My veins stick out like ropes—but I can still thread a needle or open a jar.

"Sadako, open this, can you?" Poor thing, she has to trudge halfway up the mountain from down there where she lives. Pickled greens, my favorite. Harunobu gave it to her. Sometimes he brings her stuff from the port. She always asks me if I want some. I tell her I don't like greens. She knows it's a lie. In Ogama we don't always say what we mean.

HIROKO:

People made such a fuss at first. "Ah Hiroko," they would whisper, "Hiroko is so beautiful." I wished I could be invisible. My father died when I was three. After that, my mother had to work. She worked in a cotton mill. At first she carried me on her back. But when I got bigger, I was too heavy. She told me not to make any noise. I had to sit there quietly. If I made noise she was worried they would let her go.

She used to tell me a story when she put me to sleep:

Once a man married a beautiful bride. She was like every other bride. She smiled for the photographer on her wedding day. She wore the white wedding kimono with gold-thread crane embroidery. They say you can still see her wedding picture in the photographer's window in the county seat. But when she took her wedding dress off at the end of the day, she became a normal woman like any other woman. She looked after the house, swept, gathered wood for the brazier, put the kettle on to boil. Made rice and brewed beer.

At night she swept the tatami, laid out the bedding, put on her night kimono, and dressed her hair. She lay under the quilts, resting her head on the pillow and waited for her husband. At first she noticed nothing unusual, but one day, as she gathered wood in the forest, a tanuki crossed her path. It fixed her with eyes brighter than the sun. After that, whenever she lay down for the night, although she waited, her husband no longer came. Her eyes became sleepy with waiting, and try as she might to keep them open, she fell asleep. Night after night she tried staying awake, but her days were hard, every hour filled with work. Every night she lost the struggle and fell asleep.

Her days went on marked by hard work. Her husband gathered the harvest from the fields. She spent her days pickling and drying in preparation for the winter. Every night, she tried to wait for her husband to come, but sleep overcame her almost at once.

The fall moon came ushering in the frost. (*A few measures of a harvest moon song are heard.*) At last the woman decided to investigate. She rose, put on her winter kimono. She went barefoot to make no noise. She tiptoed down the path where in the distance the light shown inside the shed. Just as she came close enough to see, she stepped on a thorn, but she was careful not to cry out, neither then nor when she removed it. She peered inside. She could see her husband sitting at the sorting table, but his back was turned toward her so she could not make out what he did.

The wind blew and she shivered with cold, but she was not afraid. Not when the tanuki came. Not even when she heard it say: "Every night he comes here—your husband—to count out your bride price. Every night he makes sure that every coin is there. And when he's satisfied, he blows the lantern out and comes to bed."

The woman became angry. She spoke to the tanuki: "For every night he no longer comes, take one coin away." But the tanuki had vanished so the woman tiptoed back to bed, walking on her heel so she wouldn't feel the pain.

In the morning when she woke, her husband stood staring at her foot.

"What's that puncture you have there?" he asked.

"Oh, I must have stepped on a nail," the woman replied. She watched her husband carefully to see if he believed her, but he seemed satisfied.

The following night—she thought at first she must be dreaming—she felt her husband lie beside her. She felt him toss and turn and thrash about.

She lay silently, pretending she was sleeping.

He tossed and turned for some time. At last he fell asleep.

In the morning, when he woke, she said to him: "Your thrashing last night woke me up. Is there something wrong?"

Her husband eyed her suspiciously. "A coin has disappeared. You must have taken it."

So the woman knew that the tanuki had come and taken one coin away.

"Look for yourself," she said to him. Her husband searched the house, but he found nothing. For one hundred nights he tossed and turned. Every morning he said to her: "Another coin is missing. You must have taken it." Every morning she replied: "Search for yourself." And every morning he found nothing.

It was cherry blossom time. *(A few bars of a cherry blossom song are heard.)* That evening as usual, her husband didn't come. At last the door slid open. Outside the man kicked off his boots. He dropped his clothes in a corner and threw himself down. He lay tossing and turning, hitting his fists against the quilts, weeping silently.

He stretched his hand to where the woman lay, but the place was empty. He called to her but received no answer. He lit the lamp. The bed was empty. The woman wasn't there.

HARUNOBU:

All this was rice when I was a boy: the whole village; that's what we did. Planting was our life.... In the paddies from early dawn, up to our knees in water. So much of the ground is level here—you can see it still despite the weeds. The meadow was so big we didn't have to terrace. Just keep the berms built up so they hold the water.

Before the spring moon, the headman would call us. We would sit in the evening studying the almanac, comparing weather reports. What day—before the full moon—what day we would prepare, what day we would lay out the shoots, what day we would plant. Everyone agreed. How many days before the full moon.

Out before dawn, our baskets full. Tuck our clothes in our waistbands. Leave our clogs on the path. Worked barefoot so our feet could feel the dirt. Plant one shoot, push in, tamp and pass on. One shoot, push in—eight inches apart maybe. Going like that from just after dawn until we couldn't see any more. Push in, tamp, and move on. Row after row.

Backbreaking! After a day like that.... But as we worked we could watch the sky reflected in the water as the sun came up over the mountains. First grey. Maybe a little blue. Then the first pink before sunrise. Flocks of geese honking across the sky. Flying north, their wings in rhythm, beating like a heart. Then the sunlight—shy at first—of the early morning, then growing warmer, warming our backs as we moved down the rows.

Sometimes we sang. (*Tries to hum. Gives up.*) What kind of songs? I don't remember. Maybe sad songs or maybe...I don't know. No one sings them any more. You have to sing them to remember.

Then noon, time to eat our rice, back at it sometimes till past nightfall. You want to get all the fresh shoots in before they wilt. And then at dusk straightening up at last. And the whole field—the great meadow—to the west the sun setting over the sea, the geese flying south to bed down for the night. We watched them against the sunset, sometimes shielding our eyes to see them.

Then the long walk home, tired, exhausted. The evening meal, the paper, maybe read the news if I wasn't too tired. Wife scrubbing my back, then to bed. Sleep for the next day of planting. The earth won't wait. The sky won't wait, the sun and the moon, they don't wait. You have to know when it's just right. When everything is right for planting.

BUDO:

"Come, give a hand," we'd tell our kids. "Hunh? You must be dreaming. I'm going to the city. Get a job in the tofu factory." Or: "I can ride a bike delivering soba. Working in the mud all year? What kind of life is that?"

They grew up. Where they got their ideas—from the newspaper maybe. They saw the ads. They saw the pictures. They didn't want to stay. Maybe they thought working the rice was something dirty or demeaning. They used to laugh at how backward their parents were. Of course they didn't say it to me or Yuki. They were respectful face to face. But they laughed about it when they thought we weren't listening.

At first it was one or two. Sometimes they went together on their bicycles, their clothes lashed to the mud guards. But then they started to leave in droves. Riding their bikes. Barely sixteen, seventeen. They were gone, off to the city. The girls went, too. Who's going to help with the housework? Not them! Sometimes they left together, singing! They couldn't wait to live in the cities where there's games, and rock and roll. Boring, they said. The life here is boring. There's nothing to do!

We didn't think about it. There wasn't time! With the rice there's always work to do. Seeding, watching the cold frames, protecting them from frost. Listening to the weather reports. Keeping the seedlings warm. Or transplanting. Flooding them when they're established. Hundreds and hundreds of young shoots pushing up through the water. Or spraying for insects or blight. Many hands. Everyone pitching in. The weather doesn't wait. Or the season. Harvesting, bundling, drying, threshing, bagging, storing, selling, starting the new seeds: on and on it goes, year after year.

We didn't have a boss. No one to hire us. Just think! We never had to worry. We had the rice subsidies. We had the skies and the meadows and the forest and the streams. We had water as much and when we wanted it. We kept enough seed to plant the next season. Watched the cranes fly. The ducks and the geese. Listened to their chatter as they passed overhead. Chopped wood and stacked it for the fire pits in winter. My wife made our clothes, even wove the cloth. Dyed it, always in the same patterns: white and indigo for working in the fields.

We were happy if you ask me. We didn't need anything. (*Pause.*) I think we were happy.

SADAKO:

Greens! I love greens! But she has even less than me. So I don't say anything. We keep each other company. We manage. I can still open a jar. You tap it against the table edge, give a smart twist. I don't mind helping when I can.

Sometimes I invite her to sit. I offer her tea when it's ready. Or rice. "Well...maybe a little," she says. She always pretends she's not hungry.

We don't always say what we mean, Hiroko and me. We have an understanding. That's how we get along. The others live down there: three couples. Eight of us left. But we're the only widows. We're both from the city. She came here, like me, a picture bride. Poor thing, only 16! She didn't know what she was in for! She's not sure when she was born, but if you look at her hands, you'll see they're still smooth as a baby's. (*She mimics Hiroko's accent.*)

"I was so beautiful," she says. "You should have seen me in my bride's kimono. All white, a white kimono—from the city. *Very* expensive!" and she laughs and laughs.

TOSHI:

I used to stop sometimes and look at my shadow. I used to think: who is it? Who is it there, bending over the water?

"Why are you stopping?" Chieko used to say. That's my wife, always impatient. I never pay her any mind.

I don't know if the others ever thought about it. Seeing our reflection moving over the water—it could be anybody, any one of us—anyone: my father, grandfather, way before—bending over the water. One, two, three, maybe hundreds of years of us. In the water, our shadows all look the same—a long line of people like us, bending over the rice.

We're still here in the high meadow overlooking the sea. People must have seen it then just as we see it now. Nothing has changed. Nothing much has changed.

ISHIO:

(Hands stuffed up his sleeves): You can't tell: it's winter now. Snow everywhere. No sign of green. But even in winter you can see the signs: the rice paddies, the orchards...everything's overgrown, the forest, the fields of stubble inching closer year by year.

First it was the Morizawas. That's when they started leaving. The Morizawas in the thatched house at the bend in the road. They were the first. One son already gone, then the youngest: the start of the slow march to the city, to the center of the prefecture. I guess it must have given other folks ideas. "What are we doing here anyway? The government's cutting the rice subsidy every year. We could be in Kanazawa." So the Hajiro's left and the Hijikata's. And pretty soon there were others.

I never thought it would affect us. Our families were farming here for generations, me and Keiko, and Ayaka and her husband Kazuo, the four of us. But when they told us they were leaving.... We always worked together—a team, like any other team. I remember the day they came to tell us. I didn't say anything. Kept my face like a stone.

It gets colder every year. And with the snow.... I can't seem to thaw, even with the kettle steaming all day on the hook. Tell the truth, these days I'm thinking of leaving, too. And the winter's worse than ever! See these mittens, threadbare now—she knitted them for me— when Keiko was still alive.

"Here," she said, "keep your hands warm—when I'm no longer here."

TOSHI:

You don't notice at first. Your strength is just the same. You can carry all the firewood you have to. But you go to sleep earlier. You're too tired at night to read the paper. Too tired to eat. And the neighbors! You notice how old they look. And bent. The way they rub their backs. You think how much they've aged. But not you. You can lift and haul. Draw out the plow, load the cart with heavy sacks.

All those houses in the woods. Going to ruin. The thatch decaying, covered in mold and damp. Doors and windows out of plumb, thick with spider webs. Home to mice.

Five households left. And no one strong enough to keep them up, no one left to tend the graves. Not anymore. Three hundred of us. Used to run thousands of sacks of rice up to the cooperative every harvest.

I don't want to leave here. Where would we go now? This is my life. My mother and father, their mothers and fathers, all buried here. If we go we have to take them with us.

SADAKO:

No sign of Hiroko. Maybe the cold got to her. Maybe she ran out of firewood. Maybe she's down there sitting by someone else's fire pit. When I'm done sweeping, maybe I'll put on my snowshoes, go down to look for her, maybe take the long way round. *(She mimics Hiroko's accent.)*

"So beautiful" she says. And when she laughs, I think—at first—I always think it's funny. But maybe it's not so funny. Maybe that's why she disappeared that time. I don't think anyone slid a screen open or watched through the slits. No one said anything, but everyday people saw her husband trudging along the path, his hoe slung over his shoulder but they made like they didn't see. Or they passed him scratching away, pretending not to notice. People brought him things, salt fish. Eel, even. Nothing, nothing cheered him up. Maybe all that attention made him feel worse, I don't know. She was so beautiful, his picture bride come up from the city.

NOON

The actors occupy separate spaces, isolated one from the other.

KAZUO:

When I was a young man kids were everywhere: running and jumping and yelling to each other. Over great distances, you could hear their shouting. School building down the road? How it's fallen into disrepair? Boarded up. But kids used to be everywhere, hiding in the alleys, between the houses and behind the outhouses. Morning to night, playing tag in the school yard. Chasing the ball when it flew over the fence, running to catch it.

In school you could hear them reciting all together. Some afternoons—when they weren't working in the fields—their mothers came to get them. Other times they walked home, some of them hand in hand, their school bags on their shoulders.

In summer they even joined us in the fields. It was fun for them to think they could work with us—like the grownups did. In fall, after school we let them help bundle the stalks. They'd pass them along for hanging on the drying racks.

Sometimes after harvest when the racks were bare they tried climbing the supports and hanging upside down by their knees. We always told them not to. But when you're a kid you never listen. What do grownups know?

That was until Yukiko fell that time. Even though they took her to the hospital she never got better. She never said anything—as if she forgot to talk.

After that no more climbing on the drying racks. That's when we got together to build a playground outside the school. It cut into the plot poor Goto used to farm. But we couldn't help it: he had to give it up.

GOTO:

My mother left me her garden plot—right next to the new schoolhouse they built right after the war.

She knew I was born like this. She said my head was not quite right. That's what she told me. She always felt bad about it. "Make the best of what you have." That's what she said.

I used to go out there, scratch a little in the dirt. Harunobu always gave me milk—and the best manure. My garden was as good as anybody's, as good as Ichiro's. I grew pumpkins, fall pumpkins and squash. Yuki used to keep rabbits and chickens. When she killed them, she gave me the blood—for my roses. My roses were the best, the reddest in the whole village.

I used to go out there early in the morning to watch the kids coming to school. I kept wondering what it was like because I didn't ever go to school. I had too much trouble reading and writing. I could write my name. Goto. But I couldn't always find the kana.

I used to stand by the fence and listen. I could hear everything they were saying inside. Sometimes when they sang songs—you know, school kid's songs—I would sing along with them. Then when they stopped singing, I wouldn't stop. They would laugh, the whole school would laugh. They could hear Goto singing outside.

At recess the little girls would line up. The outhouse backed up against my fence. Sometimes they had to go so bad, they would be jumping up and down, holding between their legs. I used to watch them.

I thought maybe if I made a hole in a certain place, I could see inside. After that I watched all the time. I watched the hands pulling up their skirts and pulling down their little panties. They had such nice rosy cheeks! I could play with myself and nobody could see.

One day I'm pressed up against the hole, trying to see. I can't make it out because this time something wasn't the same. I didn't know what it was at first. Then it blinked! It was an eye. And it was looking back at me. I was really scared. But then I could hear giggling inside.

Every morning I would wait for the eye to be there. Then as I watched, she would stand where I could see and show herself to me. And all the time she giggled. I never could tell which one it was. It could be any girl. There were lots of them.

But then when Yukiko fell, they took away my plot to make a playground. After that I started going in the woods, winter and summer. Sometimes I would see tanuki. Especially in winter when it's hungry. I used to sell wood to people. Only sometimes they wouldn't pay.

"You don't need money," they would say, "what would you do with it anyway?"

HIROKO:

A series of disappearances—that's my life! One after another: my father, my mother. Living with my aunt in the city. Who needs an orphan with no dowry? Who wants to marry her? Even if she's supposed to be pretty. Maybe a farmer up in the mountains, a plain man. At least with the war on she'll get enough to eat. That's what she thought. Maybe a farmer. Someone who grows rice.

Oh, I didn't like him. No. To tell the truth. I was born in a time when there was little a girl could do. Now—they go to Tokyo and marry who they please; work in department stores or noodle shops. Or even worse!

I didn't like him. Oh, No! When he touched me, oh! My skin would crawl! At night he pumped, quickly over, thank you. Maybe that's why. Maybe because of that...five children, all dead in infancy, all five! Every one of them. None of them alive long enough to give them a name.

One day in the forest...I was gathering mushrooms. I must have gone a long way. In the deep shade, it was...a wild dog crossed my path...as if it didn't see me! Here they call it the tanuki. Not a fox. It's not a fox and not a dog. Something in between. It passed so near, it almost touched me! Such a shy creature! Was I scared? Oh, no! Startled maybe: it made me drop my basket. All my mushrooms—I had a whole basket full—all my mushrooms fell and tumbled down the slope. I saw them bouncing as they hit the rocks down below. I felt so helpless! I didn't know what to do....

YUKI:

It's an animal. People see it sometimes at dusk—if they stay in the woods too long. You have to be very careful. Never let it cross your path. Eiko, the one who lived down in the hollow, Eiko saw one once. After that she had nothing but bad luck: Fourteen births, thirteen of them stillborn.

I must have passed the place many times—without noticing. Or maybe it changed because of the moss growing on it: It looked like the paw of a big animal. You could see the knuckles and the claws. I looked up, and there it was: a leg tall as a tree. And then I saw the other leg, a leg just like the first, like a tanuki was crouching there. I don't know how I did it: I ran up the hill. I didn't even stop for breath.

AYAKA:

It's not a dog exactly, and not a fox. It looks like something in between, with black gloves and stockings, tawny fur. It lives in the trees. The first time I went there, I didn't notice anything because I was so bent on getting to the top. If you look up, you get tired, but if you look sideways at whatever grows beside the road, you get to the top and you're not even out of breath.

Sometimes people make offerings. They leave something between the giant paws—rice or an orange for it to eat. That one will eat anything and if you don't feed it, it will go after other things. It comes out at night. It sleeps during the day. That's why you have to keep the doors firmly shut especially if there's a newborn in the house.

CHIEKO:

When my first one got sick, they told me about the tree. I went deep into the woods. You can see two trunks next to each other like the legs and paws of a gigantic dog. You can even see the toes and claws covered in moss—green—like fur.

That's the place. I brought fruit like people said—and rice. I put them there between the paws.

My son got better right away. But I didn't tell anyone, not even Toshi—so tanuki would go somewhere else and take someone else's child. And stay away from mine.

When they're hungry, they go hunting. That's why people bury stillborn children near there, close to where it lives. People say if we keep him satisfied, he'll leave our kids alone.

SADAKO:

I kept worrying. What happened to Hiroko. I kept listening to the weather reports. I couldn't sleep a wink. By morning it was snowing so hard I took the back way. Even so, it was tough going, even with snowshoes. I had to watch for icicles, the wind was so fierce. It whistled around the corners of her house, it knocked patches of snow down off the thatch. My hands were frozen but anyway I took my mitten off, gave her door a smart rap.

No answer. Just the moan of the wind.

I called to her: "Hiroko! Hiroko!"

No answer. Maybe the wind muffled my voice. I took my snowshoes off. I opened the door and went in. The tatami was swept, the bedding was neatly folded and piled on the chest. High up in the rafters the baskets groaned with all the things she must have stored up there when she could still climb up the ladder. But no sign of Hiroko. The fire pit was cold, the kettle still hanging on the hob, black from the fire, but the ashes were long past their glow.

That's strange. Where could she have gone?

It was getting dark. I strapped my snowshoes back on. I wrapped my head scarf around my face. I pulled the door shut tight against the wind.

I was about to start the long climb back when I saw it. It was a comb. Half buried in the snow. I picked it up. It was the comb she always uses to hold her hair. That's strange I thought. And then I saw a footprint, and another. It reassured me, I don't know why. Of course. She's gone down to sit by Yumi's friendly fire, except Yumi always resents it when Harunobu brings her stuff.

People forget even when they can't forgive. They don't remember how terrible it was: seeing Hiroko like that, the men carrying her out of the gorge where she tried to drown herself. It was Harunobu pulled her out. She fought so hard, he nearly drowned himself, so they say. They took her back to her husband's house. Laid her down before the threshold. Ichiro was standing there in the shadow of their doorway with the fall sun beating down. Everyone turned away. No one stayed to see.

I followed her footprints but when I reached the corner of the house there wasn't anything anymore, no trace. Like everything else, buried under snow. I had her comb in my hand. I didn't know what to do.

It was growing dark. Maybe by now the drifts were too deep to even reach the houses down below. Another blizzard was coming or so the radio said. I thought I'd better get back before everything went white. I decided there was no more time to look for her.

If I'd known, would I have done things differently?

EIKO:

Something must have been wrong from the start. I always had a midwife, every time. But this time, Masako wanted me to try to wait till the doctor came. But the doctor never came.

When he was born, she didn't want to let me see him.

"What is it?" I said.

"A boy. A boy," she said. I could hear. He was screaming. He wasn't stillborn like the others.

"Why can't I see him?" I said.

She pretended she didn't hear me.

"Why can't I see him," I said.

KAZUO:

That was a bad one that time. It wasn't like that most other times. Most other times it was easy. People expected it. Everyone agreed. Most times the midwife saw to it. But not this time. Because this time the midwife let her keep it.

Budo didn't want to do it. "Now she has it, let her keep it, damn it." But we both said no.

"Then count me out. Do it yourself," Budo said. No stopping Budo any time, even if he was headman. No way to convince him taking it away was something we had to do. Not Budo.

We watched him trudging down the road. His boots kept sticking in the mud. "Clumsy, bow-legged bastard," we joked. He never walked very well anyway. None of us do. Not since the war when we were kids and there wasn't much to eat. So then it was just me and Ishio.

We caught her in the doorway, trying to escape. We rushed her.

It was everyone's decision. She knew it. Sooner or later she knew we would come to get it.

ISHIO:

We needed to act fast before Eno got back. Kazuo got hold of her. She wailed. She struggled. She tried to scream. She didn't want to let it go, but Kazuo pushed her head covering into her mouth. She was strong, that one. She nearly knocked him over. But it didn't do any good.

I went inside. It was dark in there. I looked everywhere. Nothing. You can't spirit a kid away. It was in there somewhere. I had to hurry. Kazuo couldn't hold onto her forever. She kept trying to break loose. But it got quieter once he stopped her screaming. That's when I heard it. The faintest little snuffle. I listened again. Can you believe it? She found a place for it up in the rafters. She made a little nest up there. I couldn't tell how she could get up there—until I saw the ladder. You never know what a woman will dream up.

She had it wrapped in a little blanket—wool—to keep it warm.

She was going to run after us if we didn't tie her up. We trussed her over the roof beams—like she did the kid—sooner or later Eno would find her when he got back. We took away the ladder.

That was the worst one we had. Usually people agreed. Everybody knows: there's no way we can keep kids like that anyway, the work is too hard.

People from the outside always say how healthy farmers are. It must be the hard work they say. But we know better. We just don't talk about it.

HIROKO:

The slope was so steep, I didn't know what to do. Then I saw if I left the basket on the path, if I lowered myself going backwards, maybe I could get down there. Moving slowly. Slowly going down, holding on. A rock here or a branch. Far below I could hear the stream, but I couldn't see it. Then I spied the first mushroom—just beyond my reach. If I scrambled sideways I could just grab it. I put it inside my kimono. It felt cold against my skin.

I was so intent getting what mushrooms I could, I never thought I'd reach bottom where the low path follows the stream. I stopped there for a while. Except for the water rushing against the rocks there was no other sound. I leaned back against a tree. I could see upwards through the leaves clear to the open sky. I started turning slowly until the whole world seemed to turn: the sunlight, the leaves, the branches turning slowly. Far up, I could just make out the path—up there where I left the basket.

I don't know what spirit took me. I began to walk—a short way perhaps. I was looking for a place where I could wet my feet, where the rocks might form a basin and the water would go still.

Then suddenly the path which had been so shadowed burst with sunlight! The leaves shivered! I stopped. I stood spellbound as if all the golden leaves were whispering my name!

But then I heard another sound. I turned. A man stood behind me in the ditch alongside the path.

He was naked. I could see drops of water shining in his hair.

I wasn't afraid. But when he came toward me, he looked as if he could read my thoughts.

He was laughing! I could see water droplets clinging to his hair.

He had me by my waist band. I remember the sound of tearing. I struck at him. Hard. Somehow I must have tripped him. He fell backwards in the deep water, dragging me in with him. Then he let go of me. My arms were beating the water. I was fighting for breath. When I came up I was gasping. Then I went down again. I didn't want to drown. No one would know what happened to me. I felt my hair starting to pull. Someone was pulling me...he was pulling me up by the hair. "Stop," he said, "stop struggling, stop flailing with your arms or both of us will drown."

KAZUO:

We took it out to the forest. Just Ishio and me. Where no one would find it, just Ishio and me. It was cold, so cold, its little face was nearly blue. I had the shovel. I'd honed the blade. We laid it on the ground, unwrapped the little blanket.

It didn't have any hands or feet. Just stumps. How could it be of any use like that? The shovel would take pity on it.

Ishio wrapped the head and body in the little blanket. Snug. So it would be warm.

We buried it there. I dug the hole. I dug it especially deep that time, so the tanuki couldn't smell it there or dig it up.

BUDO:

I could hear them back there, laughing. What did I care? Screw it! I didn't care if the mud stuck to my boots, or even sucked them off, I couldn't bring myself to do it. Not that time. I kept thinking. I kept thinking how I used to wait for her after school. I'd see her coming down the road, her school bag on her shoulders, the white knee socks her mother made her wear—high on her skinny legs. And I'd chase her all the way home, her pigtails bobbing like a little girl, and we laughed and laughed. Sometimes when I caught her, I grabbed them. The ends felt like bristles when I brushed them on my face. That was way before she married Eno.

All thirteen kids—stillborn. Dead. And this last one... Shit! Well, the midwife wouldn't say at first...but you kind of know it wasn't normal. Whatever it was, I didn't want to see it. I couldn't stand to hear her screaming when we came up there to get it.

Disgrace? So what! Ishio and Kazuo. Their faces would remind me how I left them in the lurch, especially now I got to be headman. I knew it. I didn't know what they would tell their wives, Keiko and Ayaka. Either of them, what would they think? When it came their turn to lose a kid, no one cut them any slack.

Damn it! I wish I never saw her. I wish we never went to school together. I wish I never waited for her on the road. Curse her. Curse her pigtails, curse her spindly legs. Curse the way she used to let me catch her and rub her hair against my face.

ENO:

I knew right away: something wasn't right.

The fire had gone out! I called to her. "Eiko? Eiko?"

Nothing. That's strange I said to myself. She was always ready for me with a bowl of noodles steaming by the fire pit.

I looked everywhere. She wasn't outside. She wasn't sleeping. Nothing. I kept calling. Nothing.

At last just in front of where I stood a little piece of straw fell down at my feet. I looked up.

She was strung up there in the rafters! I never thought she would resist. They had to tie her up. And gag her. She could hardly breathe. I took the ladder in from outside to get to her. They had tied her to the crossbeams. I took the gag out of her mouth.

All she could do was cry. They took it away. Even before she had a chance to name it.

EIKO:

At first I didn't even know I was pregnant. The last baby, but it was the hardest. It's not supposed to be that way—at least that's not what they tell you. They say each birth is easier than the last.

The midwife told Eno: get a doctor. Maybe the doctor was busy or maybe he got there too late. Doctors don't always want to come out so far. Not to a village at the end of the road. If we're sick we stay by the fire. We drink tea from the herbs we gather. Our sheds are full of hanging racks. Or we make a poultice of mustard seed. We use clay to set any broken bones. In the city they consider us backward.

Something must have been wrong from the start Masako said. She told me to wait, not to push so hard.

And then I could hear him wailing. "Don't tell me," I said to Masako, "don't tell me what I already know. Give him to me."

I kept asking, and begging and crying, so she placed him on my belly. I cradled him in my arms. His wailing stopped. He was perfect, beautiful. He didn't have any hands, he didn't have any feet. But I saw he was beautiful.

HARUNOBU:

We had to do something. Only eight of us left. We're old. It came to me like that. We're too old. What to do? We have to do something. I'm headman now. They count on me. I better come up with something. No future for us here. Not any longer. With the young ones gone. Old ones getting on—twenty-six families left, mostly old couples, two others talking of leaving. Pretty soon no one left to carry on. We're running out of help.

We're used to hard work. Farming rice year after year? Back breaking. It takes many hands. You work in teams. Unless you've done it, there's no way you could know. Now the fields are fallow, but growing our own food, it's still up at first light; harness the cow. She's getting old, too. We've had her 16 years. An old lady. She complains. She's deaf. "Pull!" I have to shout at her. She lurches forward, snorting.

The plow is heavy. Steel. (I still keep it honed.) She's lurching forward. Down we go. Down the first row.

It's dawn. A yellow sky over the mountains. The earth turns, I say to myself. It grinds on; no stopping. And there's its shadow to the west—under the thin gauze of pink, there's that shadowy horizon before the sun comes up.

It was like that—plowing just before sunrise, alone with the cow and the sky and the dirt—when it first came to me: that's what we have to do, we have to try to sell Ogama. And I'm behind the plow guiding it. You can watch it cutting the earth, and how it rolls over on itself as the plow goes forward. Like waves. It forgets it's dirt. And I think: it's melting into water. The soil of Ogama! And—I don't know why—I never cry—it's the same dirt we have always plowed from time long ago—but I cry for us, for our forebears who lived here before us. For our children in the cities who will have forgotten this life, who will have traded it for colored lights and noise—this soil, this way of living. Will have forgotten it entirely. And for the mountains to the north and east and for the forest with all the abandoned houses to the south and for the view of the sea from certain elevations. And the flights of ducks and geese making their way south in the early morning light. And the hum of bees drunk in the cherry blossoms. The sway of branches in the spring breeze, and the endless green of summer and the shock of rain pounding the earth into life. And the leaves, fiery in autumn and the icy winds of winter and the never ending snow.

And I'm watching the blur of the cow's hooves raising clods of dirt as she pulls the plow forward. Thinking what will we do with the cow? Whatever will become of her if we have to go?

AFTERNOON

The feeling in this movement is restlessness, leave taking, coming apart. The actors must be given leave to move about.

EIKO:

By then everyone was going. All the forest people were moving to the city. Even Masako. I found out she was going and taking her old mother with her.

I kept wondering about it: that time, why did she let me have my child? Why did she give in? Why didn't she just take it away? I went out there to say good-bye. She was stiff with me at first, formal. "I don't hold it against you," I said. "I don't want you ever to think that."

At first she made like she didn't understand.

"My child," I said. "I know they had to take it away."

"Was I wrong to let you have it?" she said.

I couldn't help it. I started to cry.

"Stay," she said. "Stay for a minute. The tea is still warm." Everything was wrapped in matting, ready to go. But she cleared a place for me.

So I sat, composing myself. She handed me a handkerchief. I apologized.

"That's all right. Here." She pushed the cup toward me.

That sound of tea pouring. It reminds me of my mother—how kind she was. And how she died during the war.

"Where will you go?" I asked her.

"Kanazawa, probably. Like everyone. It's near enough. At least in the city they'll have work for me."

We sat sipping silently. Outside a wind had come up. You could hear the trees sighing. At last I got my courage up. "What made you let me keep him? That time? What made you change your mind?"

I didn't think she was going to answer. I could hear her mother coughing behind the partition.

"I thought it was my fault," she whispered.

"Why?"

"Because I tried to make you wait till the doctor came." She was crying. I felt so bad for her.

"Oh, Masako, you mustn't!" I passed her the handkerchief—I thought we might as well share it—"It was the stuff we were spraying, don't you know? That's what they said at the county seat. It had to have been the pesticides."

HARUNOBU:

(Harunobu and Yumi overlap each other in the following two speeches. The sound of a typewriter is heard.)

One day it just came to me. We have to sell Ogama. With all the young ones gone, if we want to survive, we have to sell Ogama. We can't outlast many more winters like the last one. The folks who lived on the opposite side—the ones in the woods—had it really bad. I started asking myself what do we have here? Grass! A landscape, maybe. But all the same, it's pretty nice. The mountains in the distance, the sea to the west. Sunlight. Maybe we could make some kind of vacation spot. With entertainment. Maybe even prizes.

I made room in the shed. Set up a table. A typewriter and a filing cabinet. I started to write letters, make inquiries. Well at first people here objected.

"We're getting on," I kept saying over and over. And then nature began to help: Kenzo fell off a ladder trying to repair the thatch. He couldn't work. His wife had to do everything. Their kids took them to the city. He died shortly after. Then Daibu's wife got cancer. He couldn't care for her. Sure we all helped. But she needed an operation. They had to leave half their farm supplies behind.

By then people didn't think it was such a wild idea. They voted to let me make more inquiries. We wrote everywhere. No one was interested. We were down to some 26 families maybe, then 16. Then I think 2 more left, and the midwife. There wasn't any point in her staying! And she took her mother with her. All those houses in the forest, no one living there anymore.

One day I read in the newspaper. There was a new company that built golf courses. They already had one in Osaka and another one near Kobe.

They came out to take a look. But when they got off the train at the county seat, already then I got the feeling it wasn't going to work. Even on the platform they took us in—country folk, plain people with our backward ways.

We drove them out here. All the way out they saw the cheery trees in bloom. Oh they were impressed. "How scenic" they said. "Beautiful vistas." They investigated the old school building and the playground. We didn't have to worry about Goto. His aunt came out one day and took him to the city. "We could set the club house here, even use the old foundations."

"We'll have to talk to management," they promised, but they were management.

I wanted to send out more letters. But people voted to wait. So we waited. We waited through the winter. It was especially harsh that year. The snow drifts—some of them—rose ten, even fifteen feet in some places. Some weren't even strong enough to dig themselves out.

Up in the hills the Kotanis ran out of firewood. They froze before anyone could get to them. That spring three more households decided it was time to go: Eiko and Eno, Ishio and Keiko. Even Kazuo left with his wife. We were left with ten.

YUMI:

(Her speech overlaps Harunobu's previous speech.) "A village isn't something you can pack up or sell. It's not like a basket of sea snails you can carry on your back..."

Budo went on and on like that. At least with some people—in spite of what happened—he could still command respect. After all, he was former headman. "If we sell, who will grow the rice? Tend the paddies?"

208

But Haru stood firm. "We hung the last crop to dry three years ago!"

He tried everything. I used to stay up late into the night typing letters he would dictate.

"Dear sirs,

"We are a small village close to Wajima near the Sea of Japan. We have lived here nearly 300 years by one estimate. The land is flat; a mountain plateau surrounded by forest to the south and mountains to the east and north. To the west lies the sea which on clear days can be glimpsed from certain elevations.

"We are too old to farm now. We are looking to sell our village.

"Won't you contact us for an appointment so you can come and have a look. Ogama would like to offer you our most honorable, respectful hospitality."

Six of us even met them at the train station. Old Budo didn't come of course. He kept giving Haru so much trouble. Every meeting complaining. We hired two expensive limousines to drive them out here—to the end of the road. But at first the drivers didn't want to; in spring the road gets pretty muddy. They wanted extra money.

We prepared things to eat—fancy, the kind folks are used to in the city, not the vegetables and rice we mostly eat out here. Eels, seaweed, raw fish, so rich some of us could hardly eat it. We offered them sake—our home brew. They didn't know it was local but all the same it made them pretty happy. But I noticed the shoes he wore. They were shiny yellow. They must be golfing shoes I thought. But somehow they didn't go with their dark suits.

BUDO:

What kind of stuff do you think they'll be using to keep their damn golf course green? Or keep it free of bugs? What do you plan on doing when all that stuff leaches down into the ground? When it starts poisoning our wells? City slickers! That's what I thought. Why couldn't people see that? They're not going to buy anything! They're just out for a day in the boonies. And some dainty pickings for lunch—free! On the house! But that sake's going to deliver some kick all right—local stuff—they won't even know what hit them. Screw them. They'll be off soon enough. Nothing will come of it. I could just see Haru's long face when he had to tell people: The deal is off. It didn't work out. Of course not! It was a bust and a good thing, too! A bust; that's what everyone will think but they'll be too polite to say it. But I wasn't going to keep quiet. No sir. I'll say something, you can bet on it. If people think you can sell Ogama—well anything goes: You might as well sell your mother. That's what I thought.

HIROKO:

He touched my breasts. Oh, how hot it was suddenly. I couldn't breathe. He lifted me and carried me into the shade where the moss grew thick. I could see his clothes scattered there where he had left them. I didn't cry out. I bit my lip. I wanted to cry out but I said nothing. I never took my eyes off him.

(There is the sound of pouring water.) After I could hear the stream, the water rushing against the rocks.

That first time he didn't speak. I waded in the stream, felt my way between the stones not to lose my balance.

I washed. Above me the golden leaves trembled in the wind. I shivered. When I came back to gather my clothes he was gone. I didn't know where he came from or where he went. I didn't know his name.

GOTO:

I saw them. By the path I used to take to gather wood. It was at the height of summer. Time between the flooding and the harvest. I always started early laying in wood to sell it for the winter.

They were lying there, sleeping, mouths slightly open. I could see the sweat shining on their skin. I watched them for a while. I didn't care what people said in the village. Never mind if this one disappears or that one argues with his wife. Never mind if the village beauty takes the afternoons to go mushroom gathering. It's no business of mine.

Their clothes were scattered here and there. They must have been in a hurry to dig in from the look of things.

After that, I went that way pretty often, whenever I could. I wanted to catch them doing it. Then I saw them. They didn't see me. They were too busy with their own chores to notice someone with a ladder on his back. I hid behind a tree. Where I could watch them doing it. Her arms were tight around his back. I could see her digging her nails in. Hard. They didn't even have a cover.

I liked watching, feeling the heat come over me, pushing against the tree bark faster and faster. Listening to them scream. Once—once I even screamed right along with them. Quite a racket we made.

Then I got scared. I know they must have heard something because they started up and looked around. I could hear their voices murmuring—but I was too far away to make out what they said.

It was pretty tricky that time, with the ladder on my back, getting away without them seeing anything.

My mother used to tell me a story: once a badger saw a beautiful woman come to the stream where he had his lair. He watched intently as she slipped off her geta, and opened her kimono. He watched her put a dainty foot into the water. He followed the water as it rose past her ankles, creeping up her legs until it licked at her sex, until it rose up to her dainty breasts. He wanted to keep her company so much he turned himself into a man. But the lady couldn't see him.

HIROKO:

I went back. I don't say otherwise. I couldn't help it. I went back. I came again to the place where the sunlight broke through. I came at the same time of day in the early afternoon. I found him in the thicket where we always went.

He was a charcoal burner. He lived in the deep woods I don't know where. All through the summer, I came back. He was leaving in the autumn.

"Take me with you" I said.

I began to store things in the woods in waterproof wrappings. Bundles of things, some warm things for the winter—not so much anyone would notice, burying them in the hollows of trees or under-neath the stones.

Once he saw me. He was laughing. He called me Little Squirrel. His little squirrel.

CHIEKO:

Crazy woman. Too much piss and vinegar! Everyone knew she was crazy, shacking up with some lowlife in the woods! But she lived. No one knows how. No one knows what happened after Ichiro dragged her in the house. Every day the carpenter made his way uphill, his adze over his shoulder, tools in his carrying cloth. Every day he knocked at the door. The door would fling open. "Who needs you! Get out! And don't come back." At last he must have gotten tired of it. Maybe he had other people to bury—or cabinets to make. He picked up a stone lying in the road and lobbed it against their house. Hideo saw him—she told me. She threw him a dirty look but she didn't say anything.

"What do I care?" he snarled at her. "Everyone knows. She's half dead anyway."

ICHIRO:

I didn't know what to do with her. At his wits end. If they knew, that's what people would have said. Ichiro's at his wits end.... She wouldn't go out. Not even for a little!

I tried to tempt her. "Hiroko, it's spring. The rain has stopped."

Nothing. Or I told her "Look at the iris—that clump you plant-ed. They're blooming. Come and see." She didn't move.

"Come smell the lilac." She opened her eyes. I caught her looking past me where I'd left the screen open to let in the sun.

She blinked. I held my breath. I was waiting to see what she would do. She sat there motionless, blinking her eyes against the glare. Moving very little, breathing, just breathing, but I saw: she was bending slightly.

She let me take her arm. Her hand felt lifeless; dead weight. I wasn't sure what she wanted. Slowly she stood up. I helped a little. Very slowly so she wouldn't change her mind. She hesitated. I stopped in my tracks. Waiting. Careful not to say anything. Another step and another and we were outside. In the spring sunlight. She moved slowly toward the lilac tree. I followed in her shadow, careful not to block her path. She stretched one hand upward as if to touch...

I reached around her to pull the branch closer so she could smell. She let out a sigh; I let go the branch. It snapped back, trembling slightly before it came to rest. Some little flowers fell in her hair. I tried brushing them away. She turned. I wasn't sure what she wanted to do or where she wanted to go, but she was making for the bench that runs alongside the house. She lowered herself slowly; leaned her back against the house.

She shut her eyes. I let her doze there for a while.

HIROKO:

Spring came early. Snow gave way to rain. The iris bloomed that never bloomed before. And the lilac! The air was heavy with the smell. I kept remembering his caresses on my body. My steps fell heavy on the ground. I remembered weight; the pull of weight. How heavy the feet; wooden the legs; dull the body as if something inside me broke. Even with no basket on my back, I felt yoked as if I carried a stone somewhere inside me, away from light, away from the fields and meadows where the sun beats down. Away from the forest where the foxes and raccoon dogs hunt their prey. And where one day, when she least expects it, when she's out hunting mushrooms some charcoal burner or some woodsman gathering wood is out there—waiting. Ready to cut her life down at the root.

Oh, how I wanted to be free! Free to wander off with no one to wonder where I went, waiting for a tanuki's glance to turn me invisible. That time, that time by the stream where the water pooled between the rocks. When I stopped to cool off. That time I slipped off my kimono, I could have passed unseen. That man. He wouldn't have seen anything. Never, never. Never to have had my life cut off, cut off at the root. I never think of him. I erased him, limb by limb. I forgot his hands, I forgot his legs, his belly, the dark root of his sex, his smoky nipples, forgot everything, even his face. His eyes were the last to go. Wiped out.

People kept saying, "Ah Hiroko, how fine you look. How beautiful." But I know they knew. They just pretended they couldn't see the emptiness inside. As if they couldn't see the ugliness. As if I was somebody entirely different. Sometimes I remember how in the city when I was a girl before the war—my aunt and I—we used to pass a shop with a cardboard cutout. It was a lady smiling, wearing a flowered kimono. I used to ask my aunt if she was real. But my aunt always laughed at me.

That's me, that cardboard. I am standing behind it trying to make some kind of sign. Trying to say help! Help me! I can't stop drowning.

HARUNOBU:

I was disappointed. On top of all the other rejections. This one seemed promising at first, but to be honest, I have to say I wasn't really sorry. It didn't come to me at first, but I realized half of me wanted it not to work. So did everybody, but no one said anything—except Budo of course. And Toshi.

Then I read in the paper about the Tashima Company. I told Yumi, "What are we waiting for? It's autumn already, we better write them right away."

When we got the letter, we were so excited we told everyone we found a company that might be interested but we didn't say it was Tashima. Well, not at first. Maybe we made a mistake. We couldn't wait for the next council meeting. And anyway it might not work out like so many others didn't work out. But it was a good excuse: we had a celebration anyway. Home brew. We sang songs. Everyone felt pretty good!

HIROKO:

The leaves had already colored way up in the high places where the wind did its work. I lowered myself down the slope as I did so many times. I lowered myself—foothold by foothold to join the path beside the stream. Along the path I collected the small bundles I had hidden in the woods, five bundles in all. I remembered all the places I had stored them.

A wind came up. Leaves scattered everywhere, driven by the wind. From time to time I had to stop and rest. My fingers went numb where I hooked them around the knots.

I passed all the landmarks along the way: the willow bending over the stream, the circle of hidden stones. The place where the stream widened and the trees arched over it like the ribs of some animal. At last I could make it out in the far distance, the place where in the summer the path became bright gold. I began to count my steps. Only a few more.

BUDO:

The murderer of hope! The prime minister, always in bed with the bankers. Koizumi is the murderer of hope! I said it over and over. Look at the rice subsidies. Cutbacks every year. Maybe someone should tell him rice is our backbone. It's how we live. Sell Ogama! What are you thinking of? If you sell, you're playing Koizumi's game. You're just giving up! Where are you going to put the graves? You'll have to move them somewhere else. If you sell Ogama, that's 300 years. Down the crapper. And we can never get it back." At every meeting I said it but it was like some kind of spell came over them. Collective insanity! Everyone of them!

HIROKO:

He was not by the stream. At first I wasn't alarmed. He must be waiting in the thicket. I dropped my bundles. I ducked under the branches making for the mossy place. It was buried under fallen leaves, all red, and gold and yellow. No one was there. *(Sound of dry sticks rubbing; crackle of fallen leaves. Accelerating claves punctuate Hiroko's concluding speech.)*

EVENING

The tension winds so tight it explodes in this scene. At the start, the actors should be reassembling the stools in a meeting configuration during the first two speeches. Eventually they seat themselves—except for Budo whose arm and leg are bandaged. He may sit in a wheel chair.

The salarymen set up plank and saw horses which they will remove when they exit.

Yuki and Budo speak in separate spaces, but their speeches overlap.

YUKI:

Why did I have to scream? When I saw him like that—all crumpled on the ground? I screamed at him. Why did you have to get up on the roof. Couldn't you just wait for spring for the thatcher to come? I don't know what got into me. Instead of helping him. That's what I said...

BUDO:

She knows how cheap I am. Why give someone else the job when I can do it myself?

YUKI:

Now I can't run fast enough. Washing, cooking, chopping firewood—with no one left to help.

BUDO:

(He calls to Yuki in her separate space.) Get me some water, will you?

(Here the tone shifts from two people talking in separate spaces to a face-to-face confrontation.)

YUKI:

(Brings him water. She holds a newspaper in her hand.) Budo-san. Look at this. It says in the paper Ogama's being sold, all the land! Every house, every barn, every garden patch, every stick!

BUDO:

That's just shit! Give it here! *(He rips it from her hands, nearly tipping the lamp over.)*

YUKI:

(Pointing.) There. Take a look! It's Tashima Company. They even give the price."

BUDO:

What's this Tashima anyway?

YUKI:

Toxic waste disposal! *(She snatches the paper back to show him.)* See for yourself! It says it right here!

SADAKO:

(As she speaks, Yamashita and the two salarymen enter and set up plank and saw horses to prepare the scene.) We spent a week, a whole week, tidying up. Everyone pitched in, shoveling the snow—all except Budo. After that fall, he couldn't even walk.

The day dawned gray. More snow in the air. Toward noon this big-time limousine drove up. It splashed slush everywhere. It drew up at Harunobu's house. The chauffeur held the door open while the boss got out. Two flunkies followed. City people. Poor things, they didn't even think to wear boots! We watched them tiptoe through the mud with their city shoes.

We pretty much knew what to expect. *(Stage lights illuminate the whole scene. Yamashita bows formally; the villagers return his bow. The salarymen bow.)*

HARUNOBU:

Please welcome Yamashita-san, the honorable Tashima Company's Chief Operations Officer. He—and his assistants—have very bravely come to visit us today—despite the weather. *(Everyone laughs politely.)* They're here to outline Tashima's proposal to us and to answer any questions.

YAMASHITA:

(Sits down on a hastily provided chair. Removes glasses from case, polishes them on his handkerchief, puts them on. Opens his briefcase, removes documents. Clears his throat.) Thank you, Katsumiya-san*—and all the villagers of Ogama—for inviting us today. *(He clears his throat.)* If you villagers accept it, this proposal from the Tashima Development Company promises to bring you, the honorable village of Ogama, and to every one of you, the highest honor and respect. I have the contract here—which I will go over with you point by point. I will even leave a copy for you to review before you make your decision. When you agree—and of course the company hopes you do—*(He giggles nervously.)* you can sign, not just Katsumiya-san as your headman, but each of you can sign his name to show he understands the terms and everyone approves. The ladies, too!" *(Everyone laughs politely.)*

---

* He uses Harunobu's formal honorific.

SADAKO:

(During Sadako's speech, Katsumiya-san exits with the two silent salarymen who clear the board and saw horses.) He went over the main details, how much they would pay, in how many installments, how much they would allow to move all the graves from the cemetery high up by the torii gate. No one said anything.

YUMI:

We could hardly wait till they were gone to start planning what we would do with the graves. Where was the best place to move them, maybe some place near the county seat where the rest of us would go. We got to the part about the money. That's when it started. *(She steps center stage. The scene transitions to a face-to-face confrontation. The sense of a grange meeting hall takes over. The actors take their places as they speak.)*

CHIEKO:

Wait a minute. It's not clear: they're going to pay in equal shares!

BUDO:

(With contempt.) Sure...if it's just eight old geezers they want to buy—and a bunch of graves....

HARUNOBU:

(Ignoring him.) It's up to us to decide. The contract leaves it open. All it specifies is two installments, one when we sign, the other when everyone has left.

CHIEKO:

(Relieved.) Then everyone gets an equal share!

BUDO:

OK! Let's keep score! One for buying old graves and geezers...

SADAKO:

Wait a minute, I don't agree. It should be by household. *(She looks to Hiroko to back her up.)* Each *household* gets an equal share!

BUDO:

OK! So far it's a tie...

CHIEKO:

(Talking over him.) What do you know, Sadako? You're a city woman! Why should you get one-fifth? When you weren't even born here. You just came here as a bride, you and Hiroko!

BUDO:

(Keeping score.) Do I hear two now, two now for old geezers...?

SADAKO:

(Talking over him.) So what? I lived here over 50 years! I raised my kids here just like you—even if they did leave for the city. I worked in the paddy alongside all of you! I dare anyone to say I didn't pull my weight! Harunobu, with all due respect, you were never fair! You and Yumi always favor your three households! You never think of us widows except to bring us mushrooms now and then...

HARUNOBU:

...and sometimes pickled greens... *(Everyone laughs.)*

SADAKO:

(She is not swayed by Harunobu's wisecrack.) Eight shares isn't fair, no matter what you say! I'll never go for it. It should be by household. I always pulled my weight ever since I came here. So did Koji...

CHIEKO:

Maybe. While he was still alive...

SADAKO:

...especially this past week—not like some...some big mouths around here, lolling around in their wheelchairs....

YUKI:

That's no surprise coming from you: you're by yourself. There's two of the rest of us. We did twice the work. Why should you get twice as much? And maybe you raised your kids, but so did *most* of the rest of us. *(She looks at Hiroko sarcastically.)*

BUDO:

(Looking at Sadako.) Is that three for buying geezers!

SADAKO:

They wound up in the city, don't forget!

YUMI:

So what? So our kids ended up in the city. So did yours! So what? We did twice the work you did. Maybe more. And Haru's still alive....

SADAKO:

So you and Haru think it's all right to penalize me—just because I'm a widow, is that it?

BUDO:

Listen to all of you. Haggling over money. *(He spits it out.)*

HARUNOBU:

(Ignoring him.) All right. All right. Let's take a moment to reflect. The contract says nothing about how we distribute the money.

YUMI:

Why don't we take a count?

SADAKO:

I object! Of course you want to take a count. You know how it's going to turn out...

HARUNOBU:

(Ignoring her.) How many think it should be in equal shares? *(He waits. Yumi, Yuki, Chieko and Harunobu raise their hands. The widows and Budo and Toshi do not.)*

BUDO:

(To Harunobu.) It's a tie! Imagine that! We can go right on haggling!

HARUNOBU:

(Ignoring him.) Toshi? You're not voting?

TOSHI:

I abstain. *(Some exclamations.)*

HARUNOBU:

And Budo?

BUDO:

(Continuing to ignore him.) Everyone for himself. Isn't that right? And all the time you're missing the point, everyone of you!!

HARUNOBU:

You're out of order...

BUDO:

No! You're out of order. It's you. Out of order in your thinking.

YUMI:

No one called on you...

BUDO:

(Talking over her.) It's the pits you should be thinking about. What about those pits they're going to dig? What are they putting in those pits—after they line them with concrete? *(He says this with contempt.)*

CHIEKO:

I don't have to listen to this...

BUDO:

Do you know? Do any of you care? What do you imagine they're going to put there anyway?

CHIEKO:

(Interrupting.) So what? We won't even be here when it happens.

BUDO:

(Ignoring her.) Toxics, that's what. Poison. Poison for the ground and the air and when it leaches, in the water.

HARUNOBU:

No, no. *(He laughs condescendingly.)* The pits are concrete. They can't leach...

YUMI:

Haru! Just ignore him!

BUDO:

(Pressing on.) You think concrete's going to keep everything nice and tidy in those pits?

YUMI:

We can always count on Budo to find out!

TOSHI:

Let him talk...

BUDO:

What happens in an earthquake? You tell me. Ever notice how an earthquake tears up roads and bridges. And what about the soil? The soil that kept us going, and our fathers before us? What about that? And the animals and the birds and fishes even. What's going to happen to all of them?

YUKI:

He's right!

CHIEKO:

Who's asking you? You really cared about animals every time you strangled your rabbits...!

BUDO:

What happens when all the rivers are poisoned, and all the seas? You think our children in the cities are immune? Where will they get the food they eat, the air they breathe—where will it come from?

HARUNOBU:

You're out of turn: You aren't even recognized...

BUDO:

Don't try to shut me up! *(He fumbles, trying to extract a book from its wrapping with his one good hand.)* Any of you good souls ever heard of Minamata???? Where they made some kind of plastic. They let the waste spill in the sea. Pretty soon fisherman started feeling weird. Ants crawling up their fingers and down their toes. Losing their balance and falling in the water. Cats started dancing and jumped into the sea. *(Everyone laughs.)*

CHIEKO:

What does all this crap have to do with anything?

BUDO:

Children were born blind or deformed. For years people tried to stop the company. The company wouldn't listen until...

CHIEKO:

Let's get on with the vote. It's getting late...

BUDO:

...some man, some worker came to the table where all the trustees were meeting and cut his wrist. Opened up his arm! That's what it took to make the company listen.

CHIEKO:

So what? I don't give a shit for your Minamata! This is Tashima! Why should we care? None of us will be here when it happens...

HARUNOBU:

Order, order....

CHIEKO:

There's nothing we can do, anyway. There's only eight of us.

YUMI:

Maybe something will come up later to make Tashima change their mind.

BUDO:

Maybe we can slit our wrists... *(There is a shocked silence.)*

HARUNOBU:

It takes a long time anyway before.... They won't dig the pits right away. First, they have to survey the land before they bulldoze it. They build a fence around it, set up buildings and a guard house. They'll have to dig the pits and build the forms before they pour the concrete. Then the cement trucks come in. By then, none of us will be here any more. *(Everyone becomes very quiet.)* It's getting late. It's starting to snow. Everyone has had his say. Maybe we can find some compromise. Maybe we could take the first installment and divide it in equal shares, and divide the last one by households. Everyone should go home now. Sleep on it. Think about what each one of us thinks is fair. Then go to sleep and sleep on it. There's no hurry. We have thirty days before making up our minds.

TOSHI:

I've been thinking. I didn't vote. I abstained. I've been think-ing it over. OK. OK. So we take the money, we take it by household, we take it in equal shares, it doesn't matter. All this...all of it...I can't imagine. I can't imagine. Ending up, like some nameless old man, in some nameless city, living out my old age, feeding off a countryside that's dying, that's slowly being poisoned. And where I was born! And my father before me! Where we lived so many years. All the meadows, the streams, the woods.... And the graves. Everything we worked for. All the land, all the fields. It's not too late. Let's forget the money. It's our dirt, our soil. We worked for it: the meadows, the forest—all our tumbling down houses. So what if they're falling down. Let them keep their money.

BUDO:

About time we heard someone talk sense.... *(He tries propelling himself to where he can shake hands with Toshi. Yuki restrains him.)*

SADAKO:

(Ignoring Budo.) Harunobu-san has worked very hard to get this contract for us. Toshi, I don't think you're being realistic. We're too old. We can't do all the work of this village. We can't do it anymore. We can't sign petitions, we can't demonstrate, there's only eight of us left.

BUDO:

You're just playing Koizumi's game...

SADAKO:

(Ignoring him.) Anyway we don't have time. We can't stay here anymore. Everybody knows that. *(To Budo.)* Look at you! You're just fooling yourself. This way of life for us is gone. It's gone. We need to find a place where we don't have to work so hard. We're too old. We can't do any of the things we used to do. We have to accept that. Nobody's going to come out here to take care of us, not even our kids.... We have to be sensible.

HIROKO:

(She speaks the unspeakable.) What about me? Nobody cares about me. You all have family in Wajima or Kanazawa. Who do I have? Where will I go? What about me? *(All turn away. No one looks at her.)*

NIGHT

Each actor occupies his/her separate space on the stage, half reclining on a duvet of some sort, except for Hiroko, who will rise from a galvanized tub naked, and dress herself. The light is minimal. As each actor finishes his/her night reverie, he/she extinguishes a light until only Harunobu is left.

YUMI:

Where will we bury them? That's what Haru wants to know. We will have to move them somewhere. The company only pays so many yen for each grave moved.

They say people first came to Ogama more than three hundred years ago—from the beginning when this was nearly wilderness, home to eagles, bear, and barn owls people started coming, building shelter, clearing forest, planting. And burying their dead.

All those graves. Nobody really knows how many. Haru keeps worrying, "What will we do with the graves?"

"And what about the bones?" I tell him. "All the bones scattered now. Even graves have to die. Nothing lasts forever."

"Funny," he says to me, "you're quite the clown today!"

(She blows out her light.)

CHIEKO:

That idiot! Count on him to make trouble. Even in his wheelchair. I was so mad, I was almost crying. I don't know what the hell they're all complaining about? They all know they have to leave. And that Yuki!! Going on about the animals. Slaughtering her chickens and strangling her rabbits! It makes me want to wring her neck. Nobody keeps chickens or rabbits just to look at them! I could see chickens maybe for the eggs. But rabbits? What? For their pellets? What kind of crap is that? *(She blows her candle out.)*

YUKI:

Poor Budo. I feel so bad for him, laid up like that. He's been hard, it's true, all those years getting on everybody's nerves, always spoiling for a fight. The village goad, that's my Budo. But he's honest. At least he tells the truth, even if they don't want to hear it. Why can't people see how good he is? There's got to be a place. Somewhere in this world there has to be a place for someone like him. *(She turns down the kerosene lamp at her bedside.)*

TOSHI:

How can I forget all this when I'm settled somewhere in the city? Red earth. The road shady and quiet. Deserted. The squeal of the young saplings rubbing against each other in the wind? Can you hear it? Any morning, any spring morning, standing still in the roadbed. Listen! That rubbing! Like silk tearing. *(He blows his candle out.)*

SADAKO:

I'm lucky—not like Hiroko, all alone with no one. I don't want to go but I'm lucky. I know it. I have a son. My daughter-in-law, and I, we get along. Except sometimes Nobu puts on airs. Maybe she thinks because I'm from the country. She tells me the simplest things: how to sweep the tatami; how to tie my carrying cloth. She thinks maybe in my 85 years I didn't learn such things! Every time I have to remind her. "Listen, I come from here—long before you were born! My father was an alderman! I'm a city mouse—just with country habits."

When Hiroko said that, I shouldn't have looked away. I should have said something. Tomorrow. Maybe tomorrow I'll look after her. Before the snow drifts get too high. *(She extinguishes her light.)*

HIROKO:

Enough. *(Pause.)* Enough washing. (Pause.) Time now—before the bath turns cold. *(She rises from the tub and begins to wipe herself dry. She wipes under her breasts. Speaking to her breasts:)* Enough living. See how you droop and sag, poor things—tired, exhausted, falling down to earth.

(She rubs with the towel. Her voice is muffled as she wipes herself.) I don't know what happened. I never said anything like that before. Not even to Sadako. It just fell from my mouth.

(She begins to laugh. Not a laugh in the usual sense, more a rictus.) Ah, Hiroko! Hiroko, you won't need anything. You have everything you need—old hands, old legs, old eyes, just quick enough to feel the path! No one left to bother you! They'll be sleeping, the ones down below—the happy ones! And Sadako—*(She laughs.)*—alone up there where she keeps the wind company.

Put on the shirt, the sweaters, the foot coverings. All these ridiculous things on one last time. Shirt, wool knickers, sweaters. Winter kimono. Torn now, frayed a bit, aren't you, darling, sprouting tufts thick as goose feathers. Who could imagine—something once so expensive, so elegant—would anyone have guessed what it would come to—sixty almost sixty years. And my boots. *(She groans. She bends down with difficulty to put them on. Her breath comes in short spurts.)*

Can I get up there? Every step I'll have to stop to catch my breath. Past the old gate? Up there, still standing. Where my kids— where they buried them. Five kids, one after another. The drifts are even deeper now. *(She fastens the last boot. As she pulls herself upright:)* No need to worry. *(She laughs.)* No one will come looking—no one wants an old woman. A widow. No one left to bury her but snow!

(She busies herself pulling up her hair in an elaborate hairdo, fastening it with a comb.) That's all you have to do. Open the door. Push it closed to keep the snow drifts out. And if the wind tears out your comb, well.... Might stop to fumble for it in the dark. Might stoop,

feeling for it here or there till your hand goes numb with cold. *(She laughs.)* What for? To gather some piece of yourself up? *(She laughs one last time.)* Leave it there. Let it be the close—where everything comes done.

(She rummages around for her walking stick.) They say the feeling comes quickly. Because the person—because you—are so tired, so cold you want to stop. Curl up, let the snow cover you. Cover your eyes for the last time before it, before you close them. The last time. The grey light. Face to face with the white, the white. All your days, melting.

Like snow melting in water. *(She gathers herself up, slowly moving toward the exit door.)*

BUDO:

They'll have to build a guard house. A contractor's trailer; a cyclone fence. Through the links you might still see the meadow stretching all the way up to the hills beyond, but the grass is mowed, the ground bulldozed. Here and there they're digging pits, lining them with concrete.

A truck pulls up to the gate. The door to the guardhouse opens. Some employee runs forward, unlocks the gate. The door to the administrator's trailer swings open. A supervisor appears. His name is sewed to his lapel. He carries a clipboard. The driver hands him a cargo manifest. The man checks off each item one by one. He tears off a copy for himself. He hands the manifest back to the driver; points to the farther section. And waves him on.

Sure. It takes a long time. I will be gone, long gone. I don't know where. Somewhere in the city. In a room with a water pitcher. A toilet. A bath. Someone will come when I call. Someone may be waiting there to scrub my back. I don't know. Yuki maybe. I imagine the tub. It is stout oak. The steam rises. I sit in it warming myself. But no. They don't have oak tubs like that in the city. There won't be any room. Not anywhere. No water. No tub. No rising steam. No one to come. There will be no one. There will not be. I will not be. "I" will be finished... if it can be said.

Not me. No one. None. Not even. *(He puts out his light.)*
Not even none.

HARUNOBU:

In my dream I'm standing on the north side of the road as it passes to the west. I'm standing in shadow—the long shadow cast by the hills northeast of here. But the road is already in sunlight.

The ground is still wet. In the far distance I can see the night dew rising. I don't know why I'm waiting or what I am supposed to do.

A huge truck comes barreling through—a double trailer with two hoppers banging down the road, raising up a plume of dust. From the way it rattles I can tell it's dumped its load. What is it doing out here? Trucks that big never come through here. This is road's end. It doesn't go any farther. After Ogama only footpaths reach up into the mountains. But there's no road any more.

EPILOGUE

Blinding overheads spotlight Yamashita-san.

YAMASHITA-SAN:

(Reading from the Conclusion of the Tashima Company's Annual Report):
"The Tashima Corporation anticipates a year of growing profits. In response to growing demand, we continue to acquire new Waste Product Disposal Facilities. With our various contracts in development for disposal of mercury alloys, zinc and magnesium tailings, cadmium and other computer-derived hard metals such as lead, as well as asbestos and other post-industrial products, the Tashima Corporation shareholders can expect a mounting revenue stream. In addition to companies as far afield as Australia, New Zealand, China and the United States, we have already secured disposal contracts in a total of five prefectures. *(He does not name them, he counts five on his extremely large gloved fingers.)*

"We are especially proud of our latest acquisition in Kanazawa prefecture: Installation Number Five—a land tract—and its infrastructure have become the newest site of our industrial waste disposal operations." *(It is very important that no specific mention is ever made of the former town of Ogama.)*
Thank you very much.

(He bows. The stage goes dark.)

– END –

Like Snow Melting in Water is a true story. The Tashima Company acquired the village of Ogama (whose name means wash pot because many centuries prior—so local legend has it—monks stopped there to purify themselves before making the ascent to the sacred temple in the mountains far beyond) for an industrial waste disposal site. I have imagined some of the oral histories of the people who farmed rice there in a landscape that for over 300 years remained guardian of a world more sustainable than our own.

I am grateful to Fumi Sugihara, Sadako McInerney, and Donna de Neeve for their invaluable assistance.

(Note: *Like Snow Melting in Water* was written before the Fukushima meltdowns occurred.)

Critical Note: Although I didn't recognize it for some time, *Like Snow Melting in Water* was born in October, 2005, when, following the Hurricane Katrina disaster, I began taking oral histories of displaced people. What most engaged me was the transparency of the form: you could almost see and hear the people speaking long after their voices had gone quiet.

Does it make a good play? Not according to prescribed rules. There is no recognizable Aristotelian **structure**: three scenes, **exposition, rising action, climax and denouement**. And yet, beneath the words, there's some kind of knot being wound tighter and tighter, upping the **stakes**, until at last the frankly **static** scenes give way in a burst of face-to-face **confrontation**.

It could be said that the **characters** are two-dimensional, speaking ciphers. And what they have to say takes the form—at least in four of the five times of day—of **monologue** with occasional overlaps. Except for the Evening section, it lacks face-to-face **conflict**, supposedly the *sine qua non* of theater, of Western theater certainly. *Like Snow Melting in Water* takes place in a Buddhist/Shinto culture, where conflict is suppressed; in a village society so foreign to American sensibilities, that it has no choice but to be perceived as remote, as seen through the wrong end of a telescope. Which may explain why, although the work has been staged in Thailand and India, no American audience is ever likely to see it.

It is a work for the theater that won't play according to the rules. Like the Bread and Puppet Theater's "Fire," it observes no prescribed **template**. But in sensitive directorial hands, it becomes an **event**, something to be remembered long after the lights come up, because it's not quite like a routine staged performance. *The contrast between a stage play and an event parallels the earlier discussion contrasting writing* about *something vs. writing something.*

The writer always has a choice: Some scripts are dramas; but not all drama is literature. "Writing what you know" may be exactly the kind of corseting advice that keeps American writers focused on their own narrow, memoir-bound lives to the exclusion of the great world's clamor to which they are encouraged to turn a deaf ear. *I Could Tell You Stories* by memoirist par excellence, Patricia Hampl, makes a strong case that memoir is not complete until it pulls in the **public** world into the realm of the **private**. "Out of the dread ruin and disintegration [of the world] emerges a protest which becomes history when it is written from the choral voice of a nation...."

3

CODA

As the time came to prepare this book for publication, I found myself taking the precious day off. That, too, is a discipline—one I overlook to my own peril. Insist too much, and the work gets stale. I usually walk high in the hills overlooking San Francisco Bay where the eye can see forever—a landscape that clears the mind like nothing else. But now, with the hemorrhage of migrants forcing their way past national barriers, willing to risk drowning in the Mediterranean seas, fleeing the war zones where the Untied States and its Saudi ally have created uninhabitable zones, human displacement has reached proportions far beyond what I first witnessed in Katrina's day.

I found myself resting on a bench overlooking the bay. The early fog shrouding the Golden Gate was slowly burning off, but the bay shone its usual startling blue. Suddenly I imagined the blue turning the color of human flesh as millions of arms stretched up from below the surface of the water, arms of the drowning—of Yemen, and Libya, and Syria, and Turkey and Iraq and Afghanistan—in their panic pleading for rescue.

I first learned what it means to become a refugee fleeing a war zone from my husband, who fled the Nazi invasion of France with the very few possessions he and his mother cobbled together, escaping to that "Free" zone where, for the duration of World War II, they would find shelter. I learned what it means to grow old, unable to maintain my life and household or to prune my own trees as I had in stronger, younger years. I learned the meaning—and the value to a writer—of having to leave home.

GENERAL BIBLIOGRAPHY

Abe, Kobo: *Woman in the Dunes,* a metaphysical novel about a missing person which presents an insect's-eye world view. Also the subject of a brilliant film of the same name, dir. Teshigahara.

Adnan, Etel: *Sitt Marie Rose*: a Palestinian novelist explores the politics of North Africa.

Alexievich, Svetlana: *Voices from Chernobyl,* the human chorus: a song from hell.

Bachmann, Ingeborg: *Malina,* may be the definitive novel of feminist mythology.

Beckett, Samuel: Trilogy: *Molloy, Malone Dies, The Unnameable.* Event replaces narrative.

Blackburn, Julia: *Daisy Bates in the Desert.* Biography, autobiography and fiction meet.

Buzzati, Dino: *The Tartar Steppe,* a post WWII metaphysical novel presented as an allegory.

Childs, Craig: *House of Rain,* a ten-year walkabout in Four Corners Anasazi country.

Coetzee, J. M.: *Waiting for the Barbarians,* the quintessential novel of the 20th century.

D'Agata, John: *About a Mountain,* cultural critique of American "civilization," braiding together Yucca Mtn., suicide, and Las Vegas.

Estrin, Marc: *Insect Dreams.* Possibly the great American novel in which the conscience of the country is a cockroach.

Fisk, Robert: *The Great War for Civilization.* A remarkably artistic journalistic work.

Galeano, Eduardo: *Memory of Fire*: a three-volume people's history told in vignettes of the Americas from pre-Columbian times to the present.

Hedayat, Sedagh: *The Blind Owl,* a novel encountering the *Buddhacavita* and *Tibetan Book of the Dead,* which recycles some 16 tropes in a constantly transforming narrative.

Hoffmann, Gerd: *Spectacle at the Tower*, a novel featuring a repulsive set of protagonists, drawing on dream, archetype and racial memory.

Japin, Arthur: *The Two Hearts of Kwasi Boachi*, based on the true life accounts of an African Ashante prince in a colonial world: fabulously researched and deeply affecting.

Joyce, James: *Ulysses:* an explosion of disparate narrative strategies and rhetorical devices.

Kafka, Franz: *The Trial*, a pre-WWII metaphysical novel.

Kristof, Agotha: *The Notebook*. The chaos of war and wartime from a child's point of view.

Kosinsky, Jerzy: *The Painted Bird*. In the same vein as *The Notebook*.

LeSueur, Meridel: *The Dread Road*, a narrative in three co-terminal parts reflecting on the intersection of the public & personal in the life of the American oppressed & marginalized.

Lispector, Clarice: *Hour of the Star*: a novel which—like a prickly pear—offers the reader many resistances, but whose inner sweetness is worth savoring.

Llamazares, Julio: *The Yellow Rain*. A fictional elegy for an abandoned village. A shining example of presence as it applies to writing.

Lobo-Antunes: *The Inquisitor's Manual*. A portrait of Portugal under the Salazar dictatorship.

MacCarthy, Cormac: *Child of God*, a novel which presents an intensely repulsive protagonist who nonetheless manages to evoke the reader's (and writer's) empathy.

Marcom, Micheline Aharonian, *Three Apples Fall from Heaven*, a response to Juan Rulfo's *Pedro Paramo*.

Margulis, Lynn and Sagan, Dorion: *Microcosmos*, a stunning summary of Margulis' work on endosymbiosis.

Markandaya, Kamala: *Nectar in a Sieve*. An affective portrait of poverty & marginalization.

Maso, Carole: *The Art Lover*, a novel cobbled together as a collage, in which the initial narrative collapses to be replaced by a parallel narrative occurring much closer to home.

Mowat, Farley: *Never Cry Wolf*, on creatures more civilized than humans.

Mulisch, Harry: *Last Call*, a novel that starts out in the realist vein, to take a hallucinatory turn.

Nollman, Jim: *The Charged Border*. The frontier where human and cetacean communication meet.

Pandolfo, Stefania: *Impasse of the Angels*, a stunning ethnography of Southern Morocco.

Paton, Alan: *Cry the Beloved Country*. Where fiction tends to burst into song.

Pavic, Milorad: *Dictionary of the Khazars*, not so much a novel as a superb example of a post-modern spoof, very lyrical and very wise in a completely perverse way.

Pineda, Cecile: *Face* (1985), *Frieze* (1986), *The Love Queen of the Amazon* (1991), *Fishlight* (2001), *Bardo99* (2004), *Redoubt* (2005).

Robbe-Grillet: *The Labyrinth; The Voyeur; Jalousie*. Where the protagonist's presence is dictated by objects surrounding him, which he observes.

Rulfo, Juan: *Pedro Paramo*. Perhaps the most amazing novel ever written, posits an entirely different kind of protagonist, and dispenses with the conventions of fictional location of time and place through use of repeated emblematic phrases to locate the reader.

Sarraute, Nathalie: *Tropisms*. Narratives without the customary plot or character.

Schulz, Bruno: *Sanatorium at the Sign of the Hourglass; Street of the Crocodiles*. Two story collections which present a worldview in which people and objects display every kind of perversity.

Slater, Phillip: *The Pursuit of Loneliness*, a summation of our discontents.

Tabbuchi, Antonio: *Pereira Declares*, a bestselling novel of dawning political engagement.

Thomas, Elizabeth Marshall: *The Old Way: The Ju/'oansi of the Kalahari Desert*, an informal ethnography.

Valenzuela, Luisa: "I Am Your Horse in the Night," in *The Censors*.

Wakeford, Tom: *Liaisons of Life*, what happens when the rhizo-sphere interferes with Darwin's neat narrative.

Walser, Robert: *Baron von Gunten*, the allegory of a nobody who yearns to be invisible by training to become a butler. A novel (and film dir. Bros. Quai *Institute Benjamenta*) way ahead of its time.

Wilkerson, Isabelle: *The Warmth of Other Suns*, historic account of the great Black migration north.

Wright, Richard: *A Short History of Progress*, "civilization's" failing grades.

BIBLIOGRAPHY
ON THE WRITER'S ART

Madison Smartt Bell. *Narrative Design: A Writer's Guide to Structure*. New York: W. W. Norton, 1997.

Louise Dunlap. *Undoing the Silence: Six Tools for Social Change Writing*, Oakland: New Village Press, 2007.

Natalie Goldberg. *Writing Down the Bones*. New York: Shambala, 2005.

Patricia Hampl. *I Could Tell You Stories*. New York: W.W. Norton & Company, 1999.

INDEX OF WRITERLY CONCEPTS

AFTERWORD

Cecile Pineda was born in Harlem in an area called "Sugar Hill." The Black community there was very much a presence in her childhood. During the '30s, '40s and still in the '50s, Harlem was home to established Black families, where to a great degree, the family structure remained intact. In terms of its optimism, warmth and spontaneity, the neighborhood resembled the family and kinship patterns and the culture of pre-Katrina New Orleans. With her appreciation for the music of words, Pineda remains faithful throughout *Out of the Whirlwind* to the speech patterns and dialects of her speakers, respecting both their social origins and the richness of their culture.

The heart of Cecile Pineda's fiction concerns itself with hunger (*Frieze*, Wings Press, 2007) and privation (*Face:* Wings Press, 2004). The lives of the disadvantaged remains a prominent theme. Now, she brings to her non-fiction writing the ear of a writer recognized for the sparseness of her style. Of her first novel, John Coetzee has written: "*Face* still continues to haunt me...both by what is said, and what is not said."

ABOUT THE AUTHOR

Cecile Pineda is the author of six published novels: *The Love Queen of the Amazon*, written with the assistance of an NEA Fiction Fellowship, and named Notable Book of the Year by the *New York Times; Frieze;* and *Face,* which won the Gold Medal from the Commonwealth Club of California, the First Fiction Award from the American Academy and Institute of Arts & Letters, an American Book Award nomination and a 2014 Neustadt Prize nomination; and two mononovels: *Bardo99,* a journey through the 20th century and *Redoubt,* a meditation on gender; *Fishlight: a Dream of Childhood* is a fictional memoir. Her non-fiction includes *Devil's Tango: How I Learned the Fukushima Step by Step,* a criminal exposé of the nuclear industry, and *Apology to a Whale: Words to Mend a World,* an exploration of language as the root of the world's present power alignments. All books are available from Wings Press. Her archive forms part of the Special Collections Library of Stanford University. Of her fiction, John Coetzee has written: "Cecile Pineda is a novelist of the utmost artistic integrity."

Prior to her work as a writer, Pineda founded and directed her own experimental theater company.

Visit her web page at http://www.cecilepineda.com

Wings Press was founded in 1975 by Joanie Whitebird and Joseph F. Lomax, both deceased, as "an informal association of artists and cultural mythologists dedicated to the preservation of the literature of the nation of Texas." Publisher, editor and designer since 1995, Bryce Milligan is honored to carry on and expand that mission to include the finest in American writing—meaning all of the Americas, without commercial considerations clouding the decision to publish or not to publish.

Wings Press intends to produce multi-cultural books, chapbooks, ebooks, recordings and broadsides that enlighten the human spirit and enliven the mind. Everyone ever associated with Wings has been or is a writer, and we know well that writing is a transformational art form capable of changing the world, primarily by allowing us to glimpse something of each other's souls. We believe that good writing is innovative, insightful, and interesting. But most of all it is honest. As Bob Dylan put it, "To live outside the law, you must be honest."

Likewise, Wings Press is committed to treating the planet itself as a partner. Thus the press uses as much recycled material as possible, from the paper on which the books are printed to the boxes in which they are shipped.

As Robert Dana wrote in *Against the Grain*, "Small press publishing is personal publishing. In essence, it's a matter of personal vision, personal taste and courage, and personal friendships." Welcome to our world.

Colophon

This first edition of *Three Tides: Writing at the Edge of Being,* by Cecile Pineda, has been printed on 55 pound Edwards Brothers natural paper containing a percentage of recycled fiber. Titles have been set in Bordeaux Roman Bold, and Adobe Caslon type; the text in Adobe Caslon type. All Wings Press books are designed and produced by Bryce Milligan.

On-line catalogue and ordering:
www.wingspress.com

Wings Press titles are distributed
to the trade by the
Independent Publishers Group
www.ipgbook.com
and in Europe by
www.gazellebookservices.co.uk

Also available as an ebook.